Architecture and Modern Literature

Architecture

AND

Modern Literature

✦ ✦ ✦

David Spurr

THE UNIVERSITY OF MICHIGAN PRESS   ✦   ANN ARBOR

Published in the United States of America by
The University of Michigan Press
Manufactured in the United States of America
⊗ Printed on acid-free paper

2015   2014   2013   2012   4   3   2   1

A CIP catalog record for this book is available from the British Library.

Library of Congress Cataloging-in-Publication Data

Spurr, David, 1949–
    Architecture and modern literature / David Spurr.
        p.   cm.
    Includes bibliographical references and index.
    ISBN 978-0-472-07171-5 (cloth : acid-free paper) — ISBN 978-0-472-
05171-7 (pbk. : acid-free paper) — ISBN 978-0-472-02824-5 (e-book)
        1. Architecture and literature.   2. Space perception in literature.
3. Literature, Modern—19th century—History and criticism.
4. Literature, Modern—20th century—History and criticism.   I. Title.
PN56.A73S68   2012
809'.93357—dc23   2011043633

In memoriam
Elizabeth S. Ball

Contents

Preface

This is a book about the interpretation of architectural forms in modern literature. One of its claims is that literature's encounter with the built environment is essential to its definition of what is sometimes called modernity, meaning the set of material and symbolic forms that constitute the modern world and our experience of that world. In order to address this subject, I have found it necessary to pose certain larger questions of the relation between literature and architecture. The introduction puts forward the general question of how meaning is produced by architecture and literature, respectively, and how these meanings have intersected. This question is initially addressed in historical terms, ranging from what I choose to call the foundational myths of Babel and the house of Odysseus to the "house ideologies" of the early modern period. The attention then shifts to the crisis of meaning common to both arts in the nineteenth and twentieth centuries. This crisis manifests itself in a number of ways: in the aesthetics of ruin and fragmentation, in the retreat toward interiority as a space of subjective and private meaning, in the new kinds of attention given to the human body, in the development of new forms and materials, and in the conception of the past in terms of stock or reserve.

The first chapter takes up some of the points raised in the introductory essay in order to recast them within the problematic of architecture as a space of human dwelling, understood in a practical as well as an existential sense. The subject of dwelling is of central importance to this book, as it brings together a range of literary, architectural, and theoretical discourses in which the conditions of modernity are those of crisis: a crisis in human habitation, in the adaptation of human beings to the objective conditions of a world in which the question of what it means to be human is given unprecedented urgency. The question is posed equally, if indirectly, by works as diverse as Virginia Woolf's *Mrs Dalloway* (1925) and Adolf Loos's Michaelerplatz building in Vienna (1911). The specifically modern concept of dwelling seeks reconciliation with the ontological condition that Martin Heidegger names homelessness (*Heimatlosigkeit*). Homelessness in this sense is the other of the traditional concept of dwelling, along with the conditions of ruin, fragmentation, and exile. It means not just lacking shelter but not being at home in the world, including the world of language. Modern literature and architecture are the consequences of this condition, in both their formal freedoms and their respective engagements with the question of the way we live now.

The chapters that follow explore from different angles the question of dwelling and its other, beginning at the turn of the nineteenth century and ranging through the twentieth century and beyond. The second chapter concerns the space of the "demonic" in Sade, Dickens, and Kafka. The demonic is understood here as embodying both the uncanny forces within human being which the modern world has failed to bring under the control of rational mastery, and as the destructive element within the construction of modernity itself.

The chapter on demonic spaces is concerned, in part, with modernity's relation to a premodern and even prehistoric past. The third chapter, on "allegories of the Gothic," turns to the modern relation to the Middle Ages by examining the curious variety of nineteenth-century literary responses to the abiding presence of medieval Gothic cathedrals, notably in France. These responses, which range in register from Goethe's sense of the sublime to Henry James's self-deprecating irony, prove to be symptomatic of the perplexity and sense of loss with which the modern sensibility contemplates the architectural evidence of a faith that once united the European world in its collective strength and fervor. Behind this perplexity is not just the enigma of modernity's relation to the past but also the problem of the nature of aesthetic experience in a world where art is removed from its traditional foundations in ritual and worship.

The following chapter, on Ruskin and Viollet-le-Duc, pursues the general subject of the Gothic by comparing the two most important writers on architecture in the nineteenth century in their conflicting ideas concerning the restoration of medieval architecture. Once again it is a question of modernity's relation to the past. Ruskin revives the eighteenth-century aes-

thetic of the ruin in wishing to preserve the effects of time on medieval architecture, whereas Viollet-le-Duc attempts to modernize the Gothic in
order to restore it to an ideal form that it may never have actually had. The
opposition between these architectural values is compared to that which
exists in modern literature between the figures of allegory and symbol as
contrasting modes of representing the relation of the past to the present.

The chapter on Proust in Venice carries the question of the past into
the twentieth century. Whereas in a writer like Balzac, the progress of his
hero's life is defined according to his ability to negotiate the labyrinthine
ways of the social space of Paris, in Proust the narrator experiences urban
space as a kind of map of his own memory—as a metaphorical projection
of the personal metaphysics of time in which he struggles to unite his present with his past. The historical memory embodied in the architecture of
Venice thus serves as a model in the narrator's search for a way to relive the
privileged moments of his own memory. The problem of history is equally
important for Joyce: in *Ulysses* the modern city emerges as a great
palimpsest in which architectural objects built in different historical
epochs are juxtaposed with one another so as to transform their respective
meanings in a manner similar to the way this happens between the archaic
and modern elements of Joyce's language.

The chapter on architecture in Frost and Stevens returns to the metaphysics of dwelling in order to show how, in an era when the traditional
myth of dwelling can no longer be revived, modern poetry assumes the
task of defining a new relation to dwelling, as a mode of being, in the form
of poetic language itself. The difference between the two poets lies in the
respective meanings they assign to this dwelling in relation to the more
universal conditions of being. The final chapter examines the literary response to the modular, temporary, and cumulative architectural forms produced by the adaptation of building technology to the imperatives of mass
consumption and globalization—what the architect Rem Koolhaas has
called "junkspace." The works of J. G. Ballard and Michel Houllebecq
serve as testimonies to radical transformations in subjectivity and the social
fabric—transformations seen as intimately related to specifically contemporary architectural forms, such as the high-rise apartment building, the
corporate office park, the suburban shopping mall, and the highway interchange. Our reading of these works brings us back to the question of
dwelling, both in historical time and in the space of the present, and of the
need to find a way to live in a world in the absence of any necessary relation between the human subject and the built environment—where
dwelling always has to be learned or invented anew.

Acknowledgments

Parts of this book have appeared elsewhere. Chapter 1 was published as "An End to Dwelling: Reflections on Modern Literature and Architecture," in *Modernism,* ed. Astradur Eysteinsson and Vivian Liska (Amsterdam: John Benjamins, 2007). An early version of chapter 2, "Demonic Spaces: Sade, Dickens, Kafka," appeared in *Colloquium Helveticum: Cahiers Suisses de Littérature Comparée* 36 (2005). Chapter 4, "Figures of Ruin and Restoration: Ruskin and Viollet-le-Duc," appeared in *Chora: Intervals in the Philosophy of Architecture* 5 (2007). Finally, chapter 7, "Architecture in Frost and Stevens," was published in the *Journal of Modern Literature* 28, no. 3 (2005). Permission to reprint these essays is gratefully acknowledged.

In preparing this work I have had the good fortune to benefit from the knowledge, generosity, and goodwill of some extraordinary colleagues. I wish especially to thank Guillemette Bolens, Lukas Erne, Dario Gamboni, Pascal Griener, Martin Leer, Alberto Pérez-Gomez, Jean-Michel Rabaté, Markus Winkler, and the students in my seminars at the University of Geneva.

Introduction: Meaning in Architecture and Literature

I

Architektur als wichtigstes Zeugnis der latenten "Mythologie"

In the monumental collection of fragments known as *Das Passagen-Werk,* Walter Benjamin remarks that architecture bears the most important testimony to the hidden "mythology" of a society (1002). As in so many of the remarks tossed out by the German critic in his seemingly offhand manner, there is matter for a book in this idea. If we understand mythology, in this modern sense, to be the set of symbols and narratives through which society gives meaning to itself, then the idea of architecture as testimony to a latent mythology offers one way of seeing architecture in relation to literature. What Benjamin claims is not simply that architecture is passive evidence of mythic content, but also that it "bears witness" (*zeugt*);[1] in other words, it speaks a language that bears testimony to a hidden mythology by making it available to interpretation in concrete form. His examples are the commercial arcades of nineteenth-century Paris, in which the fantasy world of burgeoning consumer capitalism, with its dreams of exotic luxury and domestic bliss, can be read in the luminous passages newly fashioned of iron and glass. In architecture this mythology remains latent to the extent that its form speaks only indirectly of its content. The novels of Balzac, by way of contrast, make this mythology manifest when they expose the ruthless ambition of parvenus, the greed of would-be inheritors, and the secret crimes of the ruling class. Each of these cultural forms nonetheless bears testimony in its own way to the underlying conditions of meaning belonging to its historical moment.

There exists a philosophical tradition that puts architecture and litera-ture into relation with one another according to the particular question of what art is and how it functions. This tradition is distinctly modern and dates from a moment—roughly located in the eighteenth century—when the aesthetic dimensions of both cultural forms began to take precedence in the discourse surrounding them, that is, when architecture could be conceived as a fine art rather than essentially the science of building and *literature* began to refer to those particular forms of writing that make a claim to consideration on aesthetic grounds. For Hegel, architecture and literature are diametrically opposed in their respective manners of giving expression to the individual and collective human spirit. In his Berlin lec-tures on aesthetics in the 1820s, he says that of all the arts, architecture was the first to come into the world because the first task of art consists in giv-ing shape to the objective, physical world of nature. However, since the material of architecture is solid, inanimate matter, it remains a purely ex-ternal reflection of what Hegel calls spirit. On the other hand it is poetry, and by extension literature in general, that stands opposite to architecture as the "absolute and true art of the spirit": more than any other art, poetry has the capacity to bring before the imagination everything of which the mind is capable of conceiving. Architecture is the first art, but literature is the total art in its pure expression of inner spirit (*Aesthetics,* 2:627).

In the twentieth century, Hans-Georg Gadamer defines the difference between the arts in somewhat different terms. For him, the essence of art lies neither in the expression of spirit nor in an aesthetic autonomy ab-stracted from the world but rather in the meaning that it produces in the world. Because the architectural work is always the solution to some prob-lem, its meaning is a function of its place in the world, in the relation be-tween its form and the surrounding context. To this spatial conception of architectural meaning can be added a temporal one, for a building, as it is "borne along by the stream of history," acquires a historical meaning by virtue of its mediation between the present and the past from which it emerged (*Truth and Method,* 157). As for literature, Gadamer takes a simi-larly pragmatic view. Literature occupies a borderline position between sheer aesthetic contemplation and the material mediation in space and time represented in architecture (159). Nonetheless, literature comes into being as meaningful only by being read; our understanding of literature "is not specifically concerned with its formal achievement as a work of art, but with what it says to us" (163). In this sense the mode of being of literature, like that of architecture, is historical: it brings the past down to us in the space of the present; the reading of literature accomplishes, almost magically, "the sheer presence of the past" (164).

For the purposes of this study, we need to retain two essential points from these philosophical discussions. The first concerns the importance of both arts in defining the world in which we live. Architecture, as the art of building, gives concrete form to the external world according to the structures of imagination; whereas literature, as the art of written language, gives symbolic form to the same world. In their respective manners architecture and literature are potentially the most unlimited of all art forms in their comprehension of human existence itself, and this fact alone justifies the task of putting them into relation with one another. The second point concerns the nature of art in general as a culturally significant phenomenon—as an ordered presentation of social and cultural meanings, whether as the pure expression of mythology, as the contestation of it, or as a symptom of the contradictions inherent in the conditions under which meaning is to be produced. In all of these cases, the artwork bears the marks of its own production as something indissociable from the larger culture, here understood in the anthropological sense of a set of values and practices particular to a given place and time. In other words, we want to know what the artwork means as a cultural artifact and how that meaning is produced.

The present work explores a series of instances in which architecture and modern literature come together in ways that appear to break down the barriers between the two art forms, or at least to construct bridges between them. The particular mode of this exploration is to ask the question of how meaning is produced by architecture and literature, respectively, and by their interaction, particularly in the context of modernity. *Modernity* is used here in historically limited terms to refer primarily to the social, cultural, and economic conditions of urban industrial society in the nineteenth and twentieth centuries. Although such conditions have their origins in the Protestant Reformation, the Enlightenment, and earlier forms of capitalism and imperialism, I hold the view that beginning in the early nineteenth century the scale of such conditions was increased to proportions that could not have been imagined a century earlier, and that one of the consequences of these changes was to throw into disarray whatever harmony may have existed among the arts.

In order to seize the points of intersection between architecture and literature in the modern context, much of the material studied here consists of the literary representation of architectural forms, such as Proust's fictional impressions of the baptistery of Saint Mark's Basilica in Venice. In a case like this, the layers of meaning are multiple and interconnected. There is first of all what we might call the architectural meaning of the baptistery, itself a fourteenth-century interpretation of the various Gospel narratives of Christ's baptism and of their subsequent institutionalization as a sacrament of the Church. This space within the basilica, however, was interpreted in the nineteenth century context by Ruskin, whose work of architectural criticism informs the impressions of Proust's narrator, and by Proust himself, who visited Venice eight years before writing this passage. The literary meaning produced in Proust's work is thus itself a re-presentation of other meanings produced by architectural form, criticism, and authorial reminiscence. When we consider that the architectural form that inspires Proust's narrative is itself inspired by biblical narrative, the interdependency of literary and architectural meanings becomes most evident. In cases like this the production of literary meaning may be theoretically distinct, but in practice it remains inseparable from the production of architectural meaning.

Architectural theory, like literary theory, has many ways of approaching its subject, but one of these is to understand an architectural work in terms of three factors: *site, type,* and *architectonics.* As we have seen in Gadamer, every architectural work intervenes in a given site in such a way as to give a new shape to that space while also establishing a new relation between the newly formed space and that which remains outside it. The notion of architectural type, introduced in the eighteenth century, classifies architecture according to figures that develop independently in themselves.[2] Originally conceived in terms of basic archetypes such as the cave, the hut, or the tent, architectural typology by extension includes such universal categorical forms as the temple, the fortress, the bridge, or, in another register, the arch, the door, the wall. *Architectonics* has come to mean that aspect of architecture specifically concerned with construction, such as the interaction of the forces of load and support. Siegfried Giedion uses the word to describe Le Corbusier's definition of the relations between architecture and construction as consisting of load-bearing pillars, of the mutual independence of wall and frame, of the free-standing facade, and so on (*Espace,* 304). More recently, Kenneth Frampton has argued in favor of the term *tectonics* (from the Greek *teknè*) to designate the "expressive potential" of constructional technique, the "poetics of construction" (*Studies* 2), thereby seeking a synthesis of the artistic and the purely analytical understanding of the architectural work.

The point of this brief excursion into architectural language is to demonstrate the potential for literary analogies. The architectural site can thus be compared to the historical and cultural context, or what Pierre Bourdieu calls the field of cultural production in which a literary work intervenes. Architectural type corresponds to literary genre, while the essential question at stake in the contemporary understanding of architectonics is analogous to the attempt in literary theory to reconcile structure with style or to disengage the specifically literary quality of a given text. In both arts, the production of meaning is a function of the relations between the respective sets of vectors outlined here: in architecture among *topos, typos,* and *tectonic*;[3] in literature among context, genre, and text.

However, the study of the relations between architecture and literature needs to go beyond mere analogy in at least two respects. One is to examine the rivalry, or even the outright opposition, between the two arts in their respective responses to certain historical conditions. The closest example at hand is that of modernity itself. Many of the most striking elements of modernist architecture—its extreme rationality, its pure functionalism, its brutal break with the past—have been seen to embody precisely the objective conditions of modernity that modernist literature calls into question. Certainly the functionalist and rationalist elements of twentieth-century architecture appear diametrically opposed in spirit to the value that so much of twentieth-century literature places on subjective, nonrational experience. Suggested by this difference is the fragmentation of meaning within the realm of modernity itself, or what Theodor Adorno calls the negative dialectic between art as imaginative production and the experience of objective reality. The other way of reading literature with architecture is, as I have already proposed, to study the representation of one art by the other. If the architectural representation of literature is rare, the representation of architecture is everywhere in literature, precisely because of what Hegel identifies as literature's capacity to bring before the imagination every object of the mind's conception or the senses' perception.

Many of the cases studied in the present work identify an ambiguous relation between architecture and literature in the modern era. The story of this relation, which can be offered in only the most tentative form, can nonetheless be told along the following general lines. In the formal classicism of the eighteenth century, poetry and architecture have in common an aesthetic designed to reproduce the classical values of proportion, reason, and the justice of natural order. To the extent that this common aesthetic represents a relative harmony between the arts (at least in their neoclassical manifestations), the nineteenth century literary interest in Gothic architecture signals, in important writers, both a break with classical values and an estrangement from what these writers perceive as the objective and subjective conditions of modernity. Against these conditions stands the purity of spirit that is thought to lie at the origin of the great medieval cathedrals, marooned like great albatrosses in the midst of European industrial cities. In the twentieth century, this experience of rupture is transformed into architectural rationalism, on one hand, and literary fragmentation on the other. These two modes of artistic production constitute very different responses to the modern condition, even if they share certain aims, such as the breakdown of barriers between inside and outside. In contrast to these positions, the art more contemporary to our own time approaches a "postmedium" condition in which architectural and literary elements are combined in the same work. As Fredric Jameson has written, in a world saturated with aesthetic codes, the specificity of any artistic mode or genre is systematically put into question. The focus of the present work, then, as well as its general thesis, concerns the manner in which the relations between architecture and literature are symptomatic of modernity as a crisis of meaning. Before treating this question further, however, I first wish to look backward at certain representative instances of the relation between architectural and literary meaning in a range of cases from antiquity to the threshold of modernity.

II

Foundational Myths

In the penultimate book of the *Odyssey*, Odysseus has returned to his house in Ithaca after an absence of twenty years. The familiar story is beautiful enough to be worth retelling. Odysseus has killed the suitors who importuned his wife, dishonored his family, despoiled his household provisions, and mistreated his servants. However, at the long-awaited moment of his reunion with Penelope, she fears an impostor and is therefore unable or unwilling to recognize him. In her caution, she requires proof that this strange man, twenty years older than the husband she knew, is indeed Odysseus. She orders her servant to prepare a firm bed for the stranger, the very bed that Odysseus himself built, and to place it outside the nuptial chamber. Overhearing these orders, Odysseus is overcome with emotion. He demands to know what man could have removed his bed from its original place, where it was literally rooted in the earth. When he built the bed, there was an olive tree in the courtyard of the house, "with long leaves growing strongly . . . and it was thick, like a column (*kion*)" (340). He constructed the nuptial chamber around this tree and made a bedpost of its living trunk. The bedpost being thus immovable, Penelope's orders to the servant must be impossible to carry out, Odysseus says, unless someone has severed the trunk of the olive from its roots.

> So he spoke, and the knees and heart within her went slack
> as she recognized the clear proofs that Odysseus had given;
> but then she burst into tears and ran straight to him, throwing
> her arms round the neck of Odysseus. (340)

This scene is the culmination of Homer's epic; after years of voyage and suffering, Odysseus is finally reunited with home and family, and as if to consecrate the event, he has penetrated to the most intimate interior of the house to find the nuptial bed rooted in the earth, exactly where he left it twenty years earlier.

The constellation of symbols is powerful: the nuptial bed is the place of conception of Odysseus's progeny; thus it is the source of the continuity of patriarchal order as well as being the center of intimacy within the domestic space of the house. Its placement is therefore temporal in the successive order of generations but also spatial in two senses: in the horizontal order of the distribution of the house as arranged around the central point of courtyard and chamber, and in the vertical order that connects the house to the earth and to heaven by means of the column of the tree. To be thus literally connected to the earth is important symbolically, because in the patriarchal and agricultural world of Ithaca, the earth guarantees the prosperity of the house of Odysseus as well as its continuity in the generational sense. In another sense, the immovability of the marriage bed and of the house itself marks the end of Odysseus's wandering. It thus signifies the supremacy of a sedentary over a nomadic way of life and the security of an agricultural and domestic economy in contrast to the economy of war. Homer gives us the first figure of the *house* as a figure of stability and permanence, symbolic values it will retain even in the modern era, when the nature of human dwelling will be called into question by architects, poets, and philosophers alike. For Gaston Bachelard the house even in the twentieth century is a world unto itself from cellar to attic, a symbol of the interior life of the psyche, and the very place of reverie: "La maison est une des plus grandes puissances d'intégration pour les pensées, les souvenirs et les rêves de l'homme" (26) (the house is one of the great forces for combining the thought, memory, and dreams of man).

When Bachelard's insight is directed toward classical antiquity, what it suggests in the case of Homer is that the *oikos,* or domestic economy, of the house is the condition for the epic itself. Odysseus, in telling the story of how he built the marriage bed, compares the trunk of the olive to a column, or *kion.* This word has been used before, in Book VIII, to designate the place of the singer Demodokos at the feast held for Odysseus in the house of Alkinoös. Let us recall that in that episode Odysseus, shipwrecked on the island of the Phaiakians, is received by the "hallowed prince" of that island, whose palace is the symbol of divine favor, of the prosperity of his kingdom, and of the justice with which he rules over its inhabitants.

> For as from the sun the light goes or from the moon, such was
> the glory on the high-roofed house (*dôma*) of great-hearted Alkinoös.
> (113)

Homer lingers on the architectural detail of the interior: brass walls of rooms encircled by a cobalt frieze, golden doors with silver doorposts. The richness of the material appointments reflects the harmony and prosperity of life on the island: the leaders of the Phaiakians hold their sessions in the light of torches held by golden statues standing on their "strong-compounded bases" (113). The island is known for its bountiful orchards and olive groves and for the skill of its women at weaving. These combined elements of architectural splendor, flourishing industry, and social harmony make the house of Alkinoös an ideal symbol of domestic economy; they define the high standard to which Odysseus's house at Ithaca must one day be restored. Seeing all this, Odysseus prays that he may live to see once more "my property, my serving people, and my great high-roofed house (*dôma*)" (117).

It is at the center of the scene at Phaiakia that Homer places the figure of epic poetry. During the great feast held for Odysseus at the palace, Demodokos, the blind singer (*aoidos*) is led into the middle of the room and is seated on a silver-studded chair leaning against a tall column (*kion*). Demodokos's lyre is hung on a peg in the column above his head, where he can reach it when he has done eating and drinking. At the end of the meal Demodokos sings movingly of the Trojan War, including the quarrel between Odysseus and Achilles. Hearing the song, Odysseus himself, his identity still unknown to his hosts, quietly weeps at the story of his own sufferings and those of his companions. The scene is as richly symbolic as that of the marriage bed of Odysseus and Penelope, with the difference that in this episode Homer connects the art of poetry quite literally to the supporting structure of his architectural and social ideal. Demodokos, loved by the Muse, is also revered by the Phaiakians and given a place of honor in the middle of their assembly. In a figure joining poetic art to architectural strength, the poet's lyre is hung on the column that holds up the roof, and his chair is propped against the same support. The song of Demodokos, which takes the narrative and poetic form of the epic, provides the occasion and the house itself with a sense of history, human community, and a relation to the gods. In Hegelian terms, it gives voice to the spirit without which the splendors of Alkinoös's palace would remain little more than a show of riches. The performance of Demodokos is Homer's manner of paying homage to his own art and its capacity to endow life with meaning. When we come to the scene of the marriage bed late in the narrative, the *kion* of the bedpost sends us back to the *kion* of Demodokos in order to remind us that the restoration of order and meaning to Odysseus's universe is the work of the poet himself. Literary meaning here works in harmony with architectural meaning as the foundation of cultural memory and value, and of their transmission from one generation to the next.

The houses of the *Odyssey* need to be balanced against that other primordial architectural text, the story of the Tower of Babel in the eleventh chapter of the book of Genesis, which implicitly proposes a different kind of relation between architecture and writing. Although the story has been reinterpreted over the centuries in innumerable theological and philosophical works, perhaps I may be permitted to retell it once more in light of the particular perspective afforded by my subject. Readers of Jacques Derrida will understand that my interpretation would not have been possible without his reading of the same biblical passage in "Les tours de Babel," although his main preoccupations and his conclusions are different from mine. The dream of a universal and common language at the story's foundation—"And the whole earth was of one language, and of one speech" (Gen. 11:1)—is heretical to the spirit of the Law in that such a language establishes the strength of the human race independent of its relation to God. For the redactor of the tale, the common language is a condition for the construction of the tower, which in turn symbolizes precisely this linguistic universality. Beyond that, the tower can be considered as an original instance of writing in the broad sense of the word, as the trace or inscription of meaning in material form: "[L]et us make a name, lest we be scattered abroad upon the face of the whole earth" (11:4). The Tower of Babel is thus the concrete institution of the name erected against the permanent danger of effacement; it bears the same relation to an original human diaspora as writing does to memory. But in addition to this centripetal force through which the tower would maintain community through geographical unity, the tower is also intended to establish the temporal continuity of the name, that is, to secure a unified genealogical descent of the human race as a single nation against the declension of the race into different peoples that will meet only to wage war on one another. The building of the tower, though presented as an act of hubris, is, at least from a modern perspective, heroic in the way that it testifies to humankind's supreme effort to escape its tragic destiny. The nature of this effort is that of the *translation* of a common language into the concrete form of the tower; in other words, the story gives expression to the dream of an ideal unity of the purely symbolic medium of language with the concrete medium of architecture. The aim of this union is to endow linguistic meaning with the fixity and permanence of a solid edifice. It is in effect a dream of truth in its character both as the unity of a universal language and as permanence, as the imperishable monument to that unity. The intention is thus to make of human solidarity a truth, independent of that received in the Law, that will protect mankind from dispersion, difference, and enmity: "lest we be scattered abroad upon the face of the earth." The tragic irony, of course, is that humankind's attempt to prevent its own dispersion is the very cause of that dispersion.

The abandonment of the tower shatters not just the dream of human solidarity but also the dream of permanent meaning symbolized by the translation of language into brick. As the universal language of truth cannot be "written in stone," mankind is condemned to an infinity of approximations to that truth in the form of literary production. The story can thus be read as an allegory of the origin of literature, for in the resulting confusion of languages we find the fundamental conditions of literary meaning. The multiplicity of languages condemns humankind to an eternity of translations from one language to another. But this state of affairs also implies the multiplicity of meanings even in a single language, thus giving possibility to figuration, allegory, metaphor, ambiguity, and all the elements of discontinuity and difference, as well as the ceaseless striving for unity, that constitute literary expression. The destruction of the tower adds to this logic of difference one of incompletion: the literary work is never fully achieved, never totally unified and finished in the production of its meaning, just as the architectural work reaches its state of divine perfection in the sky only in the holy city of biblical Revelation. On earth, the artwork still strives, like the tower of Babel, to touch heaven.

And yet the meaning of the story remains ambiguous: the divine imposition of confusion that it relates is itself confusing. If, according to Judeo-Christian doctrine, the story should teach us humility before the will of God, it also fails to suppress a counterdoctrinal motif that affirms the possibilities of human solidarity based on a common language that renders humanity capable of constructing its own future. But this is not the only source of confusion. Yet another dimension of the story corresponds to a particularly modern vision of the human condition. Maurice Blanchot calls "tragic thought" that form of thinking that is conscious of all the contradictions of our existence. In his own tragic and eloquent formulation he speaks of

> le malheur d'une pensée qui n'a rien où commencer et qui se dissipe d'un infini à l'autre, cette ambiguïté dans laquelle nous nous disséminons, ne demeurant pas, allant et venant sans cesse, toujours ici et là, et cependant nulle part [. . .], c'est la suite d'une obscurité dispersée, répandue et comme errante, que nous n'avons pas eu la force de fixer. (*L'Entretien* 138)

> *the ill-fortune of a thought that, having no bearings, loses itself in one infinity after another; this ambiguity by which we waste ourselves in a coming and going without rest, always here and there and yet nowhere. . . , it comes from a surrounding, widespread, and wandering darkness that we have not had the strength to master.*

The story of Babel gives ancient expression to this tragic thought; the active presence of a jealous God does little to dissipate the sense of darkness and confusion as the people, their city and tower abandoned, are scattered abroad on the face of the earth (11:9). This tragic thought lies at the origin of poetic expression and remains as a kind of latent content that, as we shall see, comes to the surface in the modern literature of ruin, the fragment, and homelessness.

The story of Ithaca and the story of Babel are the two universal, foundational myths in the human architectural imagination. They also present two essential but distinct analogies between architecture and the literary text. In the first instance, as we have seen, Homer's epic in its transmission of cultural value has a function analogous to that of the ancestral house rooted in the earth, like the Black Forest house that Heidegger will celebrate as ordered in such as way as to "let earth and heaven, divinities and mortals enter *in simple oneness* into things" (*Poetry* 160). When we remember the *Odyssey* as a book of wanderings, we may forget that only the first part recounts the voyages of its hero, and much of it is told by Odysseus himself in the safety of the house of Alkinoös. The entire second half of the epic takes place at Ithaca, and concerns the lengthy work of reestablishing the order of patrimony, patriarchy, conjugal rights, and domesticity—in a word, the entire social order that has deteriorated during Odysseus's absence. The *Odyssey* is at the origin of a conservative literary tradition that affirms the place of the master of the house, fidelity of the wife, veneration of the elderly, peaceable succession of property from father to son, defense against foreign decadence, and respect for law and the gods. The bedchamber rooted in the earth is an architectural synecdoche for all of these values that one finds, in one form or another, in the history of literature from Vergil to Jane Austen. To borrow another formula from Heidegger, Homer gathers the world together and takes the measure of humankind's existence between heaven and earth; the epic represents an act of building (*bauen*) designed to "cherish and protect, to preserve and care for" social being (*Poetry* 147).

The implied analogy between writing and architecture in the Babel story gives no such reassurance. The construction of the tower as the making of a name may be understood as literature's fundamental project of fixing the truth of human existence as durable meaning, but the name given is Babel, confusion, a name that cancels the name and confounds the construction of language as an adequate measure for existence. Moreover, it is not just the construction of the name told by the tale of Babel that provides an analogy between the tower and writing; it is also the tale itself that remains in a sense unfinished, unable to resolve the inherent conflict between a jealous God and a people aspiring to do "everything they have imagined to do" (11:6)—unable, finally, to master the darkness toward which it gestures. In its dream of an ideal unity arising out of invention and daring construction, the story of Babel stands at the origin of a long literary tradition of revolt but also one of disillusion and exile, and of the truth of the absence of truth, from the *tour abolie* of Nerval's "El desdichado" to the ruins against which T. S. Eliot has shored the fragments of *The Waste Land.*

Analogical Constructions

My reading of the *Odyssey* sees an allegorical relation between, on one hand, the building and habitation of the house and, on the other, the recital and transmission of the epic. My reading of the Babel narrative takes the position that the abandoned tower allegorizes not just the problem of meaning in language but also the problem of truth in literature. In both cases the allegorical relation is made possible only by means of reference to art's "symptomatic" relation to other cultural forms, such as the institutions that ensure social continuity or those, more enigmatic, that express an essential uncertainty concerning the nature of man's relation to the metaphysical realm. However, another mode of the relation between literary and architectural meaning is provided by the Middle Ages. In his classic study, *Gothic Architecture and Scholasticism* (1951), Erwin Panofsky has shown how medieval scholastic writings such as Bonaventure's *Itinerarium Mentis ad Deum* (The Mind's Road to God, 1259) and Thomas Aquinas's *Summa Theologica* (1272) are written according to a set of ordering principles that makes them analogous in form and content to the religious architecture of the same period.

The *Summa,* for example, provides a systematic exposition of Christian theology in a series of treatises on subjects ranging from the Creation to the Last Things. Aquinas's work is the culmination of a scholastic tradition based on the rhetorical procedures of enumeration, articulation, and interrelation. The *enumeration* of a sufficient number of elements of the subject, for example, the various forms of fortitude and temperance, ensures the *totality* of the work in its scope. The *articulation* of the work organizes its subjects according to a system of homologous parts, whereas the *interrelation* of elements ensures both the proper distinction among things and the rational process of deduction. In the thirteenth century these elements of division were refined, so that the successive chapters of a work treated not just different aspects of a subject but also followed a disciplined order that led the reader from one proposition to the next so as to make the progress of the argument clear. Far from being a soulless machine of exposition, however, scholastic prose is often infused with rhetorical figures, suggestive analogies, balanced periods, and elegant turns of phrase. Panofsky selects for admiration the following passage from Bonaventure's *Commentaries on the Sentences of Peter Lombard* (1252), arguing for religious images to be admitted into places of worship as a way of focusing and concentrating faith, "propter simplicium rudimentatem, propter affectuum tarditatem, propter memoriae labilitatem." The brilliant condensation of these lines can hardly be rendered in English: "because simple persons have only rudimentary skills, because the affections are slow to take form, because memory is unpredictable" (*Architecture gothique* 92).[4] As these formal procedures suggest, scholastic writing was fundamentally based on the principle of *manifestatio* or the clarification of its subject. Faith itself was to be made clear by an appeal to reason, reason by an appeal to imagination, and imagination by an appeal to the senses (99).

It is at this point that the analogy between scholastic thought and religious architecture also becomes clear. The cathedrals of the thirteenth century, like the scholastic treatises, were constructed in order to make *visible* the whole of Christian faith through abundant enumeration in the form of saintly images and scenes from the life of Christ, as well as through functional architectural elements such as the baptismal font, the tombs of the faithful, and the altar on which the bread and wine of the host are placed. As Dominique Iogna-Prat has shown, this material realization and spatialization of the sacred became possible only after the long controversy over the meaning of the Eucharist was resolved in favor of its transformation into the real substance (rather than the symbol) of the body of Christ, a sacrament whose ritual nature required an edifice worthy of its miraculous nature. Thus it was not until the ninth century that the sacraments of the Church were thought to require a church building consecrated for the purpose of their celebration.[5] The interior space of this edifice had to be ordered and "ritualized" to accommodate the various elements of liturgy entailed by the sacraments (176). The Church as an institution, like its doctrine, thus became real in the "petrified" form of the church building (275). There is, moreover, a similarity between the ritual of Baptism and the ceremony for the consecration of a church, and medieval discourses on the nature of the individual Christian compare this person to the architecture of the Temple or Tabernacle (582). The relation between ecclesiastical thought and architecture is here more profound than one of simple analogy: the church building is doctrine substantialized, the word made stone.

Like the elements of scholastic thought, the architectural elements of the cathedral are articulated according to formally homologous orders such as statues, stained-glass images, arches, vaults, lateral chapels, columns, and capitals. This division of architectural space is strict and precise; chapels, columns, and windows, for example, are uniform in size and symmetrically arranged, then subdivided into smaller but equally uniform components. Finally, the interrelation of these elements is organized in order to favor the movement from one point to the next in a manner intended to reconcile the logic of reason with the mystery of faith. Let us briefly take the example of Notre-Dame d'Amiens. The principles of order and clarity are initially announced in the approach to the western facade, which is divided into three porches devoted (from left to right) to Saint Firmin as the first Christian missionary to Amiens, to Christ as Emmanuel or "God with us," and to the Virgin Mary as the figure of merciful intercession in human life. Architecturally, these three porches function as a cross section of the sanctuary, its nave flanked by arcades on either side. One enters the main portal under the statue of Christ, whose body and princely bearing signify the *way* of faith. Inside the nave, the strong vertical thrust of columns and vaulting carries the eye toward the light, whereas the forward thrust of the axis directs one's steps forward toward the altar. On the way one passes over the gravestones of Evrard de Fouilloy and Geoffroy d'Eu, the two bishops who built the edifice, thus coming into contact, as it were, with the history of the cathedral and its great examples of faith. Halfway down the center aisle, one steps onto the labyrinth of inlaid marble. In *The Bible of Amiens* Ruskin affirms that to the Christians of the thirteenth century this design was "an emblem of noble human life, straitgaited, narrow-walled, with infinite darknesses and the 'inextricabilis error' on either hand—and in the depth of it, the brutal nature to be conquered" (XXXIII:136).[6] In the narrative logic produced by this eastward movement through the cathedral, there is an element of suspense belonging to this passage "into" the labyrinth and out the other side. For once one has left this space of confusion behind, one stands directly before the altar of Saint Denis, apostle to the Gauls, and the place of the sacrament, which represents the essential function of the cathedral. The entire movement from the western entrance to the central altar constitutes a performance, in time and space, of the measured narrative and logical movement of a work like Bonaventure's *The Mind's Road to God.* In the book the spiritual journey is a figure, but in the cathedral the light of heaven shining through the clerestory literally shows the way to the place of communion with Christ.

Examples of the analogy between spiritual and natural light abound in scholastic writing, as in the verses of the Abbé Suger devoted to his renovation of the Basilica of Saint-Denis, frequently cited as the first great example of Gothic architecture. Some of these verses celebrated the brilliant light that Suger's tall new windows let into the basilica.

Aula micat medio clarificata suo
Claret enim claris quod clare concopulatur,
Et quod perfundit lux nova, claret opus Nobile.

The Church shines from its illuminated center
For luminous is that which enlightenment joins with light
And luminous is the noble edifice filled with the new light. (quoted in
    Panofsky 42)

As Panofsky points out, the richness and beauty of Suger's renovations flew in the face of the Romanesque asceticism of the monastic tradition. But figurative language of the kind employed in his verses enabled Suger to defend his architectural renovations on more than just aesthetic grounds; a formula such as *lux nova* interprets the new clarity and visibility of Gothic architecture with the new light of Christ's advent announced in the Gospel. This interpretation of architectural form in a spiritual sense belongs to the scholastic mode of "anagogical" interpretation, literally that which sees the things of this world in the light of a higher truth. Dante writes in the *Convivio* (1307) that the anagogical mode elevates the things of literal apprehension to a level beyond the senses so that they signify "le superne cose de l'etternal Gloria," the supernal things of eternal glory (II:1).

Dante's *Commedia* (1304–21) also shows its sources in the scholastic tradition through its systematic articulation of space according to an orderly exposition of divine justice that nonetheless recognizes that divine grace, like the being of God himself, is beyond human reason. In the tradition of scholastic discourse, the *Inferno* aspires to totality in its enumeration of every kind of sin, with the division of sins into different classes according to the nature of the offense against God, mankind, or self; it organizes the various forms of punishment corresponding to these sins into architecturally homologous spaces, and, by means of Dante's descent though these spaces, the passage from one point to the next figures as a series of stages in the poet's progressive understanding of divine judgment. The successive terraces of hell correspond to the deadly sins; their relative depth in the earth, or distance from God in heaven, is determined by the gravity of offense to Him represented in the sin, whereas the same sins in reverse order but repented give a similar meaning to the series of ascending terraces on the mountain of purgatory. Dante's verse is everywhere dedicated to the lucid exposition of this architectural topography, which in turn illuminates his understanding in measurable ways as he advances through each stage of his journey.

As if to emphasize its architectural otherness, the City of Dis, or lower hell, is built of mosques (*meschite*) illuminated not by the light of heaven but by that of the flames that torment its sinners—here those who have sinned not from weakness, like those in the upper hell, but wilfully, through violence, fraud, and treachery. The fraudulent suffer in a concentric series of ten ditches (*bolge*) dug into descending terraces connected by bridges over which Dante passes, marking out in architectural form his successive comprehension of each punishment. In the eighth *bolge* of this region Dante finds a Ulysses who has not returned home and who burns in hell for false counsel, that is, for convincing his men to flee from their duties in the pursuit of experience for its own sake: "a divenir del mondo esparto" (XXVI:98). As the space of hell narrows with Dante's descent, the light grows dimmer and the movement of the sinners is ever more restricted. At the very bottom, the poet Dante has put an architect: the giant Nimrod (Gen. 10:8–10) stands half buried in a ditch, from which he utters savage, incomprehensible syllables. This is his punishment for having, according to medieval exegesis, designed the Tower of Babel, through which "wicked device" the world is linguistically divided. For Nimrod, "every language is to him as his to others, which is known to none" (XXXI:80–81).[7] One imagines that the depth of his place in hell is at least equal to the height of the tower he tried to build. In hell Nimrod is one of the guards of Satan, who is perceived only through what appears to be a thick fog. Once the "bright star" of heaven, Satan is now paralyzed, frozen in the ice of Cocytus. All of these images show the extent to which the architecture of the *Inferno* constitutes an anticathedral. The space made for the sinners in hell is in every way antithetical to the space reserved for the faithful in the sanctuary of a Gothic church. The downward movement of hell into ever narrower and darker space, where the sinner has ever less freedom of movement, is in direct opposition to the freedom of horizontal movement in a cathedral penetrated by light, and the thrust upward toward the source of that light. The symmetry of these antithetical spaces, however, is entirely in keeping with scholastic writing in its comprehension of the universe as a systematic order.

In the postface to his translation of Panofsky, Bourdieu notes that the great art historian was not content simply to draw parallels and influences between scholastic thought and Gothic architecture. Rather, he identified a way of thinking common to both endeavors that existed at an unconscious level in the individual as well as in medieval culture at large. Bourdieu, however, takes a step beyond Panofsky's "synthetic intuition" when it comes to the question of how scholastic writing and architecture respectively produce meaning. Ultimately, Bourdieu says, meaning is a function of the patterns of thought, perception, and action in which the work is produced and interpreted: the *habitus*. These patterns themselves belong to a concrete system of social relations that define which objects need to be interpreted as well as the conditions under which interpretation takes place. Scholastic thought and Gothic architecture were thus intimately related movements that had a concrete, identifiable cause in the institutions that taught scholastic thinking (*Postface* 147). In contrast to the monasteries of the early Middle Ages, most of which were isolated in rural regions, schools like that of Abélard at Sainte-Geneviève were attached to bishoprics in the urban centers of Europe. The urbanity of such schools, as well as a rational way of thinking more suited to the secular world than the mystic tradition of the monks, contributed to the formation of a cultural *modus operandi* that can be seen not just in architecture and poetry but, as Robert Marichal has shown, even in the style of manuscript copying (Panofsky 152–56).

The objection that can be made to any such socially deterministic view is that art always preserves a measure of autonomy that is essential to its very definition as art. Bourdieu himself makes this objection in *Outline of a Theory of Practice,* published just four years after his translation of Panofsky, where he points out that not everything in artistic production is available to interpretation into other codes, that something in art always consists of "pure practice," as in dance or ritual, and always contains something "ineffable" and "pleases (or displeases) without concepts" (2). This objection, however, does not discredit the theory that the interpretation of art, and thereby artistic meaning, is conditioned by social relations; it only says that something in the work always escapes such interpretation. We are then faced with the paradox that modes of thinking and acting perfectly meaningful in themselves, like those of the scholastic tradition, can produce something that cannot be fully explained within the interpretative framework of those codes, like the poetic art of Dante's *Commedia* or the effect of the light that streams in through the clerestory at Saint-Denis. There need be no mysticism here; rather it is enough to recognize the fact that certain elements of the artwork escape interpretation because of their unique or exceptional nature, that is, they remain unavailable to existing models of interpretation simply because of the limitations of those modes and because of the singularity of the artwork itself. Bourdieu's understanding of individual artistic genius is similarly demythologizing: each artist occupies his own *habitus* of creative activity, whose function lies in the unification and unfolding of the ensemble of practices that constitute his or her own existence (164); the very singularity of this creative practice alone may account for whatever degree of alterity it possesses in the context of prevailing models of interpretation. Dante's singularity lies not just in the brilliance of his poetic invention but also in his singular existence at the intersection of the various systems of meaning produced by scholastic philosophy, the lay teachings of Brunetto Latini, the poetic traditions of the troubadours and other lyric poets of the *trecento,* Florentine politics, and the history of the Holy Roman Empire. If the architecture of the *Commedia* and the distribution of its inhabitants are inspired by scholastic thinking, the exceptional nature of Dante's art lies in the way he is able to combine that tradition with the world of the thirteenth century as seen from the unique vantage point of his personal trajectory through that world.

House Ideologies

The English country house poem, a minor genre best represented by Ben Jonson's ode "To Penshurst" (1612), celebrates the architectural and landed estate of a person of rank to whom the poet wishes to pay homage for his patronage. As material for examining the kinds of meaning produced by bringing literature into relation with architecture, this genre has the advantage of being limited in time and space to England in the seventeenth century.[8] In contrast to the material considered so far in this introduction, the country house poem, along with its architectural subject, represents neither a foundational myth nor an institutionalized system of thought but rather an *ideology.* The concept of ideology has its own history, beginning with Destutt de Tracy's study of "the generation of ideas" in 1796 and acquiring new importance in Marx's *Die deutsche Ideologie* of 1845. However, if we take Louis Althusser's well-known twentieth-century definition of this concept, ideology is the representation of the imaginary relation between individuals and their real conditions of existence. Insofar as this representation consists in the production of language, practice, and other concrete manifestations, ideology also has its own material existence (38–41).

Ideology differs from the universality of Homeric or biblical myth in belonging to a particular set of social relations in a historically specific context. It differs from a system of thought like medieval scholasticism, however, in its unsystematic character, its relative independence from rational thought, and its capacity to tolerate internal contradictions; as Althusser emphasizes, it represents an imaginary, not a real, relation between the subject and the conditions of his or her existence. The meaning of *ideology* here is close to the specifically modern sense of *mythology* that we find in Benjamin. The ideology of the country house poem gives literary form to an entire series of imaginary relations: between the poet and his patron, between the patron and his estate, between the estate and the natural landscape, between the estate and the surrounding social and political universe. All of these relations are real in themselves, but they figure in the poem in imagined ways made possible by an ideology to which the poem is able to appeal as something beyond its own invention. The house that the poem takes as its subject is already a three-dimensional representation of the ideology on which the poem will draw. In this sense the architecture of the house, though material in the most substantial sense, also represents the imagined relation of its owner to his world and time. A familiar problem in the study of ideology lies in what we might call the bagginess of its contents, which lack well-defined limits as to what they include and whose relative weight cannot be precisely measured. Nonetheless it is possible to identify in the country house poem a few central ideas: those, for example, of property, propriety, legitimacy, domestic harmony, and a productive relation to the natural landscape and the peasantry. In keeping with other strains in Renaissance philosophy, this little utopian world is built very much on the scale of man and has an exemplary man at its center. The house and its estate are understood to be extensions of his noble person and qualities. As we shall see, however, this representation of imaginary relations can reveal internal tensions arising out of its difference from real conditions.

Penshurst, in Kent, was in 1612 the country seat of Sir Robert Sidney, Viscount Lisle, a member of the court of King James. The original house, built by a wealthy draper in the 1340s, consisted of a feudal Great Hall, which now stands at the center of the edifice. The Sidney family was granted title to the house by Edward VI in 1552, and it was only then that were added the outer constructions, including crenellated fortifications that were more ornamental than a practical means of defense. These additions conformed to the traditional "English" style, what would later be called Gothic, while resisting the classical style of new houses like Longleat in Wiltshire (now an African safari park). In "To Penshurst" Jonson portrays Penshurst Place as the center of an ordered, harmonious world that reflects the virtues and especially the hospitality of its lord and lady. Beginning with a general survey of the property, Jonson addresses the house as an "ancient pile" not built for "envious show" but nonetheless "reverenced" while more ostentatious houses are merely "grudged" admiration. Here Jonson enumerates all that Penshurst lacks: rich materials of marble and touchstone, a row of polished pillars, a roof of gold, a noble stair and courtyard. Instead the house is made "fair" by its natural surroundings of soil, air, woods, and water, including the tree planted to celebrate the birth in 1554 of the house's most illustrious inhabitant, the poet and courtier Sir Philip Sidney. In calling the house an "ancient pile," Jonson willingly participates in the fiction that the Sidneys are a family of ancient lineage, whereas their nobility and title to the house are of recent date (1552) and the only part of the house itself that can be considered "ancient" is the Great Hall at its core. At the same time, Jonson shifts the poem's attention away from history and onto the house's favorable position at the center of a concentric universe whose spheres include garden, pond, forest, fields, and river. The principle is that the culture of an ordered English tradition emanates from the center outward, from noble house to tamed wilderness.

In a manner similar to the poem's opening apology for the house's lack of outward splendor, its construction of humble "country stone," limestone quarried nearby, finds compensation in the fact that such stones have been raised without ruin or suffering and that "There's none that dwell about them wish them down." Here we move inside the Great Hall, where the goodwill of the Sidneys is reflected in their hospitality toward neighboring countrymen and the poet himself, relieved to find that no one counts the cups he drinks and that he is free to eat his fill without having to suffer disapproving looks. The general order being celebrated is one in which distinctions between culture and nature, as well as those of the social order, are maintained without being erected as barriers: the relation between house and field or lord and gardener is certainly hierarchical, but it is also one of mutual benefit. By the same token, the largesse of which the poet so freely partakes may be measured in proportion to the praise he lavishes. The poem concludes with praise of the family's piety and domestic economy, while returning to the rhetorical mode of the opening by making a final comparison with other houses.

Now, Penshurst, they that will proportion thee,
With other edifices, when they see
Those proud, ambitious heaps, and nothing else,
May say, their lords have built, but thy lord dwells. (99–102)

The language of "dwelling" imparts a sense of permanence not otherwise obvious, while the qualities of domestic economy, hospitality, and decorum possessed by the Sidney household grant the family a legitimacy that makes up for the newness of their title. Jonson's poem belongs to an age in which personal and social merit have begun to count more than ancient lineage; we are, after all, at the home of Sir Philip Sidney, the consummate Renaissance man.

Several commentators have observed, however, that the idyllic vision of Penshurst conveyed in the poem is rather at odds with the real circumstances under which it was written, and that the poem's congenial tone is marked by subtle misgivings.[9] What stands out most clearly is Jonson's thinly veiled opinion of the mediocrity of Penshurst as an architectural structure, despite the efforts of its present and former owners to improve it. Throughout the poem, the material and design of the house are presented as difficulties to be overcome rather than as things to be celebrated in themselves. The poet's own place in the house, moreover, is evidently ambiguous. His relief at not having every cup of wine counted bespeaks his position as a guest rather humbler than those of Sidney's own rank and suggests that he is accustomed to being treated less well at other noble houses. Finally, the poem's picture of abundance and prosperity created by wise economy is directly contradicted by what we know about Robert Sidney's affairs at this time. His letters show that he believed himself to be on the brink of ruin and that in order to improve his prospects he considered enlarging his estate in the hope that the king could be persuaded to hunt there. The scheme was discouraged by his steward, Thomas Golding, who reminded him of his "great and continual wants" while observing that "this part of the country is not pleasant nor sportely" and therefore not likely to attract royal hunters (Riggs 184–85).[10] Like the poem, the architecture of the house itself represents an imaginary relation to its own history. The crenellated towers, for example, call up images of the chivalric Middle Ages, whereas they were added in the mid–sixteenth century when such fortifications were no longer needed; they are thus merely "decorative and deliberately anachronistic" (Wayne 101). Don Wayne also points out that the asymmetry of the North Front is based on Henry Sidney's decision at the same period to move the main gate and King's Tower slightly east of center in order to provide a clear view through a series of arches from the outer entrance to the Great Hall at the center of the building. The visitor is thus led to look past the relatively recent additions to the house, while directing his or her attention to its most ancient and authentic part (100–101). Finally, a coat of arms and inscription placed in 1585 above the arch of the main entrance commemorates the granting of the estate to the family by Edward VI. Wayne argues that through this device the Sidneys' pedigree and property rights are implicitly attached to those of the House of Tudor; the recent lineage of the Sidneys is metaphorically extended into the more ancient and prestigious lineage of the Tudors, thus supplying whatever degree of legitimacy might be lacking in the inhabitants of Penshurst (104). When Jonson's poem is added to Sidney's house, the ideology of the country house is shown to consist of a double-layered representation: the poem represents the house, which is already a representation of a mythic past. This representation of representation is the essence of ideology. As for the production of meaning, it takes place at two stages in two respective media. While the architecture of the house reinterprets the past in its own terms, this interpretation is reinterpreted in turn by the language of the poem. The production of meaning, however, does not move only in one direction, for as history has shown, the poem provides the basis for yet other interpretations of the house, as witnessed by the text of a modern tourist brochure in which traces of Jonson's vision remain: "Penshurst Place is one of England's finest historic houses set in the Weald of Kent's peaceful rural landscape. Built of local sandstone, the medieval house with its magnificent Barons Hall dates from 1341 and is one of the finest examples of fourteenth century architecture. Later additions have seen Penshurst Place grow into an imposing defended manor house, containing staterooms filled with a remarkable collection of tapestries, paintings, furniture, porcelain and armour."[11]

A century later, Jonson's poem served as inspiration for a variation on its genre in a more modern cultural and architectural context, in which the ideology of the country house gave way to the ideology of the suburban villa. Alexander Pope's "Epistle to Richard Boyle, Earl of Burlington" (1731) was occasioned by Burlington's publication of the architectural drawings of Andrea Palladio, but it also celebrated the spirit of Chiswick House, the Palladian villa that Burlington had recently built on his estate outside of London. The form of the verse epistle, borrowed from Latin models, was relatively new in English, but was particularly suited to Pope's subject and circumstances. Pope's epistle is both private and public, being addressed to a person of eminence but intended for publication insofar as that person is a public figure whose works and manner of life provide a model for the cultural values that the poet seeks to promote. The tone of the epistle is at once informal and philosophical. It has the character of urbane conversation, yet it remains highly ordered both in its argument and in its verse form of rhyming couplets. In these respects the verse epistle imitates both the form and function of the Palladian villa, conceived as a place of occasional retreat from the pressures of the city but also as a semipublic place where guests could be invited for enlightened conversation. Like the poem, the architecture of the villa combines informality with rational order. The design of Chiswick House was based on two of Palladio's villas, La Rotonda at Vicenza and the Villa Foscari near Venice. Burlington's villa has an air of informality in its modest size, its festively decorated rooms, its rusticated podium, and its pavilionlike openness onto the surrounding park. The rational order of the house, however, is communicated by its symmetrical distribution, its hexastyle portico in the Corinthian order, and the octagonal drum of its stately dome. In the spirit of lively conversation among neighbors, Pope's epistle is in fact written from one suburban retreat to another, as the poet himself had built his own villa in nearby Twickenham a dozen years earlier.

The ideology of the villa shares with that of the seventeenth-century country house the values of propriety and decorum, but it treats these concepts more in terms of taste and rational judgment than in those of property and domestic economy. The emphasis is on creating an architectural counterpart to enlightened human understanding rather than on a house that reflects the position of its owners in the social and natural order. In keeping with this distinction, the villa is a *maison de plaisance,* recently constructed and more visited than lived in, in contrast to the country house as an ancestral home and a durable habitation with its own economy. Chiswick House, for example, has no kitchen or proper bedrooms; in Burlington's day the business of living had to be carried on in the adjoining house, to which the villa is connected by a gallery. Finally, the neoclassical values of decorum, moderation, clarity, and reason embodied in the Palladian villa were best expressed in a suburban setting, a position of relative neutrality with respect to the ways of court, the town, and the rural countryside. Both its form and its geographic situation made the Palladian villa a fitting symbol for the values that Pope wished to convey. Architecturally, the villa was independent of traditional English style, instead combining references to classical antiquity and Renaissance enlightenment. Geographically, it stood between but outside of the traditional centers of power in London and Hampton Court. It was thus ideal for the representation of a new way of thinking and living: cosmopolitan and free of faction and thus capable of serving as the model for a new cultural order.

Formally modeled on the Horatian satire, much of Pope's epistle directs its irony at the newly rich, who follow architectural fashion without understanding or "good sense." Burlington has too many imitators who are

> Proud to catch cold at a Venetian door;
> Conscious they act a Palladian part. (70)

In what amounts to a catalog of bad taste, the most ruthless lines are reserved for the immensely wealthy "Timon," in whom some have seen a caricature of the Duke of Chandos, owner of the ostentatious Cannons House in Middlesex, built at incredible expense by five different architects and representing a barbaric union of the baroque and Palladian styles. At Timon's villa everything is grand in scale, but "Soft and agreeable come never there" (70). In this villa the poet finds a study with expensively bound books but no signs of learning; a chapel with lavish decoration but no signs of piety. The great marble hall of the dining room is the scene of abundance without pleasure or hospitality.

> Is this a dinner? this a genial room?
> No, 'tis a temple, and a hecatomb. (72)

What distinguishes Burlington's projects from this vulgarity is his good sense, in which the rational imperative of function or "use" is combined with a taste for the pleasing variety found in nature.

Thus far the poem is a particularly witty and amusing expression of neoclassical principles already put forth more soberly in Boileau, and more urbanely in Addison. However, what distinguishes Pope's epistle is the manner in which he extends the qualities of Palladianism beyond the construction of the villa in order to envision the new construction of Britain itself. Such was the purpose of Burlington's various architectural projects and publications. The conclusion to Pope's poem recommends that the principles embodied in these projects be applied throughout the kingdom to the construction of churches or "temples," public ways, harbors, moles, and other "imperial works." Such "honours" bring peace to a "happy Britain." In order to understand the implications of what in these lines may seem at best an expression of goodwill, and at worst mere flattery, we need to recall something of the context in which Pope, a Catholic commoner with Tory leanings, is writing to Burlington, a Whiggish Protestant nobleman. Britain in the early eighteenth century is slowly emerging from a violent past, recent in memory, of regicide, revolution, and disruption in the orderly succession of its monarchs. Pope's friend Bolingbroke, exiled for his Jacobite sympathies, had by 1730 returned to England, but factionalism and the threat of rebellion against the Hanoverian King George I remained real. The conflict between Hanoverians and Jacobites was complicated by those between Tories and Whigs and between traditional landed interests and the emerging mercantile class. Pope's call for "peace to happy Britain" would therefore have had a political, as well as a cultural, resonance for his immediate audience. In effect, his poem promotes an ideology of national reconciliation based on the principles of good sense and public service, with Britain itself as the new edifice to be built in the same congenial spirit that reigns in the Palladian villa. Like the villa, the nation must be free of constraining traditions, possess a rational harmony among its constituent parts, use its natural resources to advantage, and figure itself as one of the "pleasures of the imagination" defined by the genial Addison. In Pope's ideology, a peaceful and happy Britain can only be the constructed product of an enlightened understanding.

III

If a certain apocalyptic tone marks much of what is written today on architecture and culture at large, the sources of what has been called the modern crisis of meaning are commonly located somewhere near the end of the eighteenth century. One of the important urban phenomena of that time was the opening up or outright destruction of the walls and gates that divided the city from the surrounding countryside. Such formations had for centuries served the ends of both military defense and taxation by exacting tolls on countrymen entering the city to sell their produce. The French Revolution destroyed or rendered inoperative such barriers around Paris. The destruction of these barriers, along with architectural symbols of the ancien régime such as the prison of the Bastille, was accompanied by the effacement of boundaries and the dismantling of hierarchies in every sphere of modern life. Paul Virilio notes the effect of the literal and figurative "city without gates" on the writing of history, where "the grand narratives of theoretical causality were displaced by the petty narratives of practical opportunity, and, finally, by the micro-narratives of opportunity"

(389). The "crisis of modernity" thus begins with the deterioration of common values and of the notion of the universal meaning of history, giving way to narratives of individual development. In a second stage of this breakdown, the problem becomes that of narrative form itself as mode of representation capable of describing and inscribing reality. Immediate reality is replaced with a *reality effect,* and the boundary is replaced with the screen (389). Virilio's analysis resonates with that of the architectural historian Manfredo Tafuri, who locates the onset of a "semantic crisis" marked by the disappearance of "public meaning" in architecture beginning in the late eighteenth century, one which continues to plague architectural theory today (231).

In the analyses of both Tafuri and Virilio one can sense a certain nostalgia for architectural and narrative meanings whose coherence derived from their reliable reflection of established order in the realms of politics, religion, economy, education—that is, all of the conditions under which architectural and literary forms are constructed. For Derrida, however, it is precisely the constructed nature of architecture and literature as concepts that needs to be brought to light. His essay on the Swiss architect Bernard Tschumi is worth citing here for the manner in which, by deconstructing the concept of architecture itself, it contributes to an understanding of what we mean by meaning in architecture. Given that architecture must have a meaning, this meaning is experienced in four principal ways. It is first experienced as the habitation of the *oikos,* the economic law that determines the way a building is ordered, occupied, and given value. Second, architectural order, whether of a house, a monument, or a city, is organized around a myth of origin—that of the founding fathers, the gods, and so on, and this myth continues to function as a centering principle even when it has passed out of conscious memory. Third, the economy of architecture remains tied to a teleology of the habitus: it is built to further some end, to render some service toward some ultimate goal of the polity. Finally, architecture belongs to the fine arts, whatever their fashion at the moment; it must reflect the values of beauty, harmony, and wholeness (*Psyché* 481–82). Derrida's point is that these attributes of architecture are too often mistaken for its essence. The architectural object, the mass of stone or the standing arrangement of glass or steel that we take for the thing itself, is in fact a kind of inscription that we can read only as part of a massively layered text of other written signs: "le texte volumineux d'écritures multiples" (486). The realization of this condition signals the end of architecture as it has been known and its assimilation to the larger universe of textuality.

What I want to suggest here is that the first signs of this realization, and of the end of traditional forms of architectural meaning as such, go back to the period of the late eighteenth and early nineteenth centuries. Among the effects of an emerging modernity in this period are a variety of manifestations that call both literary and architectural meanings into question. These include the aesthetic of the fragment, the value placed on subjective interiority, the significance given to the human body, the development of new materials and techniques, and a conception of the past in terms of stock or reserve. I shall consider each of these subjects briefly in turn.

Ruin and Fragmentation

The cult of architectural ruins can be traced at least as far back as the excavation of Herculaneum in the 1740s. It figures prominently in the visual arts and literature of the eighteenth and nineteenth centuries, and it survives long enough to provide striking images in poems like Eliot's *The Waste Land* (1922) and films like Tarkovsky's *Andrei Rublev* (1966). On one hand, the images of ruin so widely disseminated in pictures and literature themselves provide a metaphor for the breakdown in institutional structures of meaning that is characteristic of modernity. On the other hand, architectural ruins are nothing if not ambiguous, making it difficult to assign them any universal metaphorical value. The proliferation of meanings assigned to them is symptomatic of the fragmentary condition of architectural meaning itself. What artistic interpretations of ruin generally have in common, however, is a sense of modernity's enigmatic relation to the historical past. For example, Piranesi's *Le Antichità romane* (1756), an encyclopedic series of engravings of Roman ruins, is manifestly dedicated to the archaeological project of documenting the grandeur of ancient Rome in its concrete forms. However, even here his images have a suggestive power that ranges beyond their ostensible historical and scientific purpose. In these engravings, the Roman ruins are often juxtaposed with the hodgepodge of more recent structures that constitutes modern Rome, monuments from the Middle Ages, the Renaissance, and baroque periods lacking any coherent relation to one another. Such scenes are populated with figures of merchants, laborers, and domestic animals pursuing their daily rounds in evident ignorance of the sublimity that surrounds them. The overall effect is of a chaotic and fragmentary modernity that has lost the grandeur of the Roman past.[12] However, the confusion of the modern scene has to be considered apart from the monumental fragments of the ruins themselves. Piranesi treats various fragmentary forms—ruined walls, inscriptions, paving stones—as architectural objects in their own right. These, combined with drawings of the huge pulleys and iron grips by means of which marble blocks were lifted, give his work a strong sense of weight and volume, and of the dynamic relation between masses and surfaces. This concentration on the interrelation of geometric forms, volumes, and surfaces as concrete values in themselves works against a hierarchical tradition in architecture, which subordinates all the parts and forces of a building to a single, dominant principle. It marks an interest in the pure materiality of construction that will later prove important to modern architecture.

Chapter 4 of this work treats the subject of architectural ruin in relation to literary notions of allegory. Here it will be enough to point out that ruin's product, the fragment, has its counterparts both in the literary image and in literary form. Following a formulation introduced by Lucien Dällenbach, we can identify three historical forms of the modern fragment. The *classical* fragment of the eighteenth century is what remains of a lost totality, like the broken columns that Piranesi finds littering the Roman landscape, or, in the language of Diderot's *Encyclopédie,* "pieces detached from a whole, such as a capital, a cornice, part of a statue or bas-relief, found among ruins" (7:273). According to this conception, the literary fragment similarly is a piece missing from the whole, whether of an unfinished work or a completed work that cannot be wholly reconstituted. In both cases the fragment is the product of destruction, whether of the work itself or of the creative process that has left the work unfinished. The classical fragment is the residue or the vestige of time in its character as decline, chance, and catastrophe.

At the end of the eighteenth century, a new literary genre was introduced in the form of the *romantic* fragment as it appeared, for example, in August and Friedrich Schlegel's *Athenaeum* (1798–1800). The *Athenaeum* fragment was, paradoxically, created *as* a fragment. It remains a fragment in the sense that it belongs to some greater work not yet achieved but which exists, at least potentially, either in an ideal future or in a transcendent realm of being that our condition in time and space prevents us from fully realizing. Though made to be incomplete, the romantic fragment cannot be compared to the fake ruins, follies, and *fabriques* that dotted the grounds of eighteenth-century chateaus; it gestures not out of the past but toward the future, and its function, far from merely decorative, is to signify a collective human destiny. The romantic fragment is found elsewhere than in Germany, for example, in Coleridge's *Kubla Khan, or a Vision in a Dream: A Fragment,* first published in 1816. What is important about this form for our purposes is that at a historical moment of crisis in various domains—political, religious, social—the romantic fragment puts into question the notion of the work of art as a unified object. It does so through its willed incompletion and absence of development, through its lack of any obvious connection to other fragments with which it might be put together, and through the notion that its unity lies outside the object and even beyond the somewhat chance assemblage of fragments that made up a single issue of the *Athenaeum.*

What distinguishes the *contemporary* fragment from the classical and romantic forms is the absence of a totality, either past or future, real or ideal, of which it is part. If such a whole is conceivable, it nonetheless remains enigmatic, impossible to constitute. Blanchot's essay "Parole de fragment," on the poet René Char, is practically a manifesto for this form as being the most adequate to human reality in the twentieth century. Char's sentences consist of "islands of sense" juxtaposed rather than coordinated with one another. His images are extremely condensed, and succeed one another in an order lacking in apparent sequential logic. In these lines aptly named *paroles en archipel,* "words in archipelago," the overall sense is of the breaking apart and dislocation of language, but not in a negative sense. Blanchot compares Char's language to the exile and *dépaysement,* or "disorientation of meaning," rather than its negation or alienation, often resulting in a dazzling if enigmatic brilliance: "Le poème est l'amour realisé du désir demeuré désir" (the poem is the actualized love of desire that remains desire) (Char 73). It is Char who defends the difficulty of his poetry as the only possible form of response to what he calls "la nature tragique, intervallaire, saccageuse, comme en suspens, des humains" (the tragic, intervaled, wrecked, suspended nature of human beings) (Blanchot 451). But he also asks the rhetorical question "La réalité sans l'énergie disloquante de la poésie, qu'est-ce?" (What is reality without the dislocating energy of poetry?) (452).

An architectural counterpart to this kind of fragment is to be found in the twenty-five *folies* of Bernard Tschumi that punctuate at regular intervals the vast expanse of the Parc de la Villette in Paris. These constructions, not unrelated to the pagodas, pyramids, and other decorative buildings that decorated eighteenth-century gardens, are spaced at 120-meter intervals in a vast grid across the entire surface of the park, the former grounds of the Paris stockyards. Each *folie* consists initially of a concrete cube measuring 10.8 meters across on each side and covered with bright red steel plates. This form is then split into components that can be recombined or grafted onto ramps, canopies, stairways, and so on in a series of variations on a theme (Lavalou 24). The logic of the fragment works both at the level of the deconstruction of each *folie* and at that of the 55-hectare (136-acre) site, across which the objects are scattered but also unified by their color and material composition, as well as by the geometric uniformity of their form and placement. The analogy with Char's poetic compositions lies in the archipelagic nature of the project, consisting of a series of fragments held in suspension. Derrida comments on this project: "Une force ajointe et fait tenir ensemble le dis-joint comme tel. . . . Les points rouges espacent, ils maintiennent l'architecture dans la dissociation de l'espacement" (A force joins and holds together the disjointed as such. . . . The points of red space things out, they maintain the architecture in the dissociation of its spacing) (*Psyché* 490–92). Like Char's "words in archipelago," Tschumi's follies effectively render irrelevant the conventional distinction between fragment and whole.

Interiors

Architectural historians tell us that the nature of interior domestic space underwent a significant change in the period between the Renaissance and the nineteenth century. The fifteenth-century ideal of convenience favored an interior plan that allowed as much communication as possible between parts of the house. In *The Ten Books of Architecture* (1450), Leon Battista Alberti recommends placing doors "in such a manner that they may lead to as many parts of the edifice as possible."[13] As Robin Evans observes, rooms were thus connected to one another *en enfilade;* as paths within the house continually intersected, every activity was physically open to intercession, not to say interruption, by every other. Beginning in the seventeenth century this "matrix of interconnected chambers" was completely transformed by the introduction of hallways and passages to ensure privacy and independent access (64). The ideal of convenience now was for each room to have only a single door, so that the domestic interior changed from being "an architecture to look through" to being "an architecture to hide in" (74). By the eighteenth century, the notion of the self as being fashioned through cultivated intercourse with others, one that we see reflected in the Palladianism of Pope and Burlington, for example, was challenged by the rival notion of the self as a private entity to be cultivated in itself and as being in danger of contamination by contact with others.

In the eighteenth century the most striking example of this simultaneous intensification of subjective and architectural interiority is the series of etchings produced by Piranesi entitled *Invenzioni cappriciose di carceri* (Fanciful Images of Prisons).[14] In these extraordinary images, the vast interior spaces of the imaginary prisons are saturated with a profusion of sinister objects and frenzied human figures. The frontispiece of the 1761 edition is representative: the title of the work is shown engraved in the prison wall, where it is partly obscured by the machinery of torture in the foreground (fig. 1). On the wall above the title rests a human figure chained to a ledge, perched in midair, among a forest of beams, ropes, pulleys, wheels, spikes. A disturbing sense of disorientation is produced by extreme foreshortening, by chiaroscuro effects of light and shadow, and by catwalks and stairways crisscrossing spaces of immense height and depth. It is impossible for the viewer to grasp these interior spaces in the rational form of Cartesian space understood as the measurable extension of the object-world. Moreover, the *Carceri* brought about a striking contrast between conventional form and original content, using the large-format (545 × 410 mm) plates traditionally reserved for academic architectural designs to produce images that were to become paradigmatic figures for the depths of the unconscious (Ficacci 56).

This is the space that seizes Thomas De Quincey's imagination in his *Confessions of an Opium-Eater* (1856). There, he tells of how Coleridge described Piranesi's "dreams" (i.e., the *Carceri*) to him as a series of "vast Gothic halls; on the floor of which stood mighty engines and machinery . . . expressive of great power put forth, or resistance overcome" (*Works* 2:259). This fantastic vision has Piranesi himself hopelessly climbing stairway after stairway, like some lost romantic Sisyphus in the prisons of his own imagination. De Quincey comments, "With the same power of endless growth and self-reproduction did my architecture proceed in dreams" (2:259).[15] It is fitting that Coleridge should have introduced De Quincey to this work, as the imagery of fathomless depths already belongs to the poet's repertoire in poems such as *Kubla Khan*, which evokes a dreamlike landscape with "caverns measureless to man," a mighty fountain amid whose waters burst "huge fragments vaulted like rebounding hail," and a visionary pleasure dome whose imagined construction stands as a metaphor for the ideal object of the poet's art. What Piranesi, Coleridge, and De Quincey have in common is a highly architecturalized conception of the inner world of the imagination, one that demonstrates in an ex-

Fig. 1. Giovanni Battista Piranesi, *Carceri d'invenzione di G. Battista Piranesi*, from *Carceri in Opere varie di architettura, prospettive, grotteschi, antichità*, frontispiece, 1761.

tremely vivid manner the reflective freedom of romantic art in contrast to the classical imitation of nature. In effect, this architectural imagery gives a kind of objective, concrete form to an inner world that is in fact wholly subjective and ontologically indistinct.

The oniric flights of imagination that we witness in romantic art can be understood in the general context of a modern condition based on the primacy of the individual subject in such disparate domains as those of political rights, the juridical order, philosophical discourse, and artistic creation. As Jürgen Habermas shows, however, the institution of the subject as a self-reflective entity developed in Kant's philosophy failed to function as a force of social and cultural unification. On the contrary, human knowledge was divided into the distinct realms of science, morality, and art, each with its own form of truth, while all of these "spheres of knowing" were separated from both the sphere of faith and that of everyday, practical life (19). In this sense the impulse toward an ever deeper interiority in romantic art can be seen as the effect of a more general fragmentation in the structures of human thought. In the architectural order there were analogous phenomena both of fragmentation and of the separation between interior and exterior spaces. Increasingly, for example, artisans in the cities no longer lived over a shop, but instead traveled to a factory in order to earn their daily wage. For the working class, the place of domestic life was thus to be forever separated from the place of work. For the bourgeoisie, the domestic interior was increasingly compartmentalized for its different activities, while also individualized according to a private taste designed to reflect the image of bourgeois subjectivity back onto itself and to cushion individual sensibility from the harsh realities of the urban world outside.

In his critique of Kierkegaard, Adorno finds in the work of the Danish philosopher a convergence of three forms of interiority: as philosophical construct, poetic figure, and architectural design. In works such as the *Concluding Unscientific Postscript* (1846), Kierkegaard describes subjective reflection in its search for *inwardness* (*Inderlighed*) as the condition for an apprehension of the truth.[16] In the chapter "Truth Is Subjectivity," Kierkegaard writes, "The subjective reflection turns its attention inwardly to the subject, and desires in this intensification of inwardness to realize the truth" (*Concluding* 175). The truth spoken of here is that which is "essentially related to existence," which can only be attained through inwardness or subjectivity (178n.). The substance of Adorno's critique is that Kierkegaard evaluates truth solely by reference to the thinker's subjective existence, or "inwardness." The problem is that this inwardness lacks a meaningful relation to the object-world; it is "only an isolated subjectivity surrounded by a dark otherness" (Adorno, *Kierkegaard* 29). In the form of the concrete individual, this subjectivity "rescues only the rubble of the existent," while it mourns the loss of "meaning" in the world of things (30).

The relevance of this philosophical debate to our subject is that both Kierkegaard and Adorno rely on architectural images in their respective expositions of inwardness. In the *Attack upon "Christendom"* (1854–55) Kierkegaard employs the romantic figure of the castle as a figure of inwardness: "When the castle door of inwardness has long been shut and is finally opened, it does not move noiselessly like an apartment door which swings on hinges" (Adorno, *Kierkegaard* 40). The metaphor is intended to enforce the idea of the rigid separation between the pure inner world of subjectivity, "the world of the spirit," and the debased external world of reified objects, where everything is subject to possession by worldly wealth (40). In another figure of the architectural interior, the Johannes of "The Seducer's Diary" in *Either/Or* (1843) playfully addresses the breezes outside his bourgeois Copenhagen apartment.

> What have you done all morning but shake my awnings, tug at my window street-mirror and the cord on it, play with the bellpull wire, push against the windowpanes—in short, proclaim your existence as if you wanted to beckon me out to you? Yes, the weather is fine enough, but I have no inclination; let me stay home. (354)

Even allowing for the possibly ironic distance between Kierkegaard and a personage who represents a purely aesthetic outlook on life, Adorno cites this as one of many passages in which the bourgeois interior is the real place and condition for the existence of the "subjective thinker": "Just as in the metaphorical *intérieur* the intentions of Kierkegaard's philosophy intertwine, so the *intérieur* is also the real space that sets free the categories of the philosophy" (41). In the passage cited above, the detail of the "window street-mirror" reinforces this point. In the nineteenth century this device consisted of a mirror attached at an oblique angle to the window of a house in such a way that the length of the street could be viewed from a position well inside. It was commonly called a "spy." Adorno finds it to be a perfect figure for Kierkegaard's thought, for "he who looks into the window-mirror . . . is the private person, solitary, inactive, and separated from the economic processes of production" (42). Chapter 1, on "dwelling," will have more to say on the bourgeois interior in modern literature. Here it will suffice to say that much of modern literature, from Poe and Baudelaire to Woolf and Musil, demonstrates a preoccupation with precisely this problematic relation between the inward life of the domestic interior and the external realities of urban space.

The Architectural Body

From antiquity, the human body has been both a measure and a metaphor for architectural form. In *De Architectura* (ca. 15 BCE) Vitruvius studies the form of the body and provides a detailed set of measurements derived from it for use in the construction of temples to the gods. He commends those architects who in designing temples "so arrange the parts that the whole may harmonize in their proportions and symmetry" as they do in the human body (III:1). Vitruvius's model establishes the body as an architectonic reference, while also placing it within a larger order that defines its visible relation to the constructed environment and the divine. This conception of the architectural body prevails in the Renaissance, as witnessed by Leonardo's famous drawing of Vitruvian man, as well as in Alberti's analogy between the house and the state, each of which is held together by the organic concept that "as members of the body are correspondent to each other, so it is fit that one part should answer to another in a building" (I:9).[17] However, at the time of the Renaissance there began to emerge an alternative to this visual and highly rational concept of the architectural body. We see it in the fifteenth-century *Hypnerotomachia Poliphili* (Dream of Polyphilo),[18] in which the title character wanders through a series of marvelous palaces and pavilions, where, sporting in richly decorated fountains with nymphs and damsels, he struggles to contain his erotic impulses until he meets the young woman of his heart's desire, who teaches him of love. Alberto Pérez-Gómez has written a contemporary version of the tale in which the wonders of classical architecture encountered by Polyphilo are replaced with the more modern projects of Etienne-Louis Boullée, John Hejduk, and Daniel Libeskind, and where the woodcuts of the original are replaced with photographs. Pérez-Gómez's theoretical interest in the *Hypnerotomachia* has to do with the manner in which the fifteenth-century work shows how architectural meaning is not a rational or formal question of proportions but rather something that "originates in the erotic impulse itself"(5). Architectural space is experienced by the sentient body that moves through it, whereas the making of art and architecture is ultimately a response to human desire.

This alternate conception of architecture, however, remains somewhat underground until the publication of the drawings of Piranesi and a later series of theoretical formulations in the nineteenth and twentieth centuries. One of these is Heinrich Wölfflin's *Prolegomena for a Psychology of Architecture* (1886), which argues that the human body and psychology are related to one another in their common apprehension of the ambiance (*Stimmung*) of an architectural work. Wölfflin writes that our intuitive response to architectural space comes indeed from the body's own resemblance to architecture but also from our sensory appreciation of such qualities as weight, balance, hardness, texture, and so on, because such qualities belong to the body itself. Even beyond this, we have an emotional response to architecture based, for example, on our freedom of movement through it, in the satisfaction with which we follow the contours of space in a dynamic trajectory. This principle allows Wölfflin to relate the sensory experience of architecture to the aesthetic sense: "The laws of formal aesthetics are none other than the conditions under which organic well-being seems possible to us. The expression of these laws, manifested in the articulation of the horizontal and vertical, is given according to organic human principles" (30). Wölfflin's formulation helps us to understand the bodily relations to architectural space that are particularly important to modern literature—in the taut nerves of Baudelaire's *flâneur,* in Whitman's doors unscrewn from their jambs, in Pater's palpable excitement in the Cathedral of Amiens, in the "dark freshness" of Proust's narrator's room at Combray (*A la recherche* 1:82), in the "mouldy air" of a ruined medieval abbey visited in Joyce's Dublin (*Ulysses* 189).

The phenomenological approach to architecture is again taken up by one of the classics of twentieth-century architectural theory, Steen Eiler Rasmussen's *Understanding Architecture* (1957). For Rasmussen, "[I]t is not enough to *see* architecture; you must experience it. . . . You must dwell in the rooms, feel how they close about you, observe how you are naturally led from one to the other" (33). Like Proust, Rasmussen is concerned with "impressions" of architectural spaces and materials. He tells the story of watching a group of boys playing a ball game against the eighteenth-century wall of Santa Maria Maggiore in Rome and reflects on how their physically active relation to the space must have given them, at least unconsciously, a different sense of it from that of the tourist who merely takes a picture. Rasmussen is also one of the first theorists to give systematic attention to acoustic phenomena, observing that architectural spaces resonate with sound in different ways, according to their shape and materials.

The concrete experience of acoustics, however, has always been known intuitively. For example, the enormous interior spaces of medieval cathedrals required a certain rhythm and pitch of vocal expression in religious liturgy to prevent the reverberation of spoken syllables from becoming a confused jumble (227).

If Rasmussen's work suggests that the human body is always capable of adapting freely to its architectural surroundings, there is ample evidence to the contrary in the literature of the last two centuries. A modern tradition of social critique has noted that new forms of urban space in particular—wide boulevards, tall buildings, crowded commercial centers—contributed to the deterioration of the social fabric and to the well-being of individual psychology. Readers of Georg Simmel are familiar with his notions of the "intensification of nervous stimulation" (*die Steigerund des Nervenlebens*) and the "blasé attitude" (*Blasiertheit*) (*Metropolis* 410–13) of the modern city dweller. Benjamin's analysis of shock experience (*Choc-Erlebnis*) in the same context is equally familiar (*Paris* 182). Similar analyses have been made by Marc Augé of the cheerless spaces of transient life—airport terminals, subway stations, strip malls—that he calls *non-lieux*. More recently, Anthony Vidler has furthered this discussion in his study of the relation between architectural space and modern anxiety, or the "psychopathologies of urban space" (*Warped Space* 25). Vidler shows how, since the nineteenth century, the concrete conditions of modernity have given rise to specifically modern psychic disorders related to the sufferer's perception of his or her own body in space. These include agoraphobia, first diagnosed in 1871. Originally referring to the fear of open spaces, this disorder was associated in the popular imagination with "all urban fears that were seemingly connected to spatial conditions" (30). Other symptoms of "phobic modernism" (46) have included claustrophobia, the fear of closed spaces, and the more general neurasthenia, which still figures in the World Health Organization's International Classification of Diseases as a nervous disorder involving constant mental and physical fatigue, loss of concentration, "distracting associations or recollections," and "feelings of general instability."[19]

It is worth noting that Eliot was diagnosed with and treated for neurasthenia when he was writing *The Waste Land,* that high modernist classic of warped spaces and urban alienation. This is not to suggest that the poem be read as a symptom of the disorder but rather that Eliot's documented interest in neurasthenia and its related disorder, *aboulie,* could have inspired his writing of certain scenes and personages in the poem. For example, in the assignation between the typist home at teatime and the small house agent's clerk, her complete indifference to his sexual assault could equally be a symptom of *Blasiertheit,* neurasthenia, or *aboulie*—an incapacity to act, which is how Eliot diagnosed himself (Gold 526). In any case, Eliot puts an emphasis on the scene of this unwholesome encounter as one of weakened bodies—the house agent is "carbuncular," the typist "bored and tired"—in an urban environment where distinctions between exterior and interior spaces are nullified by a general desolation.

Materials and Forms

The material transformations of the arts in the nineteenth and twentieth centuries have a doubly signifying relation to the collective phenomena of modernity: they serve both to represent symbolically a series of changes in the larger social and economic orders and, in large measure, to embody those changes. This is particularly true of the two arts under consideration here. In the first part of this essay I advanced the notion that the relative harmony between architectural and literary forms of meaning characteristic of the neoclassical period later broke down in such a way as to constitute diverse if not formally opposed responses to the modern condition. This notion gains considerably in nuance from a more pointed consideration of material forms. Even a simple enumeration of certain formal changes in architecture and literature can suggest the extent to which these changes themselves are productive of meaning, or rather of the crisis of meaning that I have designated as the sign of modernity.

If transformations in architectural form historically have been driven by social and economic forces, this principle was never more true than in the machine age, which for our purposes begins with the nineteenth century and extends into the twentieth. Among the terms in which these transformations can be documented are those of typology, materials, construction techniques, function, and context. To take the first of these categories, the last two centuries have seen the proliferation of types of buildings that never existed before: commercial arcades, railway stations, large-scale industrial plants, office towers. Many of these types have been made possible by the introduction of new building materials such as cast and wrought iron, steel cables and sheeting, plate glass, reinforced concrete, and more recently, synthetic materials made from polymers, resins, ceramics, cement composites and metal alloys. The availability of new materials favored new construction techniques. Joseph Paxton's Crystal Palace, centrepiece of the first international industrial exhibition in London (1851), was prefabricated of fully modular iron and glass sections that allowed the immense structure to be assembled at Hyde Park in eight days and later to be dismantled and reassembled at Sydenham Hill in southeast London. The invention of reinforced concrete slabs allowed Le Corbusier to design open-plan houses without interior load-bearing walls or posts. Steel frame construction, along with Elisha Otis's safety elevator, made the urban skyscraper possible, as well as such elegant structures as Philip Johnson's Glass House at New Canaan, Connecticut (1949), "a steel cage with a glass skin" (Johnson 223). In the electronic age, computer software such as Conception Assistée Tridimensionnelle Interactive Appliquée (CATIA), originally developed for aviation, has enabled architects like Frank Gehry to design sculptural forms for buildings such as his Guggenheim Museum in Bilbao (1997), which consists essentially of a smooth, curvilinear titanium sheathing over a metal frame. The movement away from traditional materials like stone and wood toward more technologically complex synthetic materials has obviously increased architecture's possibilities, while it has also been cause for alarm by conservative art historians like Hans Sedlmayr, who writes that "the shift of man's spiritual centre of gravity towards the inorganic . . . may indeed legitimately be called a cosmic disturbance in the microcosm of man" (cited in Frampton, "Rappel" 91). Although such a statement needs to be read in the context of the place, time, and circumstances under which it was written (Vienna, 1941, under the influence of National Socialist doctrine), it serves nonetheless as an example of how building materials themselves can be loaded with enigmatic meaning.

The proliferation of new types in modern architecture has been accompanied by a remarkable adaptability of traditional forms to new functions. The geometrical forms of neoclassical architecture, for example, proved perfectly suited to the demands of new commercial and industrial construction. Early in the nineteenth century, the French architect Jean-Nicolas-Louis Durand developed a system in which classical forms were treated as freely combinable modular elements in the construction of military barracks, covered markets, or libraries.[20] Many factories and warehouses were modeled on the Renaissance *palazzo,* with four or five stories of brick masonry stories rising symmetrically in a block punctuated by rows of large, uniform windows and topped with a cornice and balustrade. A particularly fine example is H. H. Richardson's Marshall Field Warehouse (1887) in Chicago, where one can see the efficient use of space and relative openness to air and light made possible by a modern adaptation of neoclassical form.

In a rival spirit of formal adaptability, nineteenth-century Gothic architecture represented a liberation from the geometric orders of the classical. George Gilbert Scott did more than any other architect to extend the Gothic style to nonecclesiastical building. His *Remarks on Secular and Domestic Architecture, Present and Future* (1857) is a manifesto for this extension, defending the Gothic style as the most adaptable to contemporary materials, as closest to nature in its decorative detail, and as most in keeping with native English traditions. Gothic architecture was seen as modern in its freedom of structural form, as well as its use of materials, allowing for the great variety of invention that we see in a building like Scott's St. Pancras in London (1868–74), which combines the specifically modern functions of hotel and railway station.

Whereas neoclassical architecture was concerned with geometric volumes and surfaces, neo-Gothic architecture was concerned with structural support and the exposed armature of form. The great strength of the modernist movement of the early twentieth century was that it successfully combined these two approaches, affirming the values of surfaces and open volumes while articulating a visible supporting armature. In the catalog that accompanied the 1932 International Exhibition of Modern Architecture in New York, Alfred Barr defines four principles that unite architects as diverse as Frank Lloyd Wright, Walter Gropius, Le Corbusier, and Ludwig Mies van der Rohe. They are (a) *volume* as space defined by planes and surfaces rather than as mass and solidity—"a skeleton enclosed by a thin light shell"; (b) *regularity* as opposed to bilateral symmetry; (c) *flexibility* and repetition as opposed to fixed form; and (d) a fourth comprehensive principle that combines technical perfection, proportion, composition, and absence of ornament (14–15). The use of steel frames, glass walls, and flat roofs to realize such construction suggests a modernist aesthetic that is materially based on "standardized construction made possible by mass production" (Eisenman, "Introduction" 15). Should we see this reliance on industrial production as an inherent tension between modernist aesthetics and pragmatism or is this a false distinction to make in judging an aesthetic according to which form follows function? The answer to this question is far from being made clear even in the 1896 essay by Louis Sullivan that made the latter expression famous. In that essay Sullivan poses the architect's problem of imparting a higher sensibility of beauty and culture to the modern office building as the product of the "new grouping of social conditions" that constitutes modernity itself, where "all in evidence is materialistic, an exhibition of force, of resolution, of brains in the sharp sense of the word" (105). Sullivan's solution to the problem lies in a romantic version of natural law itself, "the pervading law of all things organic and inorganic, or all things physical and metaphysical, . . . that the life is recognizable in its expression, that form ever follows function" (107). However, if this law applies to the material functions of modernity, described by Sullivan as "this crude, harsh, brutal agglomeration, this stark, staring exclamation of eternal strife" (107), there is no sublimity of form without the architect's artistic intervention. Paradoxically, Sullivan wants form to follow both function and the architect's higher aesthetic sense.

The tension in architectural modernism lies not just in the difference between aesthetics and pragmatics but also in that between, on one hand, the utopian social aims of such movements as Bauhaus, *das Neue Frankfurt*,[21] and *die Neue Sachlichkeit* and, on the other hand, the emphasis on artistic genius, originality, and uniqueness that characterized the design of elegant private homes for members of the bourgeoisie. As Eisenman puts it rather cuttingly, when the modern movement was reconceived as the international style, "a pluralistic conception of the good society" was transformed into "an individualistic model of the good life," thus reducing the potential cultural alternative represented in modernism to "a stylistic nicety" (16).

Although architectural postmodernism is beyond the scope of this study, it will not be irrelevant to my general thesis to make one or two remarks on this most recent stage of modernity's crisis of meaning. A quarter century ago Fredric Jameson translated his own sense of bewildered immersion in the lobby of the Los Angeles Westin Bonaventure Hotel into a definition of *postmodern hyperspace,* something that transcends the capacity of the individual human body to orient itself in space. This latest historical transformation in the nature of space he diagnosed as a "mutation of the object . . . unaccompanied by any equivalent mutation in the subject" (*Postmodernism* 38). What appears to differentiate this kind of experience from that of Vidler's "warped space" is that the latter produces pathological disorder, whereas the condition described by Jameson is perfectly normal in the cultural logic of late capitalism.

For Jameson, John Portman's hotel, in its banal self-referentiality, as well as its discontinuity from the surrounding urban context, stands as a perfect embodiment of that essentially consumerist logic. Some of these same issues are revisited in Hal Foster's 2001 essay on Frank Gehry, which makes a qualitative distinction between Gehry's early work—the provocative edginess and funky materials of his Santa Monica house, with its implicit challenge to the notion of architecture as a monumental form of capital—and the later stage represented by the Guggenheim Museum in Bilbao. The latter is ironically characterized as an example of "gestural aesthetics," with its regressive notion of architecture as corporate-style sculpture, its slick opacity, and its antagonistic relation both to the surrounding context and to the works it is designed to house. The difference between the early and late Gehry, Foster writes, is that between a material rethinking of form and space and an architectural ingratiation of a public "projected as a mass consumer" (3).

The contemporary success of architecture as consumer spectacle, as a kind of monumental image in itself, has opened a new chapter in the perpetual contest between literature and architecture for the title of primary and most enduring form of human expression. In *Notre-Dame de Paris* (1831), Victor Hugo famously addresses the general problem of meaning in terms of the traditional rivalry between the two arts. Interrupting his story at midpoint in order to contemplate the meaning of his own art in relation to that of the great cathedral, Hugo claims that architectural monuments are at the origin of writing. In ancient civilizations, when the burden of human memory became too much to bear and the spoken word could no longer hold it in place, it was inscribed in the earth in the most visible, durable, and natural manner: "On scella chaque tradition sous un monument" (Every tradition was sealed by a monument) (281). Architecture became the great book of humankind, such that every religious symbol and even every human thought had its page in this work. Until the age of the printed word, architecture was the principal and universal form of writing; the temples, fortresses, cathedrals, cities, tombs, and other buildings were the register of humanity, and of its cultural memories and aspirations. Hugo's claim that since the fifteenth century the printed word has "killed" architecture is based on the difference in modality, if not in essential cultural function, between literature and architecture.[22] Compared to a cathedral, a book is readily made, costs little, and can be disseminated widely with ease. No wonder, Hugo writes, that since the invention of print the great tradition of human thought has taken the form of literature instead of stone. Today, however, Hugo's judgment needs to be overturned. In the twenty-first century, culture at large has been transformed into the production of images, so that a new building by a star architect like Frank Gehry or Daniel Libeskind, to say nothing of the destruction of the towers of the World Trade Center in New York, creates a much greater symbolic and perhaps more lasting impact on the public consciousness than any new literary work can hope to achieve.

The postmodern notion of architecture as image is a natural consequence of Robert Venturi's definition of the "decorated shed," which recalls the Ruskinian idea of architecture as the support for ornament, but
without Ruskin's ethical fervor or his historical sense. Venturi's celebration
of consumerized kitsch, both in his influential *Learning from Las Vegas*
(1972) and in the playful adornment of architectural works such as the
Gordon Wu Hall at Princeton University (keystones, heraldic patterns, Tu-
dor-style bay windows, stone balls), comes closer to Jameson's idea of pas-
tiche as "blank parody" (*Postmodernism* 17) than to Victorian ideals of historical revival. Still, one of the fiercest attacks on postmodernism comes
from Frampton, who sees behind the play of design a will to destroy style
and cannibalize form in the name of architecture as large-scale corporate
packaging (326–27). In another register, J. G. Ballard's novel *Super-Cannes*
(2000) portrays the gated communities and office parks of contemporary
corporate life as sinister architectural environments where high salaries and
sexual license are granted at the cost of more essential human freedoms. In
the corporate park of a multinational holding company, "the buildings
wore their ventilation shafts and cable conduits on their external walls, an
open reminder of Eden-Olympia's dedication to company profits and the
approval of its shareholders" (8). In what might otherwise be interpreted as
a postmodern aesthetic borrowed from original designs like Renzo Piano's
Centre Pompidou, Ballard finds the raw expression of a globalized capitalist ideology. If this assessment is valid, it may be that the most imaginative
possibilities for architecture lie in another direction, one represented by organizations like Philadelphia's Slought Foundation, which seeks to
redefine the built environment in response to changing populations, mi-
grations, uneven economic development, natural disasters, and climate
change. At the 2008 Venice Architectural Biennale, Deborah Gans, one of
Slought's architects, displayed her House with Roll Out Core, in which
columns of bamboo and reinforced cardboard support a light roof over a
frame of hay-bale walls. In such designs made to shelter the homeless, the
use of lightweight and flexible construction materials takes on new meaning, reviving the utopian ideals of the 1920s while seeking to address the
urgent needs of the present.

Although surpassed by architecture today in its immediate public importance, literary form has also proven adaptable to the empirical conditions of modernity, even when that adaptability takes the form of an implicit critique of those same conditions. One way to describe these
conditions is to name what Adorno calls "the reification of all relationships

between individuals, which transforms their human qualities into lubricating oil for the smooth running of the machinery, the universal alienation and self-alienation" (*Notes* 1:32). Balzac's *Illusions perdues* (1841) is the first literary work to document both the technical changes that made the mass production of literature possible and the social and economic contexts in which this production took place. The novel opens with an exposition of the iron Stanhope press, which in the early nineteenth century replaced the old wooden presses, making the process of printing cheaper, faster, and less labor intensive. In Balzac's novel, the mechanization of printing is accompanied by the wildly accelerated commercialization of literary production. Lucien de Rubempré, the callow but ambitious young writer newly arrived in Paris from the provinces, quickly masters the system, which links authors, publishers, booksellers, and reviewers in an unholy alliance of speculation, manipulation, and mutual betrayal. The center of the new book trade is in the Galeries de Bois, the prototype of the commercial arcades explored in Benjamin's *Arcades* project with so much insight into the commodity fetishism of modernity. The trade in new books (*la librairie dite de nouveautés,* 370) thus occupies commercial space alongside other shops of *nouveautés,* while the arcades also provide space for yet another kind of traffic, that of prostitution. Throughout the novel, Balzac compares the literary to the commercial product and literary work to prostitution. Lucien realizes, for example, that books to the booksellers are like cotton to bonnet makers: merchandise to be bought cheaply and sold at a profit (218). The publisher Dauriat, who "speculates in literature," tells him that a book is a capital risk, and the more beautiful a work the less are its chances of being sold (287). As for literary reputation, Lucien discovers the extent to which it is justly allegorized by different classes of prostitutes: popular works are like the poor girl shivering at the side of the road, secondary literature resembles the journalist's kept woman, whereas *la littérature heureuse* is like a brilliant but capricious courtesan who treats great men with insolence and skillfully puts off her creditors (261).

The novel, as the literary form specific to the bourgeois and industrial age, is particularly suited to the task of representing this society in which "human beings have been torn from one another and from themselves" (Adorno 32). Jameson writes that what differentiates the conditions of modern literature from those of the traditional epic is that the object-world of the epic was already endowed with meaning, which it was the function of the artwork to transmit in whole cloth. The problem for modern literature is that the object world, including the constructed environment, eludes the grasp of individual consciousness and undermines the quality of human relations. In modern art, therefore, "the elements of the work begin to flee their human center" (*Marxism and Form* 160). A centrifugal dispersal takes place "in which paths lead out at every point into the contingent, into brute fact and matter, into the not-human" (160). The novel, in its capaciousness, as a form that continually reinvents itself, as a process without formal guidelines given in advance, in its scope and its preoccupation precisely with the question of alienation—all these qualities make the novel better adapted than any other form to the task of restoring a semblance of coherence to the modern world. Georg Lukács calls it "the epic of a world abandoned by God" (87).[23] The best example of this role assumed by the novel is Balzac's own immense project, which attempts to embrace the totality of the modern social world. But unlike the *Divina Commedia,* the 137 works of the *Comédie Humaine* add up finally to a series of brilliant but discrete fragments of this world, which cannot be seized as an integral order emanating from a metaphysical center. The final verdict on the novel as a source of meaning for the modern world may already have been pronounced in 1923 by Eliot, for whom "the novel, instead of being a form, was simply the expression of an age which had not sufficiently lost all form to feel the need of something stricter" (*Selected Prose* 177).

The modern fragmentation of literary form can be understood as a consequence both of the material pressures of the conditions under which literature is produced and of literature's function as a critical response to those conditions. An initial form of this fragmentation was to segment literary production into parts of a series published over time. *Illusions perdues,* for example, was published in three parts from 1837 to 1844; it is the fourth novel in Balzac's *Scènes de la vie de province* and has a sequel in *Splendeur et misères des courtisanes* (1847). The publication of novels in sequence took place at the same time as the serial publication of single novelistic works, beginning with Dickens's *The Pickwick Papers,* which appeared in twenty installments during 1836–37. Serial publication provided a monthly wage for Dickens and greatly expanded the novel's reading public, reaching a circulation of forty thousand, as readers now could pay for a one-guinea novel in installments of a shilling per month. It also provided space for the advertising of consumer products, much in the spirit of Samuel Pickwick's own leisurely adventures pursued through a modern world of club dinners, cricket matches, bachelor parties, and tourist excursions to Bath.

The invention of the modern short story represents another innovation in literary production made in response to the conditions under which literature was received. Poe, in his 1842 *Graham's* magazine review of Hawthorne's *Twice-Told Tales,* defines the "short prose narrative" as the ideal form of fiction in that it produces the greatest intensity of effect on the reader. The short story is designed to be read in a single session, drawing the reader into its magic circle for an hour or so and giving the writer exclusive command over the reader's responses. To achieve its singular effect the story must be both completely unified and rigorously economical: "There should be no word written of which the tendency, direct or indirect, is not to the one pre-established design" ("Review" 299). The circle into which Poe's reader is drawn, free from all "external or extrinsic influences" (298), conforms in the architectural sphere to the ideal living space evoked in Poe's essay "The Philosophy of Furniture," with its picture of interior repose amid thick carpets, silk curtains, plush sofas, and soft lighting. The short story's formal adaptability to the market thus coincides somewhat paradoxically with Poe's idea of reading as a private act performed within a bourgeois interior safely removed from the harshly acquisitive world outside.

There exists a certain structural similarity between collections of short stories and novels originally published in serial form: to the extent that each consists of a series of more or less discrete entities, the end product has an empirically fragmentary nature, which, in works of literary modernism, will extend to literary form in the proper sense. The composition of Joyce's *Ulysses* (1922) began as a short story in the style of *Dubliners,* the collection Joyce had published in 1914. Although *Ulysses* was extended to novel length, it retains, in its series of episodes written in different styles, the fragmentary textual character we have already noted in René Char and constitutes the most prevalent formal feature of literary modernism from Eliot to Virginia Woolf. Throughout the modern era the literary language of internal disruption and discontinuity runs counter to the narratives of personal development, moral progress, and so-called social realism—those that deliver themselves over to a world presupposed, whether naively or disingenuously, as meaningful in itself. This countercurrent should not be understood as the abandonment of meaning but rather as the interrogation of the loss of meaning. As Adorno says of the essay form, "It thinks in fragments, just as reality is fragmentary, and finds its unity in and through the breaks and not by glossing them over" (*Notes* 1:16).

A similar observation might be made of the advent of free verse in poetry. Eliot's essay on this form looks back to the "close-knit and homogeneous" societies that produced the Greek chorus, the troubadour canzone, and the Elizabethan lyric and asserts that only in such contexts could the development of these traditional forms have been brought to perfection (36). As we see in Eliot's own poetic work, free verse is then the lyric form best adapted to the unraveled, heterogeneous conditions of modernity. It is the poetic form that reflects the fragmentary nature of reality while transcending that reality in both content and form: on the level of content, it resists the pressure to naturalize reality, by objectifying the subjective experience of that reality; on the level of form, it abandons regular rhyme and meter only for a more rigorous internal composition of sound and rhythm.

How, then, do we compare modern architecture and literature in their respective relations to the conditions of modernity, however the latter are defined? The problem is that this is the wrong question, if it presupposes modernity as a third term independent of those of architecture and literature. On the contrary, the examples discussed here should have demonstrated the extent to which modernity is constituted by cultural forms and that, among these, architecture and literature are in large measure responsible for the objective and subjective elements that we refer to in the concept of modernity. Even if these cultural forms are not exactly coterminous with the ensemble of social and economic conditions in which they are made, they are nonetheless irretrievably tied to those conditions by the materials out of which they are made and the contexts they inhabit. While this is immediately obvious in the case of architecture as the creation of modern space, it is equally true of literature by virtue of its grounding in language; through the conceptual medium of language, literature is inevitably grounded in the social. Our question is therefore better approached by thinking of architecture and literature neither in terms of their aesthetic autonomy, nor in terms of their appropriation by a third, external term, but rather as alternate discourses of modernity itself, as constructions of the modern through their respective conceptual and material forms. While this question is taken up more fully in the next chapter, we may anticipate that discussion here by mentioning a few ways in which the modern discourses of architecture and literature are comparable, simply on the basis of the formal transformations just reviewed. First, both arts have broken with traditional models of a formal unity whose elements are subordinated to a single dominant principle. Instead, those models have been replaced with systems of freely combined modular elements, with emphasis on repetition and variation rather than hierarchical order. Second, this decentered notion of order has been accompanied by the breakdown of various barriers, including those between inside and outside. The glass-roofed arcades of Balzac's Paris already diminished the distinction between interior and exterior, as later the glass walls of Mies's office buildings would do. Modern literature has broken down the barriers between the objective and subjective worlds while in the latter case breaking the further barrier between the conscious and the unconscious. Third, both arts have moved toward the increased exposure of their respective inner structures, from the systems of support and armature on view in modern buildings to the various modes of reference in modern literature to its own methods of composition. Here I would include Joyce's conscious reference to the *Odyssey* as a framework for *Ulysses,* as well as Eliot's notes to *The Waste Land,* even if neither is wholly free of irony. More to the point is that both Joyce and Eliot freely expose the gaps and fissures of their compositions, refusing to paper them over with a semblance of narrative or conceptual continuity. Finally, the sense of historical continuity in both cultural forms has been replaced by a sense of historical forms as a vast warehouse from which objects can be freely chosen and combined in new ways.

In "Die Frage nach der Technik" (The Question Concerning Technology), Heidegger writes that in contrast to traditional methods of the cultivation of nature, modern technology treats nature as a vast standing reserve (*Bestand*) or stock of material from which materials and energy are drawn forcibly. The difference between an old-fashioned water mill and a hydroelectric plant is that in the former case the river drives the wheel at its natural rate of flow, whereas in the latter case the dammed river is "challenged forth" as the object of stockage, acquisition, transformation, accumulation, and distribution in a series of operations distant in form and meaning from their source (*Question* 16–17). As forms of cultural production, contemporary architecture and literature bear a relation to history similar to that which modern technology bears to nature: historical forms are there to be cited and transformed, at worst into consumerized kitsch, at best into something rich and strange. All of these cases remind us of the basic truth that the human world is literally structured as the built environment, and symbolically structured as language. The art of the built environment is architecture; that of language is literature. Here is reason enough to consider their common ground.

An End to Dwelling:
Architectural and Literary Modernisms

The Buster Keaton movie *One Week* (1920) is a possibly unintended but nonetheless effective allegory of a twentieth-century predicament. In this, Keaton's first independent film, he and Sybil Seely play the roles of newly-weds who build their new home, to be assembled according to numbered pieces delivered in a box. The honeymoon starts to go wrong, however, when Sybil's jilted lover secretly alters the numbers on the pieces, so that what ends up being built looks today like a grotesque parody of a Frank Gehry design (fig. 2): walls jutting out at wild angles, trapezoidal windows, tilting columns, and an ill-fitting roof. When a storm comes up, the house begins to spin like a top, throwing its inhabitants from room to room. The wind eventually dies down, but then disaster arrives from another quarter: the couple learns that they have built their house on the wrong lot; the right one is across the railroad tracks. As they try to tow the tottering struc-ture across the tracks, a train arrives and smashes it to bits. In the final scene, Keaton puts a "For Sale" sign on the ruined pieces.

Keaton's dark comedy brings to modern audiences a series of themes that may resonate with their lives: the commodification of shelter, the pa-thetic effort to build a "home," and the doomed attempt to sell the ruined remains of this project. His images are emblematic of a set of conditions to which both architectural modernism and literary modernism are forced to respond: big-scale industrialism, social fragmentation, the commodifica-

Fig. 2. Still from Buster Keaton's *One Week,* 1920.

tion and mechanization of everyday experience. Walter Benjamin claims in 1936 that since World War I "experience has fallen in value"; the traditional human relations that make storytelling meaningful have been subverted and contradicted by unprecedented and incommensurable developments in civilization itself. As the title character in Robert Musil's *The Man without Qualities* (1930–42) expresses it, "There's no longer a whole man confronting a whole world, only a human something (*ein menschliches Etwas*) moving about in a general culture" (234).

As art forms, literature and architecture share a profoundly ambiguous and yet productive response to these conditions. In his essay "Experience and Poverty" (1933), written the year that Hitler became chancellor of Germany, Benjamin points out that writers like Bertolt Brecht and architects like Adolf Loos are equally motivated by "a total absence of illusion about the age and at the same time an unlimited commitment (*Bekenntnis*) to it" (*Selected* 2:733). Their disillusionment is not just with political events, but with the poverty of experience itself, and with the attempts to mask this poverty by the bourgeois aesthetic values of the nineteenth century—attempts represented, for example, by the Jugendstil and Biedermaier styles in design, by the Deuxième Empire and Gothic Revival in architecture, by Victorian sentimentality and the chic aesthetic of the interiors in Oscar Wilde's *The Picture of Dorian Gray* (1891). Against these styles, the commitment of artists like Brecht and Loos lies in a vision of the age that faces unflinchingly the poverty of experience but not at all in the manner of the late-nineteenth-century realistic novel. Rather, they seek a new aesthetic relation to the world based on an unprecedented existential condition. This is the common ground shared by the modernist movements in literature and architecture.

In architecture, disillusionment with nineteenth-century aesthetics is to be found in Loos's attacks on ornament and kitsch in his essay "Ornament and Crime" (1913) and in Le Corbusier's call, in *Towards an Architecture* (1920), for order, geometry, and purity of form: "spirit of order, unity of intention" (75).[1] In literature, we find similar impulses in Ezra Pound's insistence on the clarity and economy of the poetic image. Just as Loos rejects ornament and kitsch in architecture, Pound rejects sentiment, abstraction, and rhetoric in poetry. Another point of intersection between the two arts is to be found in Le Corbusier's idea of the open plan, or *plan libre,* according to which the design of a building evolves outward according to a "primary rhythm" belonging to its inner function: "[T]he plan proceeds from inside out: the exterior is the result of an interior" (75). Developing this idea, Mies van der Rohe defends it against the charge that *plan libre* means absolute freedom: "That is a misunderstanding. The free plan asks for just as much discipline and understanding from the architect as the conventional plan" (quoted in Norberg-Schultz 366). We can compare Mies on *plan libre* to T. S. Eliot's 1917 essay on *vers libre:* free verse does not mean escape from meter, but mastery of irregular meter; it does not mean liberation from rhyme, but liberation *of* rhyme from conventional forms (*Selected Prose,* 31–36). We might say that in *vers libre,* as in *plan libre,* form follows function. These are not, however, mere questions of style: in each case, we see the reinvention of artistic form based on the conditions of human existence as it is actually lived.

If we see modernist architecture as an expression of contemporary human existence, we begin to understand why one of its great projects is the demystification of "dwelling," that idealized conception of space that promises rootedness, permanence, and a womblike removal from the experience of modernity. It is important, however, to distinguish *dwelling* from words of similar meaning such as *living* or *inhabiting*. From at least the time of the Renaissance, *dwelling* has had sacred overtones in English, as in the King James version of the opening line of Psalm 90: "Lord, thou hast been our dwelling-place in all generations." The associations of dwelling with sacredness and eternity last well into the nineteenth century. Thus Ruskin in *The Seven Lamps of Architecture* (1849): "Our God is a household god as well as a heavenly one; He has an altar in every man's dwelling" (VIII:227).[2] As so often happens in English, however, the modern meaning of a word conceals a strange history, in this case one that actually contradicts what the word has come to mean. *To dwell* comes from the Old English *dwellan,* meaning "to go astray, be misled, be hindered." This etymological ambiguity is to my purpose, for what I wish to demonstrate is that for modern architects and writers alike, the traditionally idealized concept of dwelling is a false promise, one that modern art forms reject in order to strive for a more authentic definition of human existence in its spatial dimension.

The concept of dwelling became a literary and philosophical preoccupation precisely at that moment when it was no longer possible as a way of life. The concept itself is most lyrically evoked in Heidegger's essay of 1951, "Bauen Wohnen Denken" (Building Dwelling Thinking), in which the German verb *wohnen* is given a meaning very close to the English *dwelling.* As his ideal symbol of *das Wohnen,* Heidegger presents us with the picture of a farmhouse in the Black Forest that has been the dwelling of peasants for two hundred years. Rooted in the earth, open to the sky, and furnished with the work of patient craftsmen, the house represents the ideal of human dwelling in complete harmony with its surroundings. Heidegger originally gave this lecture in Darmstadt, a city that lay in ruins after the war: a Royal Air Force (RAF) attack in September 1944 had destroyed most of the city, killed twelve thousand inhabitants, and left another sixty-six thousand homeless. Invited to speak in the *Darmstädter Gespräch* series on "Man and Space," Heidegger addressed an audience composed mainly of architects preoccupied with the practical work of rebuilding the city. For them, the *Wohnungsfrage,* the question of dwelling, was a matter of the urgent need for shelter, so Heidegger's evocation of the Black Forest farmhouse must have seemed both strange and irrelevant to the purpose at hand.[3] It is not that Heidegger completely ignored the *Wohnungsfrage* as his audience understood it. He begins his lecture by admitting that in the present housing crisis one is lucky to have a place to live; he reaffirms the need for practical and affordable housing open to the air, light, and sun. But he also asks the question whether such housing ensures dwelling (*wohnen*) in the deeper sense of man's fundamental relation to the conditions of his being, such as we might imagine to have once been the case for the dweller of the Black Forest farmhouse. For Heidegger, the Black Forest house stands as a countersymbol to the modern condition of spiritual homelessness. The real crisis of dwelling therefore lies not in the present housing shortage but in the fact that human beings are always in search of dwelling in this deeper sense and that they must ever anew learn to dwell. To this is added the problem of consciousness: man's homelessness (*Heimatlosigkeit*) lies in the fact that he does not yet understand the urgency of the real crisis of dwelling in this spiritual sense. Yet Heidegger concludes with a consolatory thought: "[A]s soon as man gives thought to his homelessness, it is a misery no longer" (161). Like his contemporaries in literature and architecture, Heidegger calls for an authentic reflection on being, in the space as well as in the time of modernity.

Heidegger's reflections find an echo in Derrida's 1998 homage to Maurice Blanchot, entitled *Demeure* (Dwelling). In this essay, Derrida points out that literature has no essence or ideality of its own; the radical historicity of literature—the fact that its identity is always only provisional and granted only by external circumstances that are themselves subject to change—means that literature has no safe dwelling place: "[I]t doesn't occupy a place of dwelling if 'dwelling' designates at the very least the essential stability of a place; it dwells only *there where* and *if* in another sense: it remains in debt (*à demeure*), having received notice to pay (*mise en demeure*)" (29). Literature has no place of its own. Wherever it resides, it is always being asked to pay up or move on. Similarly, dwelling is always both conceived of and experienced in a manner that is historically contingent. Dwelling, in other words, does not dwell in the stable essence of its own ontological place; we may say of dwelling what Blanchot says of the truth, that it is nomadic.

In this chapter I wish to explore the question of dwelling as it arises in some representative literary texts from the nineteenth and twentieth centuries. I hope to demonstrate that the literary reflection on dwelling passes from a nineteenth-century nostalgia for dwelling in the traditional sense to liberation from this nostalgia by various narrative and rhetorical means, including a new consciousness of urban space. This process passes finally to a renewed confrontation with the absence of dwelling, where modern writing strives to relieve the misery of homelessness by giving thought to it. This general movement in literature coincides historically with architecture's movement from nineteenth-century historicism through the various phases of architectural modernism. To cite just one example, according to Siegfried Giedion, the constructions of Le Corbusier are made as light and airy as possible because this is the only way to put an end to the "fatal patrimonial monumentality"—in other words, to the traditional concept of dwelling that literally weighs so heavily in the history of architecture (*Bauen in Frankreich* 85).

The kind of dwelling that Heidegger recalls nostalgically is close in spirit to the architectural visions of Victorian writers like Walter Pater and John Ruskin. For Ruskin, one of the fundamental principles, or "lamps," of architecture is what he calls the "lamp of memory." This is architecture's memorial function; it preserves the historical past, as in the great Gothic cathedrals of Europe but also in those domestic dwellings that are a memorial to the ancestral past of their inhabitants: "If men lived like men indeed, their houses would be temples . . . in which it would make us holy to be permitted to live" (VIII:226). At his first view of a "Swiss cottage," or old-style farmhouse, on the road between Basel and Schaffhausen, he finds it to be "tangible testimony" to

> the joy of peasant life, continuous, motionless there in the shadow of its ancestral turf—unassailed and unassailing, in the blessedness of righteous poverty, of religious peace. (XXXV:113).

Dwelling takes place here in deeply privileged space and time, far removed from the crowded tenements of industrial England.

As Ruskin's general views on architecture are well enough known, let us turn to his contemporary, Dickens, a writer somewhat better acquainted with the crowded tenements of London but seldom read as an architectural writer. Dickens's novel *Bleak House* (1852–53) is intensely architectural in its preoccupations. Its great panorama of Victorian society is presented as a triangular relation among three scenes of the built environment. The first is the urban legal district of Temple Bar and Lincoln's Inn, of courts of law whose institutional corruption is reflected in the smoldering tenements nearby. At the center of this district is the Court of Chancery, "which has its decaying houses and its blighted lands in every shire" (13). Second, there is the sinister country house, Chesney Wold in Lincolnshire, emblematic of a sterile aristocracy and rivaled in ghostliness only by Edgar

Allan Poe's House of Usher. Finally, there is Bleak House itself, a dreamlike refuge from these other scenes of England's ruin. It is described as follows by Esther Summerson, the novel's young heroine.

> It was one of those delightfully irregular houses where you go up and down steps out of one room into another, and where you come upon more rooms when you think you have seen all there are, and where there is a bountiful provision of little halls and passages, and where you find still older cottage-rooms in unexpected places, with lattice-windows and green-growth pressing through them. (78)

This is all one sentence whose loosely periodic structure imitates the rambling passage through this pleasing labyrinth of a house. The furnishings of Bleak House are similarly eccentric—a profusion of mangles, three-cornered tables, Hindu chairs, china closets, scent bottles, paper flowers, pincushions, needlework, velvet, brocade—in short, all of the Victorian bric-a-brac that makes this domestic space into a richly upholstered projection of the fantasy life of its inhabitants. Bleak House is the middle-class counterpart to another of Dickens's architectural wonders, the little fisherman's house in *David Copperfield* (1849–50), made out of an old boat. This eccentric dwelling is presented as the perfect realization of David's childhood fantasy: "If it had been Alladin's palace, roc's egg and all, I suppose I could not have been more charmed with the romantic idea of living in it" (28).

If in *Bleak House* Esther is the honorary mistress of her guardian's house, its resident spirit is Harold Skimpole, Dickens's parody of the poet and essayist Leigh Hunt. The aging Skimpole is the eternal child, a figure of pure enjoyment, coveting nothing and asking only that others know the joy of generosity by providing him with all the little luxuries of country-house life. The gentle irony with which Dickens treats this genius loci of Bleak House is one sign, I believe, of his ambivalence regarding the fantasy of the house itself. Dickens's social vision is keen enough to realize on some level the unreality of Bleak House. Others have remarked on the unreal, uncanny nature of Bleak House in terms of Dickens's vision of social reality, but here I would like to consider it in the light of architectural theory. In its labyrinthine eccentricity and its profusion of exotic furnishings, Bleak House serves as a kind of architectural extension and affirmation of a Victorian fantasy.[4]

However, the symbolic function of Bleak House as a privileged space is undercut at the end of the novel, when John Jarndyce, the benevolent master of the house, builds a perfect dwelling for Esther, his ward, and her new husband, Woodcourt. This new house is in fact a second Bleak House, an uncanny double of the house that up to now has been distinguished by its uniqueness. Reproduced in this manner, the ideal dwelling is in fact commodified, offered in an unacknowledged exchange for Esther's continued attachment to her guardian after she has chosen to marry a man of her own age rather than Jarndyce himself. The easy reproducibility of the house also tends to undermine its status as an ideal dwelling: unique, authentic, and rooted in a special place. The second Bleak House calls into question the myth of dwelling represented in the original Bleak House by submitting it to the logic of seriality, by permitting the thought that this "original" is in fact based on some earlier model, thereby opening up a process of potentially infinite reduplication, which in turn suggests that the ideal of dwelling is something imagined, constructed, and contingent rather than being an organic, ineluctable bond between human beings and the earth.

I find it significant that among the more than forty illustrations for this novel produced by Hablot Browne under Dickens's supervision, not one gives us a proper view of Bleak House itself. The frontispiece of the first book edition depicts the brooding Gothic manor of Chesney Wold, not bright Bleak House with its three-peaked roof. It is as if to represent Bleak House in graphic, visual form would be to destroy its immaterial, phantasmatic status. Of course, both Bleak House and Chesney Wold are products of Dickens's novelistic imagination. But Bleak House is inscribed within the narrative framework itself with a certain dreamlike status, rendering it doubly imaginary. We are thus faced with the following paradox: by producing an exaggerated idealization of the figure of dwelling, Dickens tends to subvert the bourgeois Victorian aesthetic that he appears to celebrate. To register the fantasy of ideal dwelling as such is implicitly to relegate it to the realm of the purely imaginary, just as Ruskin's own vision of dwelling, the Swiss cottage, can be realized only within the framework of a sacred space far removed from the realities of nineteenth-century England, or, for that matter, of Switzerland.

The qualities of private fantasy embodied in Bleak House are precisely those that come under attack by the modernist movement. In *Das Passagen-Werk* (The Arcades Project), Benjamin argues that the nineteenth-century private interior is the culmination of a process of alienation brought about by the Industrial Revolution. The theory is that the private individual is alienated from the dehumanizing conditions of the workplace, and so he creates a domestic space apart from and opposed to this workplace where he can freely indulge in the fantasies of his own subjectivity. Hence the emphasis on ornament, knick-knacks, and materials such as plush, designed to capture and preserve the trace of the dweller.

> The nineteenth century, like no other century, was addicted to dwelling. It conceived the residence as a receptacle for the person, and it encased him with all his appurtenances so deeply in the dwelling's interior that one might be reminded of the inside of a compass case, where the instrument with all its accessories lies embedded in deep, usually violet folds of velvet. . . . The twentieth century, with its porosity and transparency, its tendency toward the well-lit and airy, has put an end to dwelling in the old sense. (*Arcades* 220–21)

Benjamin's larger point is that the nineteenth-century womblike interior, far from satisfying the individual's desire for an authentic subjectivity, merely increased a sense of alienation from the real conditions of existence. Again, such a response is recorded by Musil, whose principal character wearily contemplates the interior of the little rococo château he has had renovated at great expense: "All these circular lines, intersecting lines, straight lines, curves and wreaths of which a domestic interior is composed and that had piled up around him were neither nature nor inner necessity but bristled, to the last detail, with baroque overabundance" (134).

The initial project of modernist architecture, then, was to break open this inner space, clean up its lines, clear it of clutter, and let in light and air. This process had already begun, in fact, in the London of Dickens's day. When Dickens was writing *Bleak House* in the early 1850s, the most popular public attraction in England was the Crystal Palace in Hyde Park, built in 1851 to house the Great Exhibition of the Works of Industry. Designed by Joseph Paxton, the Crystal Palace was basically an immense greenhouse made of three hundred thousand panes of glass supported by a skeletal framework of thin iron beams. Although iron and glass roofs had appeared in the Paris arcades as early as 1822, the Crystal Palace promised much greater possibilities for these materials, and was immediately recognized as a completely new kind of architecture.

With the twentieth century, then, modernist architecture seeks to create a new interrelation between interior and exterior. Its principles are those of open space, transparency, freedom of movement, the dissolution of mass, the disappearance of historicizing masks and symbols, and the breakdown of hierarchical and domineering spatial effects. Frank Lloyd

Wright's buildings open out into the landscape in a subtle and organic way that consciously avoids the domination of surrounding space that we see, for example, in the Palace of Versailles or Castle Howard in North Yorkshire. Many of these principles are given technical definition in Le Corbusier's "Cinq points d'une architecture nouvelle" (Five Points of a New Architecture, 1926): (1) structural weight is to be borne by pillars instead of walls, (2) flat roofs maximize interior space and preserve green space as gardens, (3) the plan of each level is independent of the others, (4) and windows extend horizontally across the facade, which (5) remains free of the weight-bearing structure (Conrads 120–21). In his writings on urban planning, Le Corbusier also introduced the notion of *trafic différencié* (differentiated traffic), according to which the built environment is designed for varying speeds and rhythms of life (Norberg-Schultz 362).

Le Corbusier made it clear that his project went beyond a merely technical program: it represented a new way of life, a revolution in consciousness. Where Heidegger finds rootedness in traditional architecture, Le Corbusier finds paralysis.

> Out of mere words, we make things whose meaning and form are arbitrarily fixed and immobilised—a glossary of themes appealing to the most permanent ideas, which we then petrify into immovable attitudes: roof, village, belltower, house, etc.; stone, rock and earth; hands. (*Manière de penser* 18)

We need no clearer statement of the intended continuity between architecture and language, and of the symbolic economy in which certain materials signify a profoundly conservative ideology, which Le Corbusier calls "le culte du souvenir," the cult of memory (18). If the building materials of stone, wood, and earth or brick carry the symbolic charge of hearth and fatherland, then an entirely new set of values is implied in the new materials of steel, glass, and reinforced concrete. Giedeon called these materials the "subconscious" of modern architecture; they allowed for a new conception of architectural space, one no longer concerned with representational facades and monumental volumes. Rather, the traditional mass of the house was dispersed into a more loosely connected design of rectangular planes. This redesign brought into play an unprecedented degree of interpenetration between the interior and exterior space, as well as between the varying levels of a building (*Espace* 30). The consequence in symbolic terms was to diminish every traditionally hierarchical order governing the use of space and materials. Architecture, then, transcends notions of *patrie* or *Heimat* in order to become international; it embraces open space; and it decenters axial order, moving the dweller away from the hearth and putting him or her at the window, where the gaze is naturally directed outward.

If we look at modernist literature in the light of these ideas, it is true that we do not see much interest in the kinds of houses being built by Wright and Le Corbusier. However, we do see what I believe to be a more fundamental correspondence of certain principles as formal and thematic features of literary modernism: transparency, the interpenetration of interior and exterior, the rejection of historicizing symbols, and the breakdown of the hierarchies that traditionally order human experience and, by extension, the structure of works of art. An important dimension of literary modernism is the mise-en-cause of the nineteenth-century notion of privileged space—whether this notion is applied literally to architecture and landscape or figuratively to the nature of the subject. In one work after another, from Proust to Beckett, the subject is opened up and exposed to the elements of modernity. What is revealed in this process, however, is not the inner Xanadu of romantic poetry but rather a space essentially continuous with the outside, itself composed of the elements of a symbolic universe that exists independent of any subject. The inner space of the subject turns out to be a constituent part of the symbolic universe to which the subject is just that—subject and not sovereign. The point is not merely to expose the modern subject as a mere automaton jostled this way and that by forces beyond the subject's control, like Poe's "The Man of the Crowd." Rather, it is ultimately to come to terms with this condition, to work through it toward a more authentic relation to existence. In this respect, literary modernism is like psychoanalysis—there is no question of a cure, but at least we can learn to live with our symptoms.

It is in this light that I would like to consider Marcel Proust's *A la recherche du temps perdu* (In Search of Lost Time), 1913–27, a work whose excavation of modern subjectivity is carried out through a richly architectural system of figuration. If the "cathedral" nature of Proust's work has become a critical commonplace, the proper sense of this metaphor has nonetheless been frequently misunderstood. Adorno observes that in Proust's work the relation of the whole to its parts is not that of an overall architectonic plan to its realization in concrete detail. Rather, Proust revolted against "the brutal untruth of a subsuming form forced on from above" (*Notes* I: 174). Proust has a predilection for the Gothic precisely because, unlike classical architecture, it cannot be apprehended in its unity;

too much of it is hidden away in an irregular and asymmetrical profusion of elements. Proust thus puts his faith in the *non confundar,* the "uncombined," in his unreserved surrender to things in their natural coherence (*Zusammenhang von Natur*) (174). On one hand, this quality as a formal principle would seem diametrically opposed to Le Corbusier's call for the "spirit of order, unity of intention." On the other hand, the natural coherence of Proust's work is perfectly in keeping with the architectural principle of a "primary rhythm" and a "plan libre" that takes form from the inside out and breaks down the conventional divisions between inside and outside. The effect of such a procedure is to destabilize the traditional notion of dwelling, in fact to redefine dwelling in a modern sense, as a continual process of displacement.

From the very first page of his work, Proust creates a multiple analogy of the book, the self, and architectural form. The narrator tells how as a child falling asleep at night his reflections on the book he had been reading would take a peculiar turn: "[I]t seemed to me that I myself was the subject of the book: a church, a quartet, the rivalry between François I and Charles V" (1:3). The idea of the self as a church introduces the notion of the narrator's rich inner life as a space to be entered and explored in all the complexity of its structure. From this point on, he will return frequently to the topos of architecture in his analysis of human subjectivity.

In Proust, the structures of desire are rendered in terms of architectural space: on the level of narrative, interior spaces provide a refuge for the expression of forbidden desires, while on a figurative level they allegorize both the hidden nature of such desires and the manner in which they are brought to light through a process of penetration and exposure. I am referring here to the numerous scenes of voyeurism in Proust's novel. In the opening volume, the young narrator finds himself outside Montjouvain, the country house of the deceased musician Vinteuil. Through a lighted window, he watches Vinteuil's daughter making love to her female friend before her father's portrait, an image the two young women take pleasure in abusing as part of a sadistic ritual (1:159–61). In a later volume, *Sodome et Gomorrhe,* the narrator watches from a window of his parents' house as, in the courtyard, the Baron de Charlus engages in an elaborate flirtation with the waistcoat maker Jupien. When the two men go into Jupien's shop, the narrator moves to an adjacent room in order to hear the violent sounds of their sexual encounter (3:6–16). Again, in the final volume the narrator finds himself on an upper floor of an obscure hotel where, hearing muffled

cries from an isolated room, he peers into the room from a hidden opening. What he sees inside is a lurid scene of sadomasochism, in which Charlus is being vigorously flogged with chains and whips (4:394–96).

Each of these scenes depends for its effect on the arrangement and
above all the interpenetration of architectural spaces. In each case, an act
of transgression is made possible by an interior space thought to be concealed, but which is in fact open to view from an adjoining space, the space
of the voyeur. It is true that scenes like this are not new in literature. They
are well known to readers of eighteenth-century fiction, they belong to the
repertoire of the licentious novels of Sade and Laclos, and they occur in
lighter form as the "bed-trick" scenes in the works of comic authors like
Fielding. But Proust's voyeurism goes beyond these precedents in that it
does not rely wholly on the vices of the secret witness and his stealthy gaze.
These belong to a conventional voyeurism that depends for its gratification
on maintaining the distinction between inside and outside, concealed and
revealed, and so preserving the frisson of scandal. Proust's voyeuristic
scenes, however, are rendered in such a way as to undermine these distinctions by a process of analysis, by working through the dynamics of transgression. And so in each instance the narrator arrives at an understanding
that allows him to see sexual transgression as something more than mere
vice. In Mlle Vinteuil's profanation of her father's portrait, he sees an essentially respectful daughter because the pleasure of sacrilege can belong
only to those who hold sacred the things they profane: virtue, the memory
of the dead, daughterly duty. In Charlus's seduction of Jupien, what at first
appears grotesque is rendered intelligible and even natural by the narrator's
sudden realization that Charlus is in essence "a woman," that is, one of the
secret race of men whose temperament and desires are feminine. Finally, in
the scene of sadomasochism, Charlus's vice comes to be interpreted as having a certain virtue; the country boys whom Charlus hires to whip him
bear a striking resemblance to his estranged lover Morel. By thus preserving the figure of Morel in these sad rituals, Charlus remains in his way
faithful to the memory of that young man.

In addition to the interpenetration of spaces represented by these
scenes and the narrator's interpretations of them, Proust also thought of
these passages in a more figurative manner related to the form of his composition, as supporting the architecture of his work as a whole. According
to Proust, the poet Francis Jammes advised him to suppress the infamous
Montjouvain scene, an episode he found shocking. But as Proust explains

in a 1919 letter to François Mauriac, "I have so carefully constructed this work that this episode in the first volume explains the jealousy of my young hero in the fourth and fifth volumes, so that by tearing away the column with the obscene capital, I would later on have brought down the vaulted ceiling" (*Lettres* 21–22).

More generally, the figurative dimension of Proust's use of architecture can be seen as a modern extension of the classical *ars memoria,* in which a complex object of knowledge could be safely stored in the memory by assigning its parts to the respective rooms of an imaginary house. In Proust, however, this model undergoes a twofold transformation: first, its organization is based not on the assignment of discrete categories to a correspondingly divided series of inner spaces but rather on the mutual permeability of such spaces and categories. Second, the memory to be reconstructed is not an object of merely intellectual knowledge but rather a profoundly disturbing experience—in effect a primal scene—the traumatic elements of which the narrator must recombine and reinterpret as a form of insight into the workings of human nature. In doing so, he acquires a deeper knowledge, as well as an altered sense of what it means to be at home in the enigmatic world that he inhabits. The effect is both cathartic and salutary in ways not unrelated to the liberating effects intended by the masters of modern architecture.

If architecture figures in Proust as a metaphor of inner desire, it figures in Joyce as the concrete embodiment of modernity itself. *Ulysses* is a work that gets its characters out of the house and into the street, where they are confronted not with dwelling in its domestic sense but with their existence in urban space, the very scene of modernity. Le Corbusier's notion of an architectural space designed for differentiated speeds and rhythms echoes a remark made by Walter Gropius on his design for the Bauhaus School in Dessau in 1926: "The imposition of axial symmetry gives way to a vital equilibrium of free and asymmetrical groupings" (quoted in Norberg-Schultz 370). This is not a bad way to understand Joyce's Dublin, as well as the structure of *Ulysses.* Joyce shows us a single day in which his characters wander through the space of the city at their respective speeds and rhythms, their paths intersecting occasionally and as if by chance. This plan allows for a break with conventional narrative development, while it also diminishes social distinctions and class difference. In the street, persons of all classes stand at the same level, equally subject to the gaze of the other. At the same time, the space of the city becomes continuous with that of consciousness itself, effacing the distinction between subject and object. Here is a passage from chapter 8, which Joyce designated informally as the "architectural" chapter.

> Trams passed one another, ingoing, outgoing, clanging . . . squads of police marching out, back: trams in, out. Those two loonies mooching about. Dignam carted off . . . Cityful passing away, other cityful coming, passing away too: other coming on, passing on. Houses, lines of houses, streets, miles of pavements, piledup bricks, stones. (8:484–86)[5]

Almost imperceptibly, these lines shift from an anonymous, objective point of view to the consciousness of the novel's main character, Leopold Bloom, thus performing on a textual level the interpenetration of inside and outside, of the subjective and objective universes. At the same time the shifting, associative flow of consciousness in Joyce is shown to be a function of the ceaseless movement of the city, whose traffic comes and goes, whose structures rise and fall like the formations of thought itself.

Joyce's profound loyalty to the scene of modernity as one of ceaseless reconstruction leads him to a merciless parody of the traditional myth of dwelling, exposing it as something that can only be realized in a banal and commodified form. The penultimate chapter of *Ulysses* reveals Bloom's "ultimate ambition" to be the ownership of

> a thatched bungalowshaped 2 storey dwellinghouse of southerly aspect, surmounted by vane and lightning conductor, connected with the earth, with porch covered by parasitic plants (ivy or Virginia creeper), halldoor, olive green, with smart carriage finish and neat doorbrasses, stucco front with gilt tracery at eaves and gable, rising, if possible, upon a gentle eminence with agreeable prospect from balcony with stone pillar parapet over unoccupied and unoccupyable interjacent pastures and standing in 5 or 6 acres of its own ground. (17:1504–12)

Bloom's dream house, with its imaginary address of "Bloom Cottage. Saint Leopold's. Flowerville," is the twentieth-century real estate agent's update of Bleak House or of Ruskin's Swiss cottage. In Joyce's deconstruction of the myth of dwelling, its true nature in the twentieth century turns out to consist not in the righteous joys of peasant life but in the frantic pursuit of middle-class leisure activities: snapshot photography, gardening, tennis, do-it-yourself carpentry, the reading of "unexpurgated exotic erotic masterpieces," and the "discussion in tepid security of unsolved historical and criminal problems" (17:1599–1600). The roots of dwelling are exposed as being not in the earth but in the accumulation and circulation of capital; hence this passage is followed by a long paragraph, written entirely in contractual language, stipulating the terms of a mortgage loan from the "Industrious Foreign Acclimated Nationalised Friendly Stateaided Building Society" (17:1658–59). The point is that Joyce's parody of dwelling ends by affirming another, more vital relation to architectural space, that represented by the city itself as the scene of encounter with the reality of experience.

Joyce's representation of urban space in terms of multiplicity, seriality, and circulation finds a counterpart in Virginia Woolf's *Mrs Dalloway* (1925), published three years after *Ulysses* and based on a similar structuring principle: the movements of a series of characters through the space of a city (in this case London) on a single day in the middle of June. In contrast to Joyce, however, Woolf is more precisely concerned with a dialectic between domestic space and the urban landscape, especially as this dialectic implies the freedom of feminine consciousness. In Woolf, the recurring motif of this relation between inner and outer space, as well as of conscious freedom, is the figure of the window.

One can hardly underestimate the importance of the window and glass in the discourse and practice of modern architecture. Already in his 1909 essay *Brücke und Tür* (Bridge and Door) Georg Simmel finds in the very nature of the window as a human artefact an object whose symbolic significance goes beyond its practical value. The window is ordinarily made for looking out, not in. Like the door, it marks the transition from a spatially limited interior to an unlimited exterior, and so in an existential sense it symbolizes the place of the uniquely human, poised on the border between finitude and the infinite. In a more concrete sense, the modern innovation of non-load-bearing facades meant that they could be entirely transparent, thus solving in a quite natural way the problem of interior illumination that had existed since the beginning of human history. Among the early modernist visionaries of architectural transparency was Bruno Taut, who designed a Glashaus for the 1914 exhibition of the German Werkbund. This in turn inspired Paul Scheerbart's novel *Glasarchitektur* (1914), where glass construction symbolizes the society of the future. Scheerbart argues that a higher culture can only come about through architectural transformation, which for him means the introduction of glass, "which admits the light of sun and moon and stars not only through a few windows, but through as many walls as possible, walls made of glass" (Kruft 372). Later, the great master of the medium proved to be Ludwig

Mies van der Rohe. His buildings in the form of glass boxes and towers embody an almost spiritual approach to construction, in which the material of glass unites surface and light, the material and the immaterial (Frampton, "Modernisme" 44).

The architecture of *Mrs Dalloway* is the dull stone masonry of Westminster, with its eighteenth- and nineteenth-century houses. Woolf has no interest in modern architecture as such, and the utopian manifestos of modern architecture in particular should not be confused with the aims of modernist writers like Joyce and Woolf. However, Woolf shares with her architectural contemporaries a passion for the dematerialization of solid boundaries and for the interpenetration of interior and exterior space. The impulse of the novel's opening passage is that of, precisely, an opening out and a dissolution of the barriers to desire. Clarissa Dalloway stands at the open window of her house and reflects that for that evening's party "the doors would be taken off their hinges." This architectural image opens simultaneously onto the exterior space of the city ("what a morning—fresh as if issued to children on a beach") and the interior space of her memory, for the scene recalls to her how, as a girl, "she had burst open the French windows at Bourton into the open air" (3). The door between memory and actuality, inner and outer spaces, is taken off its hinges. Both the remembered gesture and the present one, however, stand in contrast to the tomb-like hall of the house, "cool as a vault" (37), or to the confined space of the attic room where she sleeps alone on a narrow bed: "There was an emptiness about the heart of life; an attic room" (39). As Clarissa ventures forth into the city to buy flowers, she embodies the freedom of movement enjoyed by middle-class women in the modern city. The nearly ecstatic pleasure she derives from the sensations of urban space serves to compensate for the sterility of her domestic life.

If the window stands for this opening out of feminine desire, it also serves to affirm the "odd affinities" (200) that unite Clarissa on a profound and mysterious level with the people and things around her. Near the end of the novel, she stands at the window once again, alone for a moment during her party. It is dark now, and she has just learned of the suicide of a young stranger whom we know as Septimus Warren Smith. The young man has thrown himself out of a window in an act that Clarissa imagines as one of defiance, of "an attempt to communicate" (241–42). Across the street, in the room opposite, she is surprised by the sight of an old lady staring straight at her from another window. The old lady is going to bed; at last she puts out the light. Clarissa, now contemplating the darkness that passes over the house opposite, thinks of the young man who has killed himself by throwing himself out of a window; she feels "glad that he had done it, thrown it away while they went on living" (244). The scene is rich in the way it uses architectural space to stage Clarissa's confrontation with the conditions of her own existence. She stands in a room apart from her guests, but her gaze is directed outward, toward a female figure opposite who returns her gaze, as if in a mirror image. It is a remarkable moment in which the gaze of the other appears as Clarissa's own gaze directed back at her: however, the old woman's gaze is neither entirely Clarissa's own nor that of the other. The point is that the window scene creates a moment in which the difference between self and other is suspended, thereby effacing this boundary in a kind of revelation that also effaces the boundary between life and death. Then the light goes out in the house opposite, and in that sudden darkness Clarissa sees her own death. But death here is not the confinement of the tomb; rather it is the final suspension of difference, the breakdown of barriers. The thought of death unites Clarissa with both strangers, the young man and the old woman: "There was an embrace in death." I find it significant that this vision is seized through the enframing device of the window, by a feminine gaze directed outward and away from the patriarchal order of the domestic interior—the house of Mrs. Richard Dalloway, hostess to the prime minister. The gaze that passes through one interior, across open space, and into the inner space of the other, stands as a figure for Woolf's ideal of a unifying feminine consciousness.

The figure of a woman standing at the window is symbolic of a certain feminine stance that we find elsewhere in Woolf. Here we are reminded that the traditional ideal of dwelling is inseparable from a certain idea of the feminine—the *femme au foyer,* herself a bodily extension of the warmth of the hearth, yet one that is confined to the walls of the dwelling. Woolf's novels consciously subvert the notion of dwelling that includes the *femme au foyer* while seeking a sense of permanence that does not depend on the enclosure of domestic space. Her characters represent the attempt, however fleeting and tentative, to be at home in the world. The opening section of *To the Lighthouse* (1927) is called "The Window." It is here that Mrs. Ramsey, wife and mother, has the occasion to reflect on the world of social difference: "The real differences, she thought, standing by the drawing room window" (14). These are differences of rich and poor, high and low, "things she saw with her own eyes, weekly, daily, here or in London, when she visited this widow, or that struggling wife" (15). Woolf's emphasis here is on the feminine consciousness of the feminization of poverty, one that can be acquired only by a gaze directed outward from the purely domestic sphere. Mrs. Ramsey, however, is not merely an observer of social reality. She also bears witness to a sense of the permanence of being, a sense confirmed by the light reflected in the window: "something, she meant, is immune from change, and shines out (she glanced at the window with its ripple of reflected lights) in the force of the flowing, the fleeting, the spectral" (142).

As an opening onto exterior space, Woolf's window joins the domestic sphere to the social; as a reflecting surface, it serves as the place of fusion between the material and the immaterial dimensions of Woolf's world. Finally, it is through an uncurtained window that the narrator of *A Room of One's Own* (1929) surveys the London streets (124). In order to write, Woolf says, a woman needs money and a room of her own. But the point is worth making that this celebrated essay is not about feminine self-enclosure. Rather, it is about creating a position from which the world at a given historical moment can be observed and rendered by a feminine consciousness. And so she looks out her window to see what London is doing on the morning of 26 October 1928. Woolf makes it clear, however, that the glass is transparent both ways: as she observes the world, she also exposes herself to its view. The window has no curtain. The woman wears no veil. She looks at London face to face.

At this point I want to return to Benjamin's essay "Experience and Poverty" in order to lay the groundwork for discussing a rather different response to the conditions of modernity from that which we find in Joyce and Woolf. In that essay, Benjamin speaks of modern civilization as composed of people "who have grown tired of the endless complications of everyday living . . . to whom the purpose of existence seems to have been reduced to the most distant vanishing point in an endless horizon" (*Selected* 2:735). An important artistic response to this state of things has been that of the tabula rasa, the ruthless clearing away or emptying out of all forms of value so that the creative spirit can begin again. This art of "insight and renunciation" is found equally in architecture and literature. Rather than idealizing the material of glass in the manner of Scheerbart, Benjamin finds it to be something cold and sober, "a hard, smooth material to which nothing can be fixed" (2:733). Scheerbart with his glass and the Bauhaus school with its steel create rooms in which the human being leaves little or no trace.

This idea has been taken up more recently by the Italian theorist Massimo Cacciari, who sees the history of twentieth-century architecture as the concrete embodiment of the spirit of nihilism. Architectural nihilism, in Cacciari's terms, is an even more radical renunciation of the myth of dwelling than my examples have shown up to this point. It annihilates the spirit of place in favor of an abstract geometrical conception of space, it destroys all that is "collected," and its movement is one of "universal displacement" and "radical uprooting." Cacciari finds this architectural movement to be essentially necessary given the historical conditions it expresses. He admires, for example, the antiornamental effect of Loos's 1911 Michaelerplatz building in Vienna, with its bare, stripped-down facade (161). This building, with its simple windows and bare, whitewashed walls, was regarded by Loos's contemporaries as "nihilistic" (Heynen 91), just as they called his Café Museum (1899) "Café Nihilismus" (Cacciari 111). Cacciari also admires the glass towers of Mies, of an absolute transparency that no longer violates the interior but "appears henceforth as the meaning of the thing that it has helped to destroy" (190). Quoting Rilke's Seventh Elegy, Cacciari renounces the possibility of being consoled for the loss of dwelling and place, finding instead, in the empty space left by the destruction of these things, "das atmende Klarsein," breathing clarity (174).

The literary counterpart of the architecture of nihilism is the austere, lucid work of writers of the second generation of modernists such as Jean Rhys and Samuel Beckett. Their deliberate flatness of style, their renunciation of lyricism and "fine writing," is the literary equivalent of Loos's relentless antiornamentalism. In this particular respect they show the influence of Eliot more than of Woolf or Joyce. The deadpan voice is the authentic expression of a world emptied of dwelling and bereft of place. Eliot's 1920 poem "Gerontion" revives the metaphor of the house as an inner space of memory, but here, unlike what happens in Proust's work, memory no longer bears fruit; it has the lifelessness of "reconsidered passion." Only vanity now guides the mind through the house of memory, with its "cunning passages, contrived corridors, / And issues," and the only remaining "Tenants of the house" are "Thoughts of a dry brain in a dry season" (*Collected* 31–33). In the voice and the architectural setting of this poem, Eliot has set the stage for the later work of Beckett.

Before examining one of Beckett's plays in this light, I would remark that the theater is the perfect hinge medium between literature and architecture. That is, in the theater, a dramatic text is performed in an architectural space specifically adapted to this text, in the form of stage set, backdrop, lighting, and so on. When the scene represented is the Battle of

Agincourt, the actual theatrical space may be nothing more than a limitation to be overcome. But in the case of an interior scene, what is represented is pretty much what is in fact there: an architectural space represents itself. Consider the opening stage directions of Beckett's *Endgame* (1958).

> Bare interior.
> Grey light.
> Left and right back, high up, two small windows, curtains drawn.
> Front right, a door. Hanging near door, its face to wall, a picture.
> Front left, touching each other, covered with an old sheet,
> two ashbins.
> Centre, in an armchair, on castors, covered with an old sheet,
> *Hamm.*

One could hardly conceive of a better expression of architectural nihilism. The bare interior is the literal staging of an architectural tabula rasa that resists all traces of human dwelling, while doing away with every "collected" object to which an aura still clings: the picture, for example, is turned to the wall. In the course of the play, Hamm will throw away his toy dog, the last object to which any of his affection still attaches. The gesture is reminiscent of a scene in Rhys's *Voyage in the Dark* (1934) where Anna Morgan, the down-and-out woman of the streets, smashes a picture of a little dog entitled "Loyal Heart" (137). These little dogs are the last survivors of the kitsch objects that once abounded in the Victorian interior.

In *Endgame,* whatever qualities of shelter or domesticity are suggested by the very notion of an interior are here negated, not only by this bareness but also by the absence of difference between interior and exterior. Hamm, who is blind, directs Clov to look out of the windows, which can only be reached by means of a stepladder. The windows are placed above eye level because they serve no purpose, there being nothing on which to open out. Modern architecture's destruction of the barrier between inside and outside here is given a new, if entirely negative, meaning. Thus at the window stage right, Clov reports, "Zero . . . all is . . . corpsed" (25). At the other window, a featureless sea. There is literally nothing to see in the sense that what Clov sees is the landscape of nothingness, which as such is indistinguishable from the bare interior.

The sense of displacement and uprooting defined by Cacciari is likewise enacted on Beckett's stage. It has, for example, no traces left of place—of an identifiable landscape or setting with its own location and history: all of this has been abstracted from what is now just space. The sense of displacement, which here means the annihilation of place, is enacted in the constant if pointless movement about the stage, and by Hamm's obsessive attempts to occupy the exact center of the room. The notion of rootedness, meanwhile, is parodied in the figures of Nell and Nagg, literally rooted in their ashbins. To portray rootedness as consignment to the dustheap is implicitly to assert a profound sense of uprootedness. Finally, the overall structure of the play is one of a systematic evacuation: it begins with a bare space that is emptied out even more completely, with the extinguishing of Nagg and Nell, the discarding of various props, the hesitant departure of Clov, and the veiling and the silence of Hamm, who is finally frozen in a brief tableau.

How are we to understand this negativity in terms of the problematic of dwelling that Beckett and his architectural contemporaries have inherited from the nineteenth century? An answer to this question is suggested by Slavoj Žižek in *The Fragile Absolute,* where the negativity of empty space constitutes, paradoxically, a fundamental component of the structure of sublimation. His version of this structure consists of two elements: a sacred space, cleared out and exempted from the circuit of everyday economy; and a positive object, which, by virtue of filling this space, is elevated to the dignity of the sublime. In Lacanian terminology, these two elements are designated respectively as the Void and the Thing. In traditional, premodern art, the problem was to find an object sufficiently beautiful to occupy this sacred space, thereby fulfilling the conditions of the Sublime. Vestiges of this premodern aesthetic are to be found in Ruskin, for example, where the "righteous poverty" of Swiss peasant life takes place in a similarly sacred space of dwelling.

Today, however, we can no longer count on the existence of any sacred space, either in the concrete physical sense or in the structure of our symbolic universe. If the problem for traditional art was to fill in the Void, the problem for modern art is one of creating the Void to begin with, this clearing in the midst of a world hostile to anything sacred. The space of modern art, according to this logic, can only be occupied by the most minimal, leftover object: the remainder, the piece of trash. A more sublime object is not available and in any case would not be possible without an adequate space of the sacred; only an object utterly devoid of the sublime can "sustain the void of an empty place," whose purity depends on its being distinguished from the elements that fill it out (Žižek 26–27).

Here I think we have a key to understanding the trash that occupies Beckett's theatrical space: the characters in ashbins, the soiled handkerchief, the sawdust, the fleas, the urine, the stink, the dialogue of asides and throwaway lines. The point is to create a space emptied of all value as the necessary condition for the sacred in a world where no actual object or discourse can fulfill that role. As we have seen, modern architecture, too, has cultivated empty space as well as open space. What might be seen as the fulfilment of nihilism, however, should rather be seen as an essential move in the dialectic of the Sublime.

> *Clov:* Do you believe in the life to come?
> *Hamm:* Mine was always that. (35)

Hamm replies to the question of faith with a wry confession of failed expectations in his own life, on which the curtain is about to close. His reply expresses a hopelessness to which the emptiness of the stage set, and the austerity of the play as a whole, are perfectly adapted. But it would be an error to interpret Beckett's art of negation in a purely nihilistic sense. It is more properly seen as a work of ascesis, in the tradition of the *via negativa* that goes back at least as far as Saint John of the Cross. However, the difference between sixteenth-century and modern forms of ascesis is that the latter have an essentially social character. As Adorno argues in "Trying to Understand *Endgame*," modern forms of ascesis, whether literary or architectural, are related more to the spirit of the age than to the Holy Spirit (*Notes* 1:241–75). Such works constitute a form of resistance to the oppressive character of modern social reality. In the very purity of their negation, they therefore carry an element of promise, the promise implied in the courage of an unswerving commitment to the age combined with a total absence of illusion about it. It is in this negative way that modern art finally refers, however distantly, to the promise of that other, as yet uncreated world, the life to come that always was.

2

Demonic Spaces:
Sade, Dickens, Kafka

In the eighth chapter of the book of Matthew, Jesus travels in the land of the Gadarenes, where he is confronted by two men possessed by demons (*daimonisomenous*), who have come from the tombs of the dead. "Art thou come hither to torment us before the time?" they ask Jesus, in the King James translation. In the next verse Matthew makes it clear that it is the demons (*daimones*) themselves, speaking through the possessed, who beseech Jesus: "If thou cast us out, suffer us to go away into the herd of swine." Jesus casts the demons from the men into the herd of swine, who then, seized with frenzy, rush headlong into the sea to perish in the waters (Matt. 8:28–32). For our purposes, this episode is emblematic for more than one reason. First, it gives a local habitation and a name to the demonic. If the demons inhabit the men, the men possessed by demons inhabit the tombs of the dead (*mnemeion*), like their counterparts in Mark 5:1 and Luke 8:27. In Luke, the man long beset by demons wears no clothes, nor does he live in any house, but "in the tombs." The habitations of the possessed are places of concealment, but they are also, perhaps not incidentally, monuments to the dead. If we consider that the precincts of the tombs are the ritualized and architecturally constructed space of ancestral memory, these scenes from the New Testament take place as if there were a hidden demonic possession within the space of memory itself, so that, metaphorically, the emergence of the possessed from out of the tombs figures as the unveiling of a terrible secret. The possessed who interpellate Jesus represent a kind of return of the repressed from the depths of cultural and tribal memory.

The biblical passage also shows us that in the Christian dispensation, the ancient Greek notion of the *daimon,* which Homer used to denote a divine being, has been degraded to the status of an evil spirit. From a modern perspective we can see this as an intermediate stage in the evolving relation between the demonic and the human. Homer's *daimon* was a divinity, independent of mortal being. Matthew's *daimon* inhabits men in the form of an evil or unclean spirit, but only in a relation of exteriority to the human; the *daimon* may speak through the person it possesses, but it can also be cast out. Modern literature brings us to the final stage of this evolution: demons no longer inhabit or possess human beings; they are human, and the space of demonic habitation is the world as constructed by human beings.

In this chapter I want to show a number of different ways in which modern writers make a space for the demonic in the constructed world. The three writers I have chosen belong, respectively, to the past three centuries of the modern era, each having a conception of the demonic that reflects a particular historical context within the larger framework of modernity. Insofar as the constructed world of modernity is the concrete manifestation of human will and desire in an age of rational enlightenment, the manner in which the demonic inhabits this world has the function of calling into question the precise nature of that enlightenment. The implicit question posed is not so much whether the post-Enlightenment world continues to be haunted by uncanny forces that defy rational understanding. Rather, it is a question of whether the increasing dominance of reason does not reveal, the more completely it prevails, the secret space of the demonic at its center. The quite different ways in which this question is negotiated by the literary works I propose to examine here reflect a plurality of responses to a common preoccupation that is symptomatic of modern literature in general.

From an architectural perspective, the notion of demonic spaces raises the question of architecture's ethical function. The question is inherited from Vitruvius, who stressed the importance of moral philosophy in the architect's formation and the essential propriety of architectural form in its relation to nature and use (Book I, chapter 2). In the modern period this question takes on a degree of urgency such that both Ruskin and Adolf

Loos speak of crime in architecture and Giedion devotes one of his chapters to "The Demand for Morality in Architecture." Karsten Harries begins his *The Ethical Function of Architecture* (1997) by asking, "Should architecture not continue to help us find our place and way in an ever more disorienting world?" He defines the function in question as that of architecture's task to help articulate a common ethos, a way for human beings to exist in the world (4). The ethical function of architecture is that of a concrete interpretation of the question "how to live." I shall argue that the presence of demonic spaces in the modern literary imagination can be understood as symptomatic of the lack of any reassuring answer to this question.

Among the dynamics already present in Matthew is one that proves essential to the demonic spaces that lie at the center of the Marquis de Sade's narrative in *Justine, ou les malheurs de la vertu* (1791): that of concealment. In Sade, the demonic takes the form of the instinctual violence of human passions, which require a space of secrecy in order to be fully unleashed. In psychoanalytic terms, such spaces can be compared to the mechanisms that seal the subject off from the realm of the real in order to give full rein to the delirium of sadistic fantasy. One of the many trials of Justine begins when, having escaped from the tortures of the surgeon Rodin, she seeks refuge at Sainte-Marie-des-Bois, a Benedictine monastery hidden in the midst of a vast forest somewhere south of Auxerre. In the church attached to the monastery, the monk Dom Severino receives her confession and, on discovering that she has no protectors, seizes her for service in the seraglio of the monastery. Justine is taken behind the altar into the sacristy and from there through a secret door into a dark and narrow passageway. Inside this passage, she is driven through "détours dont rien ne peut me faire connaître ni le local, ni les issues," labyrinthine passages that made it impossible to know either the place she was in or the way out. In the course of this subterranean transfer, the monk stops her from time to time in order to perform preludes to the acts of sodomy to which she will henceforth be subjected daily. In this way, her introduction to the mysteries of the institution through a secret tunnel corresponds to the penetration of her own body through the orifice that one of her earlier tormentors has referred to as "l'antre obscur" and "le temple le plus secret," the dark lair and most secret temple (92–93). Sade registers the experience of the constructed environment as itself obscenely erotic, based on certain elements that this environment has in common with the architecture of the human body. The analogy between body and building follows, however perversely, in the tradition of architectural discourse dating from Vitruvius, which understands and measures the built environment according to the proportions of the human body.

At the end of the tunnel, Justine finds herself in a hidden annex, which is revealed to her as the site of the monks' orgiastic rituals. It is a building of four stories, half underground and surrounded by a concentric series of six hedges thick enough to conceal it entirely from any exterior view. A deep, circular ditch renders it even more secure from those who might wish to enter or escape. The principles of isolation and concealment are repeated inside the structure: Justine and her fellow captives are held in isolated cells and can communicate with one another only at the monks' pleasure. When, after several months of captivity, Justine finally escapes, she is able for the first time to look from the outside in, through the windows of the floor below the one to which she has been confined. It is at this point that she discovers, to her and the reader's horror, *another* scene of debauchery, identical in kind to those in which she has been forced to take part, but with other young women, until now unseen by and unknown to her and her companions: "d'autres malheureuses inconnues de nous" (other sufferers unknown to us). To the principles of confinement and isolation, Sade adds that of spatial repetition corresponding to the temporal repetition of orgiastic ritual.

In her notes to the Gallimard edition of *Justine,* Noëlle Châtelet points out that the monastery is the perfect site for Sade's immorality. As a religious institution, it is the ideal place for sacrilege, so that the very objects of the sacrament are here made instruments of torture and debauchery. Moreover, as an ordered and enclosed space, it lends itself to the staging of erotic rituals of the kind that Justine and her female companions suffer at the hands of the monks. Sade's choice of a monastery for these scenes can also be read as a phantasmic vision of the Church's doctrinal and historical mortification of the human body, especially in its monastic tradition. It is as if the Crucifixion had to be reenacted on an endless series of sacrificial innocents and reinterpreted in an endless series of erotic variations in a frenzied desire to feel the full weight of its meaning, both for the crucifier and the crucified. However, if one asks, as Justine does, how men could abandon themselves to such depravity, the answer is to be found not merely in the libertine tastes of the monks but also in the architectural form of the monastery. The strange tastes of the monks may be the cause of their vice, but the equally strange design of their habitation—unseen, unknown—is the condition necessary to its full indulgence. More than this, Sade implicitly poses the question of the natural consequences of human power and desire in a space whose absolute secrecy confers absolute freedom on those who to whom it belongs. The concealed and buried seraglio is an architectural figure for the demonic unconscious in its unbridled freedom to make happen whatever it desires.

The difficulty in reading Sade is that any ethical perspective on his world is both anticipated and opposed by the force of violence, which, in Sade's thinking, lies at the heart of reason. This problem applies to the ethics of architecture, which in his work is reduced to the function of serving the logic of power and desire. Sade's hidden prisons and underground horror chambers are reminiscent of Piranesi's *carceri:* both architectural imaginations destabilize the classical values according to which the construction of a building reflected the ideal nature of human society. Nonetheless, Sade's design for Sainte-Marie-des-Bois, like that of the Château de Silling in *Les Cent vingt journées de Sodome,* corresponds to an eighteenth-century debate over truth and ethics in architecture. Theorists such as Jacques-François Blondel had elaborated the notion of *caractère* or the expressive function of a building as distinct from its purely utilitarian function: *caractère* "announces the building to be what it is" (2:229). Thus, for Blondel, the proper character of a temple is that of *décence,* of public buildings *grandeur,* of monuments *somptuosité,* of promenades *élégance,* and so on. The architectural style of a building is "true" when it conforms to its natural expressive function, or *caractère*. Alongside this essentially classicist doctrine, Marc-Antoine Laugier developed a theory based on a Rousseauian vision of a benevolent Nature as the model for all human constructions. The primitive hut is the original and truest of shelters, from which all architectural principles must be derived. Architectural crimes, then, are those that deceive, such as the pilaster, which presents the false appearance of a column. This conforms to a later formulation by the English architect John Soane, a contemporary of Sade, for whom every building "should express clearly its destination and its character, marked in the most decided and indisputable manner" (126). Whether judged by the theories of Blondel or Laugier, Sade's imagined buildings would have been deeply troubling to architectural theorists of his own time because, part of their function being to conceal themselves and the truth of their functions, these buildings place in opposition to each other the normally inseparable principles of truth and function. On one hand, the monastery of Sainte-

Marie-des-Bois is perfectly functional, if one admits that its true function is that of imprisonment, torture, and rape. On the other hand, its deceitful appearance as a place of spiritual refuge, its secret passages, and the concealment of its monstrous prison-cum-pleasure dome—all of these make it, from the classical perspective, an architectural crime as well as a place of demonic transgression. In the wider historical context, Sade's spaces register the uncertainty of architecture's ethical function in a social world in which such notions as character, grandeur, decency, and truth no longer have the meanings assigned to them by classical value.

Roland Barthes has pointed out that architectural closure in Sade serves the practical purposes of isolation, but also that the utter secrecy produced by this isolation produces its own sensual thrill, a *volupté* based on the momentary desocialization of crime (20), on the pleasure derived from committing crimes in the knowledge of absolute impunity. Within the confines of his secured space, the Sadean figure is free to act without restraint and without limits—without meaning, even, if *meaning* implies the need to answer for one's words and actions to the other, to some coherent symbolic order. One of the many paradoxes of Sade's work, however, is that his demonic utopia of unrestraint, though predicated on an ideal isolation from the social world, reveals itself to be wholly preoccupied with the conditions of his own time and place. It is no accident that Sade wrote the manuscript of *Justine* in a prison cell of the Bastille: his text serves in large measure as a nightmare version of the ancien régime. We know as well that, for at least the years 1792–93, during the height of the Terror, Sade displayed a great deal of republican fervor as president of the revolutionary *section des Piques*. The sadistic monks of *Justine,* members of the richest and most powerful families of the ancien régime, seem designed to fuel revolutionary hysteria in general and anticlericalism in particular; they could only add to the reputation of provocateur that Sade had gained during the storming of the Bastille when he harangued the crowd, falsely crying out that the guards were slashing the throats of his fellow prisoners (Bataille, *La littérature* 122).

It has been pointed out more than once that Sade is at best an ambiguous spokesman for revolutionary ideals. Georges Bataille sees the scene of the Bastille as a sign of Sade's fascination with the unchained passion of the crowd. For him, revolutionary ideology is only an alibi here for the destructive impulse lying at the heart of Sade's work: his desire is to destroy not just the object-world and its victims but also himself and his own work. In contrast to the good news brought by the Gospel,

Son œuvre porte la *mauvaise* nouvelle d'un accord des vivants à ce qui les tue, du Bien avec le Mal et l'on pourrait dire: du cri le plus fort avec le silence. (118)

His work brings the bad *news of a pact between the living and what it is that kills them, of Good with Evil, and, one might say, of the most piercing scream with silence.*

Writing on this subject six years after Bataille, Blanchot also cautions against identifying Sade too closely with the Revolution: if Sade saw himself in the Revolution, it was only to the extent that by overturning one law after another, the Revolution for a time represented the possibility of a lawless regime (*Lautréamont et Sade* 24). However, the ambiguity of Sade's writing is such that it can neither be fully identified with nor fully distinguished from the ideology of the Revolution. On one hand, Sade is quoted as saying that the reign of law is inferior to that of anarchy. On the other hand, the interminable discourses that accompany Sade's scenes of cruelty and domination are entirely preoccupied with the fundamental concerns of revolutionary thought and the motives of revolutionary destruction: power, freedom, the laws of nature, and the pursuit of happiness. One of the many paradoxes of Sade's work is that these values are defended by fictional characters who, historically speaking, belong to the feudal and monastic orders of the ancien régime. In fact Sade's anarchic impulses are directed both against the ancien régime and against the Enlightenment ideals of the Revolution, insofar as the rational order of the Enlightenment represses the instinctive energies of the human while it conceals this same repression. Here Sade has certain affinities with William Blake, for whom, in the *Marriage of Heaven and Hell,* "Energy is the only life and is from the Body." Sade's philosophy is elaborated in relation to contemporary theories concerning liberty and the equality of individuals before nature and the law, but without the categorical imperative that, according to Kant, should determine a consciousness of right and wrong. It is as if Sade wished to expose the Kantian moral imperative as a mask that concealed the destructive forces of an unbridled rational mastery of nature that he saw as a consequence of the Revolution and its industrial counterpart. But Sade's thinking is like the chapel that, seen from another angle, becomes a prison: it is strangely anamorphic. In his philosophy there is no place for what Blake calls Soul, and for this reason the elaborate machinery of Sadean imprisonment and torture, as well as the total objectification of its victims as both the raw material and the laborers in this machinery, prefigures the social and philosophical conditions of modernity that will be more explicitly, if more sentimentally, exposed in Dickens.

The monk ironically named Father Clément is a perfect representative of this rationality. After having worked himself into a lather by whipping Justine, Father Clément explains to her that nothing is more natural than this subjugation of her body to his desires, however strange they may seem to her.

> Lorsque, préférant son bonheur à celui des autres, [l'homme] renverse où détruit tout ce qu'il trouve dans son passage, a-t-il fait autre chose que servir la nature dont les premières et les plus sûres inspirations lui dictent de se rendre heureux, n'importe au dépens de qui? (244)

> *When, putting his own happiness above that of others, man overturns or destroys everything in his way, has he done anything other than to serve nature, whose primary and surest inspiration tells him to make himself happy, no matter at whose expense?*

Sade's peculiar idea of liberty is that human equality gives every person the right to pursue his own desires regardless of the cost to others, with the understanding that he assumes the risks of such a course of action; liberty is the power to subjugate others to one's will. The actual practice of this philosophy in *Justine,* however, has certain architectural requirements. As Dom Severino tells the novel's heroine:

> Jetez votre regard sur l'asile impénétrable où vous êtes; jamais aucun mortel ne parut dans ces lieux; le couvent sera pris, fouillé, brûlé, que cette retraite ne s'en découvrirait davantage: c'est un pavillon isolé, enterré, que six murs d'une incroyable épaisseur environnent de toutes parts. (192–93)

> *Cast an eye over the impenetrable asylum where you find yourself; never has an outsider appeared within these premises; the monastery could be taken, searched, and burned down, while this retreat would still remain undiscovered: this is a buried and isolated pavilion surrounded on all sides by six walls of unbelievable thickness.*

Severino's assertion that no outsider has ever penetrated the precincts is later supplemented by Omphale, Justine's fellow prisoner, who concludes her more detailed description of the prison with the words "la mort seule rompt ici nos liens" (only death breaks our bonds here) (195). Omphale, who is in a position to know, explains that this inescapability guarantees for the monks absolute impunity for their actions, which, because they are unpunishable neither in this world nor the next, no longer have the name of sin. It is precisely this absolute impunity that inflames the monks' imaginations and incites them to cruelty and tyranny.

The testimonies of both Severino and Omphale recall the scene in the *Inferno* where Guido da Montefeltro, one of the "evil counselors," takes Dante for one of the damned, since "già mai di questo fondo / non tornò vivo alcun" (never from these depths has anyone returned alive) (xvii:62–63). The similarities between the fictional space of Dom Severino's pavilion and that of the Inferno itself—another concentrically walled, buried series of torture chambers, has much to suggest concerning the medieval aspect of Sade's imagination and the feudal world from which he emerged. In Guido's case the absolute inescapability of hell, as in Severino's the absolute impenetrability of the *pavillon,* allows for a complete and fearless freedom of expression. In the event, Severino's account will turn out to be a slightly exaggerated description of his building's inescapability. But an imagined architecture serves his purposes just as well as a real one: it is enough for Justine to believe in the utter impossibility of her deliverance to make her the perfect object of her tormentor's *jouissance.*

In her relentless innocence and her role as perpetual victim, Justine can be compared to the character of Little Nell in Charles Dickens's early novel, *The Old Curiosity Shop* (1841). Both young heroines are homeless, both are wanderers, and both are sacrificed to the powers of a world that reduces human beings to the status of objects. However, in Dickens's novel, the space of the demonic is inspired not by the feudal and monastic orders of the ancien régime but by the ravages of capital, which take concrete form in the urban industrial landscape. In this landscape there is no place for Nell and her old father, both of whom are exiled from a more humane object-world of the past, that of the old curiosity shop. This shop, with its ancient suits of mail, fantastic carvings, tapestry, and strange furniture "that might have been designed in dreams" (14), has a more aesthetic and human significance than any commercial importance. It is particularly related to the baroque aesthetic of the Renaissance *Wunderkammer* or "cabinet of curiosities," where objects were related to one another as respective emblems of the wonders of God's creation.[1] The old curiosity shop is thus a vestige of a premodern world in which objects, nature, and human history held in common a universal meaning.

The difference between the old shop and the newly forged world into which Nell and her father are thrown corresponds to the antithetical scenes of A. W. Pugin's *Contrasts* (1841), a polemical work of architectural theory that juxtaposes images of medieval England with those of the Victorian industrial environment. Pugin's paired etchings show England "before" and "after" it was reduced to an industrial wasteland. For example, on one hand is shown a "Catholic town of 1440," with its dreaming spires and echoing greens; on the facing page, this is pictorially opposed to "The Same Town in 1840," a place of dark satanic mills, soot-blackened air, and polluted streams (105). Pugin's book has a strongly moral and religious tone: for him, the Gothic architecture of the Middle Ages was the spontaneous expression of Christian revelation, whereas the tenements and factory chimneys of the present testify to the decline of authentic (Catholic) moral and religious values. Although Dickens is no Catholic and is not the polemicist that Pugin is, his novel tends to confirm Pugin's sense that the Industrial Revolution is the modern form of the demonic. The architect's "after" images could have served to illustrate certain scenes from *The Old Curiosity Shop*. In one such scene, Nell and her father seek shelter in "a large and lofty building, supported by pillars of iron," which houses an industrial forge. An infernal din arises from "the beating of hammers and roar of furnaces," while

> in this gloomy place, moving like demons among the flame and smoke, dimly and fitfully seen, flushed and tormented by the burning fires, and wielding great weapons, . . . a number of men laboured like giants. (329–30)

One of the furnaces burns perpetually, watched day and night by a man who has spent his entire life with no other aim. Dickens's illustrator, George Cattermole, shows him as a haggard, wild-eyed figure, mesmerized by the flames of an industrial hell, as Nell bends over him in an attitude of mute interrogation (fig. 3). In contrast to the Gothic cathedrals admired by Pugin and Ruskin, Dickens's industrial mill is a kind of anticathedral: large and lofty, but with pillars of iron instead of stone, filled with deafening noise and gloom instead of silence and light. At the center of its rituals, there is not the altar but a furnace fire, tended by a strange devotee who confides in Nell, "Such as I, pass all our lives before our furnace doors, and seldom go forth to breathe." The repast he shares with his visitors is not the consecrated bread and wine of the host, but "a scanty mess of coffee and coarse bread" (332). In his duties the furnace watcher resembles the "filles

Fig. 3. George Cattermole, illustration for *The Old Curiosity Shop.*

de garde" (girls of the watch) in Sade's monastic prison; each of them must stand watch day and night over one of the monks, ready at any moment to administer to his caprices. In other respects as well, Sade's universe prefigures the industrial system of labor: the women of the monastery are in fact highly regulated sex workers who conform to a strict spatial and temporal regimen in which even the gestures by which they gratify the monks' desires are made uniform and repetitious.

In an essay on *The Old Curiosity Shop* written in the early 1930s, Adorno finds that its strongly allegorical quality belongs to a "dispersed baroque" aesthetic, a "prebourgeois form" in Dickens's novels that serves to "dissolve the very bourgeois world that they depict" (*Notes* 2:171–72). In other words, Dickens's universe contains vestiges of a world in which the individual has not yet attained either full autonomy or the isolation that goes with it; the destiny of the fictional character is determined not by individual psychology but by a fate tied, however obscurely, to the objective nature of the world itself. This essentially "baroque" world is dispersed throughout Dickens's work as a ghostly presence. According to this reading, social reality in Dickens is not merely represented; it is invested with the mythical power of the demonic. By retaining a premodern sense of estrangement from the modern world, Dickens is able to convey the horror of social reality without resigning himself to it as the natural order of things. This is what distinguishes Dickens from a merely naturalist writer like Zola. What Adorno calls Dickens's "dispersed baroque" can also be described in terms of narrative technique, as the contrast in Dickens between a naturalist background and a surface narrative composed in the register of the fantastic. Although Raymond Williams rightly remarks that Dickens was able to perceive "the critically altered relationship between men and things, of which the city was the most social and visual embodiment" (163–64), this is not what makes the particularity of Dickens. What needs to be added to this reading is a recognition of the allegorical nature of a realism that in Dickens is pushed to the limits of the surreal. Dickens's urban landscape is not just modern and realistic; it is a timeless space of desolation, a "cheerless region," where

> Dismantled houses here and there appeared, tottering to the earth, propped up by fragments of others that had fallen down, unroofed, windowless, blackened, desolate, but yet inhabited. (335)

Moving through this space of ruined habitation, Nell and her father appear as a dark parody of Dante and Virgil touring hell; in this respect they are allegorical figures of the second degree, as the persons of the *Divina Commedia* are already allegorical. Against Dante the pilgrim Dickens puts Nell the wanderer. Dante is accompanied by Virgil, spirit of reason; Nell by her father, beset with madness. But there is no Beatrice to watch over Nell. Her destination is a lost paradise: the place where she dies is an ancient tenement attached to a Gothic church; but its oriel windows and stone arches have fallen into ruin and are fast being reclaimed by the surrounding vegetation. In his nineteenth-century rewriting of the *Inferno*, Dickens is able to revive an ancient sense of the demonic by allegorizing the modern object-world as the concrete manifestation of evil, created by the spirit of capital.

If Dickens's oppressive mills are the modern manifestations of capital or, more precisely, the sites of production in the industrial capitalist order, he chooses, curiously, to allegorize the spirit of capital in a premodern and even folkloric figure. In *The Old Curiosity Shop,* this spirit is personified by Daniel Quilp, the malicious moneylender whom Dickens calls a dwarf.

Adorno argues that Quilp is more accurately called a kobold: a mischievous familiar spirit who haunts houses or lives underground, a gnome. As such, the figure of Quilp allows us to see the origins of modernity in a figure out of fairy tale who, like Nell and her father, has been surpassed by the world in which it survives as an uncanny remainder of the past. The habitations of this spirit are flimsy, precarious structures: Quilp stays in a moldy cabin where he sleeps in a hammock, and where, as he says, "I can be quite alone when I have business on hand, and be secure from all spies and listeners" (373). He entertains his rare visitors at a place called the Wilderness, a wooden summer house "in an advanced state of decay, and overlooking the slimy banks of a great river at low water" (381). This is the imagery that Eliot will later employ in *The Waste Land* (1922) as symptomatic of a modern spiritual wilderness. In Dickens, the leaking, weatherblown habitations of Quilp suggest that, if the means of production of modern capital are powerful enough to create a modern Inferno, the spirit of capital nonetheless remains poor—poor in spirit, badly housed in a world created after its own image. Quilp is but an early version of that weightier, more modern Dickensian capitalist Paul Dombey (in *Dombey and Son,* 1848), whose bourgeois mansion crumbles around him in a stony allegory of his own spiritual desolation. The fate of all of these characters, however, is determined by their relative power to master an object-world that takes its toll on the human through poverty, homelessness, disease, and starvation: suffering on a much greater scale than that inflicted by Sade's torturers. Nell is powerless in the face of this newly demonic character of the world. This fatal powerlessness is signaled early in the novel, when Quilp turns her and her father out of their home: "There were some trifles there—poor useless things—that she would have liked to take away, but that was impossible." Adorno remarks on this passage, "Because she is not able to take hold of the object-world of the bourgeois sphere, the object-world seizes hold of her, and she is sacrificed" (2:177).

In Sade and Dickens we are given, on one hand, a vision of the demonic inspired by the architectural spaces of the Church and, on the other, an equally demonic vision inspired by the architecture of modern industrial production. By adding Kafka to this scheme, we obtain a threefold vision of the demonic spaces of modernity: historically, they range through the eighteenth, nineteenth, and twentieth centuries; institutionally, they implicate the Church, bourgeois capital, and the state; architecturally, they are figured in the monastery, the factory mill, and the Castle as bureaucratic office space.

Kafka is close enough in spirit to Dickens, to his sense of the uncanny and to the ghostly presence of the dispersed baroque, to want to mark his distance from the older writer. In a notebook entry of 1917 he complains of Dickens's extreme prodigality and the barbarous impression created by the "extravagant ensemble" (*unsinnigen Ganzen*) of Dickens's novel, qualities that Kafka himself has been able to avoid, he says, thanks to his relative lack of vigor and his status as an imitator (*Epigon*) (*Tägebucher* 841). But the obvious difference in style is symptomatic of a more substantial difference between Dickens and Kafka concerning what might be called the ontological condition of the demonic. For if Dickens has transported elements of the premodern baroque universe into the modern industrial world, he does so in order to redefine the demonic in terms of the inhuman social conditions created by that world.

The meaning of Dickens's allegory is thus relatively clear, whereas Kafka presents us with something else entirely. Benjamin observes that Kafka's writing takes the form of a parable, like the story of Jesus and the demons in the land of the Gadarenes. But unlike the parable, the meaning of Kafka's stories does not unfold for us; we do not have the doctrine, if there is one, that is being interpreted (Benjamin, *Illuminations* 122). There is an unbridgeable gap in Kafka between material form and doctrine, and this accounts for the sense of impenetrability that Kafka rehearses as an element of his fictional universe. In contrast to the figures that inhabit Dickens's work, however ghostly and uncanny they may be, Kafka's fictional universe implies a much more enigmatic relation of the demonic to the human and object worlds. The nature of this enigma has been defined in various ways. Roberto Calasso remarks that Kafka finds his narrative substance in an archaic state of being that precedes the separation of demons from gods (54), that is to say, before the symbolic repartition of being into the ontological distinctions necessary to assign meaning, or even to formulate a doctrine of good and evil. Benjamin says something similar by observing that "laws and definite norms remain unwritten in [Kafka's] prehistoric world" (*Illuminations* 114). Such observations go a good way toward explaining the way things in Kafka are both familiar and strikingly other, but how can we take into account the specific modernity of Kafka's work? In order to do so, we need to consider the degree to which Kafka was instinctively in tune with, and even in advance of, the philosophical currents of his own time, especially those concerning ontology, the question of being.

My reading of demonic spaces in Kafka starts from a passage in Heidegger's *Introduction to Metaphysics* (1935) that specifically addresses the condition of Europe in the twentieth century. This condition is characterized by what Heidegger calls *Entmachtung,* the destitution of the human spirit (*Geist*): the flight of the gods, the destruction of the earth, the transformation of the people into the masses, the disintegration of spiritual forces, the refusal of any original questioning of the fundamentals of being, and finally, the concealment and denial of this state of affairs (*Einführung* 49). Somewhat cryptically, Heidegger attributes this disintegration of spirit to the invasion of what he calls the demonic (*das Dämonische*) in the sense of a destructive malevolence (*zerstörerisch Bösartigen*). A problem for readers of Heidegger has been that he does not name the source of this demonic malevolence toward the human spirit. Derrida, however, finds this source in Heidegger's very conception of spirit, which is capable of a torment that turns it against itself: the spirit is double and therefore capable of destroying itself (*De l'esprit* 102). The demonic, which in antiquity stood for an intermediate form of being between the human and the gods, is now that which confounds and obscures the real relation between consciousness and being. As Ned Lukacher puts the matter in his Heideggerian reading of Shakespeare, the demonic is "the figure for the incontrovertible ghostliness, the familiar strangeness, that dwells between the perceptions and reflections of consciousness and the enigmatic ground of Being itself"(2). This space of the demonic, as the unbridgeable gap between consciousness and being, is the space occupied by Kafka's writing.

While Heidegger's notion of the demonic provides a historical and metaphysical context for the conditions of Kafka's writing, my own reading of Kafka takes place on a more practical level, where the terms of consciousness and being are replaced by those of meaning and material form. More precisely, I wish to show that in Kafka there is a studied lack of fit between what things are, materially, and what they mean, in functional or symbolic terms, and that this lack is made manifest in the figuration of architectural space. The consequences of this lack, moreover, are a generalized sense of homelessness, an absence of shelter in every sense of the word.

Kafka often described his own writing in architectural terms. A notebook passage written in 1922, at a moment when his progress in writing *The Castle* was at a standstill, begins with the statement, "Das Schreiben versagt sich mir" (writing refuses itself to me). He then speaks of his writing as a process of construction (*aufbauen*) but in a way that also makes this a construction of the self. I want to construct myself (*will ich mich dann aufbauen*), says Kafka, like someone who has an unsafe house and who wants to build a new one next to it by using the materials of the old house. But it is bad (*schlimm*) if while he is doing so his strength gives out, so that now instead of having an unsafe but fully built house, he has one that is half destroyed and another only half built, and so nothing (*Nachgelassene* 2:373).[2]

The first thing to notice about this passage is the degree of intimacy between writing and the self, as if only through the constructive process of writing could Kafka himself come into being, not just as a writer but as a human being. The second thing is that Kafka is testifying to a kind of spiritual homelessness. The metaphor of the unsafe (*unsicher*) house suggests that, fundamentally, his being lacks a secure shelter and that in attempting to construct a new one through writing he risks losing whatever meager shelter he had to begin with. The constructive process of writing is therefore, paradoxically, a leap into the void because for its materials it must deconstruct the unstable architecture of a prior mode of being, with the danger that the very process of this deconstruction will exhaust the writer's resources for beginning anew. Earlier Kafka spoke of his weakness (*Schwache*) compared to Dickens, while here he compares himself to a builder whose strength gives out (*Kraft aufhört*). It is as if Kafka saw his role as a writer as one of giving testimony not just to his own homelessness but to the spiritual destitution that Heidegger would later define as symptomatic of an entire civilization. The problem for Kafka is that this fatigue, this destitution, has robbed him of the strength necessary for the task of self-reconstruction. In the notebook passage on the two houses, what follows the destitution of the builder is an insanity (*Irsinn*), which Kafka compares to a Cossack dance between the two houses in which the Cossack's boot heels scrape and throw up so much earth that his grave takes form beneath him. This frenzied Cossack dance is the demonic figure for Kafka's own writing, inscribed in the empty space between unbuilding and building, the unsafe and exposed space of shelterlessness.

The Castle (*Das Schloss*, 1926) becomes a parable for precisely this space, as its main character is repeatedly driven from one place to another in an endlessly frustrated attempt to find shelter, in both the material and the spiritual senses. Let us recall that this personage, K., is by profession a land surveyor who arrives in the village with what appears to be a commission from the Castle. In the normal order of things, he would make contact with the proper authorities, have his commission confirmed, and begin employment according to what he understands to be the work of a

surveyor. Let us for a moment consider exactly what a surveyor is. The
professional activity of a surveyor is to make measurements that define
clear boundaries and limits; these in turn serve to establish legal rights
and responsibilities concerning property, while they are also designed to
prevent conflict in claims of property rights. Most of all, they determine
what the property is: its nature, precise location, and dimensions. Land
surveying is thus an essential preliminary to architectural construction.
Although the concept of land surveying is fairly simple, in fact it depends
on a complex set of institutional and even ontological conditions: whereas
the surveyor must enjoy complete professional independence in measuring an object, the juridical value of these measurements depends on the
surveyor's authority as determined by the state. Finally, the property to be
measured must in fact be measurable; it must be localizable, visible, and
stable, and there must be reliable instruments with which to measure it.
Surveyors live in a relatively fixed world of empirical certainties. The
problem for K. is that none of these conditions is met in the strange village where he hopes to begin his work. Simultaneously recognized and ignored by the authorities, he fails to receive an actual assignment, to be
given any surveying to be done, at least in the sense of professional surveying for which his training has prepared him. On the contrary, he is
thwarted at every turn in his attempt to *survey*, take the measure of the
constructed space of the village from the vantage point of empirical
knowledge; the village, and above all the Castle, will not be reduced to his
gaze. The trials of K. are thus determined by two apparently simple but in
fact insurmountable problems: to master the space into which he has
wandered and to find a habitation. Both of these problems are presented
in architectural terms.

As a building, the Castle stands as a figure of impenetrability, but the
nature of this impenetrability is strangely out of keeping with its architectural form. Kafka's Castle is neither a feudal fortress nor a remote, hidden
complex of the kind found in Sade. Far from being an imposing structure,
the Castle is designed to disappoint, in every sense of the word. When K.
first sees the Castle at a distance his expectations are satisfied, but as he approaches nearer:

> enttäuschte ihn das Schloss, es war doch nur ein recht elendes. . . .
> Städtchen, aus Dorfhäusern zusammengetragen, ausgezeichnet nur
> dadurch, dass vielleicht alles aus Stein gebaut war, aber der Anstrich
> war längst abgefallen, und der Stein schien abzubröckeln. (17)

he was disappointed in the Castle; it was after all only a wretched-looking town, a huddle of village houses, whose sole merit, if any, lay in being built of stone, but the plaster had long since flaked off and the stone seemed to be crumbling away. (Muir 15)[3]

The source of disappointment here is that the Castle does not stand as a distinct object. It is only a nondescript group of village houses, distinguishable from its surroundings only by being made of stone. But even if there is a material difference between stone and wood or brick, it fails to make the Castle architecturally distinct from the rest of the village, thus reinforcing the impression of indeterminacy concerning the Castle and its architectural context. The sense of disappointment is renewed later in the tale, but in a different form, when K. gazes on the Castle in the gathering dusk. The problem this time is that the more K. concentrates his gaze on the Castle, the less distinct its contours become: "[T]he longer he looked, the less he could make out and the deeper everything was lost in twilight" (97). Taken together, these two passages tell us something about the function of the Castle in the labyrinthine space of the novel. On one hand, the utter ordinariness of the Castle, in its situation as well as its architectural form, makes all the more strange the fact that K. never finds the path to it and all the more incongruous its absolute ascendancy over every aspect of life in the village. On the other hand, the tendency of the Castle to elude the gaze of the onlooker is a sign of the impenetrability of these very mysteries concerning the nature of its relation, physical or institutional, to its surroundings. The impenetrability of the Castle lies not in its solidity but in the curiously insubstantial nature of its presence as an object. As castles were originally military structures, a military analogy might not be out of place here: Kafka's Castle has the impenetrability not of a fortress, but of a village all too easily entered, where not only is it impossible to determine the difference between enemy forces and peaceful inhabitants; it is also doubtful whether such a difference exists. "There is no difference between the peasantry and the Castle," the schoolteacher says (17).

There is, however, a tower. In one of the few references to his place of origin, K. compares in his mind the church tower of his native town to the Castle tower before which he stands. The church tower was "firm in line, soaring unfalteringly to its tapering point." It was "an earthly building (*ein irdisches Gebäude*)—what else can men build?—but with a loftier goal than the humble dwelling-houses (*niedrige Häusergemenge*), and a clearer meaning than the muddle of everyday life" (15). The tower before K. now is actually the tower of a house, "graciously mantled with ivy" but pierced with small windows that produce a kind of maniacal (*etwas Irsinniges*) glitter in the sun. The battlements at the top are "broken, irregular, and fumbling, . . . as if a melancholy-mad (*trübseliger*) tenant who ought to have been kept locked in the topmost chamber . . . had burst through the roof and lifted himself up to the gaze of the world" (16). The contrast is between the homely native village and the *unheimlich,* unhomely world in which K. has found himself. Kafka's word for home, *die Heimat,* resonates in German with all the force that Heidegger will later give to his ideal of the authentic, if no longer possible, being of the human between earth and heaven. The church tower is above all firm in its architectural and spiritual definitions; visible in form, clear in outline, and lofty in purpose, it gives meaning to the everyday muddle of life. The Castle tower, by contrast, is demonic in form and character, its deceptively gracious ivy offset by the maniacal glitter of its windows, and by the half-destroyed, crazed aspect of its battlements. Despite his interest in Dickens, Kafka is unlikely to have borrowed an image from Dickens's contemporary, Charlotte Brontë, and so one must suppose the resemblance between the imaginary madman of this attic and his female counterpart in *Jane Eyre* (1847) to be merely accidental. It is nonetheless worth noting the ways in which this madman is more demonic than Bertha Mason. The worst she can do is to burn down the house, maim her husband, and kill herself as prelude to a Victorian happy ending. The maniacal spirit of Kafka's tenant, on the other hand, inhabits every corner of the village and endlessly defers any satisfaction that might be derived from an apocalyptic denouement.

Given the inaccessibility of the Castle and what turns out to be the infinitely hierarchical nature of its structures of authority, one might suppose that its own precincts were divided within themselves by boundaries more definite than those of the town. However, Kafka destabilizes the facile opposition reflected in such a notion. Most of K.'s information about the workings of the Castle come from the servant Barnabas, who is admitted into certain rooms of the Castle but may or may not be admitted into others depending on the uncertain state of the boundaries dividing them. His sister Olga tells K. that there are indeed barriers (*Barrieren*) inside the Castle but that these do not necessarily form dividing lines (*Grenzen*). The barriers Barnabas can pass at the entrance are not really different from those beyond which he has never passed, which makes it seem as though one ought not to suppose that the bureaus behind the last barriers are any different from those Barnabas has already seen. "Only that's what we do suppose in moments of depression (*in jenen trüben Stunden*). And the doubt doesn't stop there, we can't keep it within bounds" (*man kann sich gar nicht wehren*) (165). In such passages Kafka constructs a complex network of relations among power, architectural space, and psychological effect. The bleak (*trüb*) feelings of Olga connect them to the gloomy (*trübselig*) tenant in the attic of the castle, as if this fantastic figure set the tone for the entire village. The unbounded melancholy of the villagers, however, is more directly inspired by doubts about the meaning and function of particular architectural spaces, and particularly about the definition of their boundaries. Olga's doubts are such that she asks herself whether Barnabas is in fact in the service of the Castle: "[G]ranted, he goes into the bureaux, but are the bureaux part of the real Castle? And even if there are bureaux actually in the Castle, are they the bureaux that Barnabas is allowed to enter?" (165). The supposition is that the key to the code governing the form and distribution of these spaces would clarify the nature of the power that, by inhabiting them, casts its pall over the entire village. But this key is no more within the grasp of Olga, a native of the village, than of the stranger K.

Olga's account of the inner precincts of the Castle recalls Kafka's parable *Vor dem Gesetz* (Before the Law, 1915), the text of which also appears as part of *Der Prozess* (The Trial, 1925). In this story, a countryman appears "before the law," but the way into the precincts of the law is barred by a doorkeeper who tells the countryman that he cannot grant admittance "at the moment," although it is understood to be possible that permission may be granted later. Despite this discouragement, the countryman "stoops to peer through the gateway into the interior," but he is warned by the other.

> [I]ch bin nur der unterste Türhüter. Von Saal zu Saal stehn aber Türhüter, einer mächtiger als der andere. Schon den Anblick des dritten kann nicht einmal ich mehr ertragen. (*Drucke* 267)
>
> *I am only the least of the doorkeepers. From hall to hall there is one doorkeeper after another, each more powerful than the last. The third doorkeeper is already so terrible that even I cannot bear to look at him.* (Complete 3).

The countryman decides to wait outside the door until he has permission to enter. He waits for his entire life, growing old before the door. In his last moments it occurs to him to ask why no one else has ever sought admittance. The doorkeeper replies, "No one else could ever be admitted here, since this gate was made only for you. I am now going to shut it."

In Derrida's essay on this story, he remarks that the interior (*das Innere*) is not concealed from view. The door is open even if access to what lies beyond it is not verbally granted; it allows a view onto "interior spaces that appear empty and provisionally forbidden" but is not physically impenetrable. What prevents the countryman from entering is what Derrida calls the *topique différantielle* of the law, its organization into a time and space that perpetually defers access to its essence: year after year one waits for the permission that would, if granted, allow one to pass from room to room toward an ever deferred, never penetrable essence. Derrida's notion of *différance* here takes the form of an insidious spatial effect that in fact conceals the essence of the law, which is that the law has no essence: the law is "the nothing that forbids itself" ("Before" 209). Its forbidding power, however, relies on an effect of spacing. The door before which the petitioner stands, like Barnabas in the Castle, looking in toward room after room, guardian after guardian, is "an internal boundary that opens on nothing, before nothing, the object of no possible experience" (212). For the countryman, it is the door of his own life as endless deferral, brutally closed as an interruption, not an ending, at the moment of his death.[4]

In *The Castle,* this condition of endless deferral belongs to K.'s attempts to enter into the confidence of its authorities, as well as his efforts to gain access to the actual precincts of the Castle. Among the architectural figurations of this deferral is the scene in which K. follows the main street of the village, which makes toward the Castle without ever getting nearer to it. Increasingly weary, K. is amazed at the length of the village, which seems without end. "Again and again the same little houses, and frost-bound window panes and snow and the entire absence of human beings" (17).

The failure of the spatial form of the village to conform to rational expectations of direction and distance has its counterpart in the interior spaces of the village, where an uncanny relation exists between the conventional nature of these spaces and their function in Kafka's narrative. Let us enter, for example, the taproom of the Herrenhof, the inn where functionaries of the Castle come to do business with members of the public, in order that the latter not be admitted to the precincts of the Castle itself. Frieda, the girl who works there, is one of Kafka's strange women—alternately fierce, comical, and sentimental. When the servants of the functionaries linger too late in the bar, she takes up a whip and, with cries of "into the stall, all of you!" drives them out like cattle, "across the courtyard and into their stalls" (44). The metaphorical value of this formula is indeterminate, for there is nothing to suggest that the servants are not literally housed in cattle stalls. In the comic scene that follows, K., who is also present, slides under the counter of the bar to hide from the landlord while Frieda playfully conspires with him. In a few moments K. and Frieda are locked in an embrace "amid small puddles of beer and other refuse gathered on the floor" (45).

In addition to working in the bar, Frieda is the mistress of the revered functionary Klamm. But now she has suddenly "in a state of unconsciousness" (*Gesinnungslosigkeit*) become the mistress of K., in an act of sexual promiscuity that belongs to the more general erasure of boundaries in the scene. In each of the details of this scene, architectural figures—the taproom, the stall, the counter, the floor, the quasi-sacred precinct of the Herrenhof itself—provide the framework for a narrative of multiple transgressions: between the literal and the metaphorical, between the human and the animal, between consciousness and the unconscious, between public and private space, between the object of desire and that of waste. The sense of impermeability inspired by the Castle is accompanied by an equally frustrating sense of the excessive permeability of limits of every kind. At one point, K. has no sooner driven his bothersome "assistants" from his room at the Bridge Inn than they climb back through the window, an occurrence so routine that it is mentioned without further comment: "The assistants had pushed their way in too, and on being driven out came back through the window. K. was too weary to drive them out again" (47). For K., the cumulative effect of such conditions is one of profound homelessness; he is haunted by the feeling that he has wandered into a strange country, farther than ever anyone had ever wandered before. It is

> eine Fremde, in der selbst die Luft keine Bestandteil der Heimatluft habe, in der man vor Fremdheit ersticken müsse und in deren unsinnigen Verlockungen man doch nichts tun könne als weiter gehen, weiter sich verirren. (55)

> *a country so strange that not even the air had anything in common with his native air, where one might die of strangeness, and yet whose enchantment was such that one could only go on and lose oneself further. (46)*

Even the air is strange. The interior spaces of the village are intolerably stuffy, literally driving K. out-of-doors. The maids' room at the Bridge Inn, where he finds temporary lodging with Frieda and the two assistants, is "dirty and stuffy" (*schmutzig und dumpf*) so that K. is glad to escape from it (33). The tiny, windowless rooms in the Herrenhof where the gentlemen from the Castle work are "too stuffy," so that one of them sits outside in the low, narrow, noisy passageway (228). The maids of the Herrenhof are packed away in a small room, "actually nothing more than a large cupboard," in "stuffy air, with the heating always on" (276). The landlady's small private office is overheated and almost entirely given over to her bulging wardrobe of outmoded, rustling, wide-skirted dresses. These interior spaces of stifling closeness serve as microcosms of the village as a whole, both in its measures of exclusion directed toward the stranger and in its internal promiscuity, where everyone is too closely involved in the affairs of everyone else, where vicious rumors circulate unchecked, where a look or a misplaced word can cause the ruin of an entire family. The putrid, overripe air of the village is, according to Benjamin, the air of exile: "This is the air that Kafka had to breathe all his life. . . . How was he able to survive in this air?" (*Illuminations* 126).

When K. does not instinctively flee from these too intimate spaces, he is driven from them into spaces of an opposing character—too cold, too public, too exposed. It is as if in the general anxiety reigning in this world, space could inspire only feelings of either claustrophobia or agoraphobia.[5] An example of the latter is the schoolhouse scene. Having been turned out of their room at the Bridge Inn, K. and Frieda take up lodging in the schoolhouse where K. has been hired as a janitor. Together with the troublesome assistants, they move into a schoolroom, also used as a gymnasium, where they set up makeshift domestic arrangements. With only a single sack of straw for bedding, they spend a fitful night on the floor, only to awaken the next day to find themselves, half naked, surrounded by curious schoolchildren and the angry teacher. To avoid the gazes of the children while dressing themselves, they must construct a little shelter out of a blanket thrown over the parallel bars and the vaulting horse. However, they have forgotten to clear away the remains of their supper from the desk of the teacher. The teacher is a young woman named Gisa, "fair, tall, beautiful, but somewhat stiff" (125). Noting her blond beauty, her cruelty, and her hardness, Adorno sees her as a demonic figure stemming from "the pre-Adamic race of Hitler *Jungfrauen*, who hated the Jews long before there were any" ("Notes on Kafka," 226). Clearing her desk of the fragile possessions of K. and Frieda, she sends them all shattering onto the floor with a single stroke of her ruler. Like Little Nell forced to abandon her poor useless trifles, K. and Frieda, "leaning on the parallel bars, witnessed the destruction of their few things" (125). This violent end brought to a pathetic attempt at domesticity is characteristic of a world where the stranger is never allowed rest.

K's sense of exile is heightened by the fact that he does not understand the protocols governing certain spaces that are easily penetrated in the material sense but whose meaning and function remain mysterious to the stranger.[6] Seeking an interview at the Herrenhof with a functionary from the Castle called Erlanger, K. finds himself in "a low, somewhat downward-sloping passage," not unlike that which leads to Justine's place of imprisonment in Sade's novel. This is the passage between the little rooms where the functionaries work during the night. It is just high enough for one to walk without bending one's head, with rows of doors close together, almost touching one another, on either side. This description of the passage itself already consigns it to the logic of minor spatial distortion, in keeping with the way gestures and speech in Kafka are always slightly *off*. A particularity of this passage, apart from its closeness and narrowness, and somewhat in contrast with these features, is that the walls do not quite reach to the ceiling, so that noise sounds throughout the passage and the adjoining rooms. In the early morning hours as the files are being distributed, a babel of voices begins to stir, while heads, oddly masked with scarves, suddenly appear in the space between the partition walls and the ceiling, only to disappear just as quickly. K. witnesses this scene with increasing anxiety and fatigue but remains standing in the passage, a bit incongruously, in the vain hope that some light may be shed on his own bewildered destiny.

The situation corresponds to Benjamin's analysis of the disconnection in Kafka between the gesture and its coding according to a system of signification: "He divests the human gesture of its traditional supports and then has a subject for reflection without end" (*Illuminations* 122)—except that here the principle applies to architectural space as well. Only slowly does K. begin to understand, from the furious remonstrances of the landlord, that he has been the cause of the disturbance around him, that his presence in the passage has been a grave impropriety, that he has visited untold distress on the gentlemen from the Castle. But even now K. is allowed no rest. He collapses onto the beer barrels in the taproom, only to be once more accosted by the landlord and landlady, and in his fatigue their talk takes on an exaggerated significance: "To be driven out from here again seemed to him a misfortune surpassing all that had happened to him hitherto" (270).

For Adorno, the logic of Kafka's world makes it seem as if the philosophical doctrine of categorical intuition, according to which human consciousness has a fundamental perception of things in themselves,[7] had been "honored in Hell" ("Notes on Kafka" 219; "Aufzeichnungen" 263). What he means is that the process of "demolition" enacted in Kafka's writing replaces what in previous forms of literature registered the consciousness of reality in terms of metaphor, significance, or meaning. Here we need to make a distinction between what we have been calling the demonic in Kafka and its manifestation in Dickens. In Dickens, figures like Daniel Quilp personify the demonic allegorically, and this allegorical representation itself implies a rational consciousness of reality. To a certain extent this is equally true of figures like Dom Severino in Sade: the demonic figure is contained within structures of meaning as produced by a rational consciousness of reality. In Kafka these structures themselves are demolished, so that the source of the demonic in being cannot be concentrated in a single figure. To do so would be to render the demonic banal and to imply the possibility of transcendence over it, both of which Kafka implicitly refuses. That is, Kafka refuses the distinction between the demonic and its other because he assigns the demonic to being itself. Thus one can speak of the demonic in Kafka only by adapting this concept to a novelistic universe in which in which the traditional distinction between good and evil does not hold and by referring to a doctrine whose relation to the language, gestures, and spaces of this novel is undecidable. In Sade and Dickens such doctrines do exist as a way of generating meaning. Sade, in fact, stages a contest of doctrines between the unshakeable faith of Justine and the purely instrumental reason of her tormentors, whereas Dickens posits a doctrine of humanism against the logic of capital. Both authors test these doctrines on a "good girl," an innocent victim who figures as an example of virtue against which the demonic can be defined. In Kafka there is no such person. Even K., for all his trials, hardly attains this status and instead occupies a kind of neutral position between the abject submission of the villagers and the inhumanity of the authorities. Moreover, there is a certain inverted demonism in the extreme shyness and delicacy of these authorities, who are willing to receive petitioners (*Parteien*) only by night and in artificial light because the sight of them by day would be unbearable and so that the ugliness of these brief, nocturnal interrogations can quickly be forgotten in sleep. K's transgression at the Herrenhof, which consists of occupying the passage in what is regarded as an unbefitting manner, is made all the more offensive in that, according to the landlord, the authorities themselves are too kind and sensitive to comprehend such perfidy.

> Sie wissen nicht oder wollen es in ihrer Freundlichkeit und Herablassung nicht wissen, dass es auch unempfindliche, harte, durch keine Ehrfurcht zu erweichende Herzen gibt. (444)

> *They did not know or in their kindness and condescension did not want to admit there also existed hearts that were insensitive, hard, and not to be softened by any feelings of reverence. (266)*

In any other writer this would be pure irony, but it is part of Kafka's diabolical humor that he gives us precious little ground on which to make the distinction between irony and earnestness. Just as physical gestures in Kafka are either absent when they might be expected or exaggerated out of proportion to whatever occasions them, so the distribution, function, and use of built spaces in Kafka bear little relation to known repertoires. In these spaces K. finds himself perennially *de trop,* his very existence a matter of indifference or offense to others. The demonic in Kafka consists, finally, in its demolition of human value, perhaps in the name of a more secure edifice toward which his writing gestures but for the construction of which his strength, like ours, fails.

3

Allegories of the Gothic in the Long Nineteenth Century

"The gothic gets away," writes Henry Adams, musing on the Cathedral of Chartres in the summer of 1904: "No two men think alike about it, and no woman agrees with either" (87). Over a hundred years later, it is fair to say that medieval Gothic architecture still eludes us, not just in its own spirit and form but also as the object of such intense, even fanatical interest in Adams's own age. Gothic religious architecture produced such a variety of responses in writers of the late nineteenth and early twentieth centuries that one struggles to come to terms with the simple question of what made it so interesting and important to that moment in history. This chapter undertakes a preliminary answer to that question by proposing that, despite the variety of responses to the Gothic, one can nonetheless discern two general movements, both of them symptomatic of nineteenth-century European culture. The first is that of an inherent tension between an ahistorical aesthetics of transcendence and an emerging historical sense whereby the writer poses, explicitly or not, the question of what the aesthetic experience means in terms of contemporary social forms. In other words, the aesthetic sense is put to the test of its ethical consequences, as writers ask, essentially, "What is our relation to the past?" and when the answer to that question registers an irreparable loss, it is followed by the question "How can we construct our world anew?"

The second general movement effects a kind of withdrawal from the larger cultural dimensions of these questions into an aesthetics of individual reality, immediate experience, and fragmentary perception, a point of view characterized by Pater's question as he contemplates the interior of Notre-Dame d'Amiens: "What, precisely what, is this to *me*?" ("Notre-Dame" 113). In this discourse, the sense of spiritual and historical loss registered in the modern appreciation of medieval architecture is compensated for by a valorization of the local, the contiguous, the involuntary, and the familiar, such things as will later be endowed with redemptive status in the work of Proust.

In both of these cases, medieval religious architecture stands at the center of nineteenth- and early-twentieth-century attempts to conceive of the world itself in its contemporaneity. This will seem less of a paradox if we consider, first of all, the simple fact of the imposing presence of a Gothic church or cathedral at the medieval core of nearly every European city in the nineteenth century. While standing at the center of the city's origins, it was also likely to be the city's tallest building. If writers and architects of the neoclassical age could afford to ignore these edifices, that was no longer possible in an age in which the city itself had become the object of intense political and aesthetic focus: the age of urban planning, urban landscape painting, the urban novel, and poetry like that of Baudelaire, who saw the city as a life form in itself. Apart from its concrete presence, Gothic architecture also served, of course, as a spectacular monument to the religious past, that is, to a sense of spiritual transcendence now cut off from religious experience and consigned to a purely aesthetic realm. As a constant and present reminder of that rupture and a charge newly assigned to art, the medieval cathedrals of Europe could not escape the allegorical if enigmatic meanings that would be assigned to them by writers of the nineteenth century.

The idea for this chapter began with the simple observation that several English and American writers of the nineteenth century had visited and recorded their impressions of French Gothic cathedrals, notably Amiens and Chartres. That is why this chapter is largely devoted to works of English-language literature. From the perspective of "English studies," it would presumably be possible to gain an understanding of the respective sensibilities of these writers by comparing their differing responses to the architectural monuments they had visited in common. Once this fairly modest project was undertaken, however, it became clear that even such a seemingly straightforward notion as "sensibility" could not be properly understood in this context without reference to more general cultural conditions, especially insofar as Gothic architecture was above all a cultural phenomenon. It represented a common project of the people in the Middle Ages, but it was also a cultural phenomenon of the nineteenth century, both as an object of architectural revival and as a focal point for reflections on the nature of an age that could only mark its radical difference from the Middle Ages. Architectural theory itself was too narrow a field for such reflections; they had to be given the freedom possible only in literary works, whether in the form of Wordsworth's poems or in the essays of the Victorian writers who followed him. However, one cannot do justice to the question of the importance of Gothic architecture to the nineteenth century by limiting oneself entirely to English-language sources. That is why it is necessary to show how Goethe lays the foundation for such an inquiry before turning to the writers of the English-speaking world. Even with such a foundation, and even with its resonance in Hegel's lectures on aesthetics, what follows is not so much an argument as an excursion among a series of literary occasions having in common principally their engagement with the great cathedrals of the Middle Ages.

Eighteenth-century England had its defenders of the Gothic style, such as the architect Batty Langley and the writer Horace Walpole, builder of the fanciful villa Strawberry Hill and author of the "Gothic" novel *The Castle of Otranto* (1765), where Gothic architecture serves primarily for melodramatic effect. Certain passages in Walpole's *Anecdotes of Painting in England* (1762) offer a spirited appreciation of Gothic architecture, but always in the distinctly measured eighteenth-century language of taste.

> The men who had not the happiness of lighting on the simplicity and proportion of the Greek orders, were however so lucky as to strike out a thousand graces and effects, which rendered these buildings magnificent yet genteel, vast yet light, venerable and picturesque. (1:107)

More representative of that century is a passage in Rousseau's "Lettre sur la musique française" (1753), which compares Gothic architecture to the counterfugue in baroque music. Rousseau says of the latter, "Ce sont évidemment des restes de barbarie et de mauvais goût, qui ne subsistent, comme les portails de nos églises gothiques, que pour la honte de ceux qui ont eu la patience de les faire" (173) These are obviously the remains of barbarism and bad taste that survive, like the portals of our Gothic churches, only to the shame of those who had the patience to make them.

However, by the time Hegel began to give his lectures on fine art in the Berlin of the 1820s, medieval religious architecture had already been established as the most immediately available and concrete manifestation of the Kantian principle of aesthetic transcendence. Noting that throughout the previous century Gothic architecture had been judged to be "crude and barbaric," Hegel contrasts it with what he regards as the purely functional nature of classical architecture. For Hegel, the Gothic stands at the center of "the properly romantic style" because in it "mere utility and adaptation to an end are transcended (*aufhebt*) . . . and the house [of God] is erected freely, independently and on its own account. . . . The work stands there by itself, fixed and eternal" (*Aesthetics* 2:684) and "In its grandeur and sublime peace it is lifted . . . into an infinity in itself" (2:685). The consequences of this view of Gothic architecture are no less than a redefinition of the function of art.

> The impression (*Eindruck*) which art now has to produce is, on the one hand . . . this tranquillity of the heart which, released from the external world of nature and from the mundane in general, is shut in upon itself, and, on the other hand, the impression of a majestic sublimity (*Erhabenheit*)[1] which aspires beyond and outsoars mathematical limitation. (*Aesthetics* II:686)

In this and other formulations of Hegel we can recognize several elements of romantic aesthetic theory derived from Kant: the autonomy of the work of art as such, the tension between transcendent unity and the diversity of particulars, the outward form as an expression of an inward principle, the "dynamic" as opposed to the purely mathematical sublime. But for Hegel art is already "a thing of the past" in that it no longer affords the spiritual satisfaction that earlier ages sought in it; from its earlier necessity in a spiritual and religious reality it has been transferred to the realm of ideas (1:11). As Paul de Man demonstrates, Hegel's two main theses in the *Aesthetics*, namely, that "art is for us a thing of the past" and "the beautiful is the sensory manifestation of the idea," are in fact one and the same in that the paradigm for art is now thought rather than perception, one that, in de Man's formulation, "leaves the interiorization of experience forever behind" (*Aesthetic* 103). The elevation of the artwork to the status of the sensory form of a transcendent idea, a movement at the heart of Kant's and Hegel's theories, can only take place at the expense of the stability of the category of the aesthetic as a philosophical category. In other words, once the artwork is turned loose from its traditional function in a religious or mythic context and makes its own claim to truth, the grounds on which such a claim might be made have already been undermined. De Man is joined in this analysis by Gadamer, who finds an "internal *aporia*" in art's independent claim to truth. Art traditionally derived its meaning from its function within a religious or sociopolitical framework on which it conferred splendor, beauty, and a superior existence. But wherever art seeks to impose itself only as art, it is already on the decline (*Esquisses* 191). These observations are especially pertinent to the newly discovered appreciation for Gothic architecture in the late eighteenth century, when medieval cathedrals became the object of intense aesthetic interest independent of their religious function. The precise nature of that interest, however, was rendered all the more unstable by both the inherently problematic nature of the aesthetic category and the emerging conditions of modernity of which it was symptomatic.

I. GOETHE AND WORDSWORTH: THE AESTHETICS OF RETURN

Hegel pays homage to Goethe for having inaugurated a fresh interest in Gothic architecture, crediting him with having brought it into honor again when the poet "looked on nature and art with the freshness of youth" (2:684). Hegel is referring to Goethe's essay "Von deutscher Baukunst," published in 1772 and based on the twenty-two-year-old poet's impressions of Strasbourg Cathedral. This little essay, written in a highly subjective manner, appeared in the form of a pamphlet of sixteen pages without the name of the author, publisher, or place of publication. It is unusual in two respects. First, as Hegel notes, it marks the point of departure for a widespread movement dedicated to the revival of interest in medieval religious architecture on aesthetic grounds qualitatively different from eighteenth-century standards of taste. Goethe's approach would prove to be symptomatic of the Gothic revival throughout Europe, whereas in Germany his essay found an immediate audience. It was favorably reviewed in the *Frankfurter Gelehrte Anzeigen,*[2] the organ of the Sturm und Drang movement, included in Herder's edited volume of essays by different hands, *Von deutscher Art und Kunst* (1773), and was continually reprinted for several years.

What is also unusual about this essay is its anomalous character in Goethe's career; it is both his first published piece of prose and the only unreserved statement in admiration of Gothic architecture from the writer who would later become a disciple of classicism. In what has been called a "hymn in prose,"[3] the young Goethe of this essay pays homage to Erwin von Steinbach, the cathedral's thirteenth-century master builder, while reenacting Goethe's own conversion from the received classical ideas of Laugier to a newfound faith in the Gothic.[4] This conversion takes place in a single moment of revelation as he stands before the great edifice.

> The impression which filled my soul was whole and large, and of a sort that (since it was composed of a thousand harmonizing details) I could relish and enjoy, but by no means identify and explain. . . . It is hard on the spirit of man when his brother's work is so sublime (*hoch erhaben*) that he can only bow and worship (*nur beugen, und anbeten muss*). (Gage 107; Sauder 419)

Goethe's language alternates between this purely subjective testimony and a contemplation of the cathedral itself in ideal terms: "How the vast building rose lightly into the air from its firm foundations; how everything was fretted (*durchbrochen*), and yet fashioned for eternity!" (Gage 108). His cult of genius makes this transcendence an effect of the will of the artist, who imparts an active form to the work through an "inner, unified, particular and independent feeling" (109). If the present age, no longer recognizing the genius of Steinbach, has driven its sons about "after strange growths" (109), there is nonetheless hope in youth, which is still alive to the joy of life and the beauty of the earth. But earthly beauty is not enough. The essay concludes by imagining a young artist (in whom we recognize Goethe himself) who, sated with earthly beauty, will be received in the arms of heavenly Beauty so that he may, "more than Prometheus, bring down the bliss of the gods upon earth" (111).

This is rich and moving prose, but perhaps it is not too obvious to remark that Goethe has adapted to entirely new purposes an object constructed for Christian worship in a historical context very different from his own. Strasbourg Cathedral figures here no longer as the house of God and the Roman Catholic faith but as a monument to romantic ideals of genius and beauty, which, while abstracted from any specific religious context, are nonetheless invested with the language of religious devotion and the spirit of transcendence that, in a more traditional context, obtained only in the relation between the artwork and its theological framework. Goethe's move, like that of Kant and Hegel, is in effect to remove from the work of art the theological and religious scaffolding from which it has traditionally derived its transcendent meaning, while still insisting on that meaning as derived from the material form of the work itself. The analysis of form, however, is in fact subordinated to a hastily assembled apparatus of personal impressions, figures of genius, and pagan deities. Compared to the weight of the Christian tradition, this seems a rather fragile vehicle for conveying the transcendent power of even so imposing a monument as Strasbourg Cathedral. Goethe himself seems to acknowledge this fragility in his later writings on architecture.

Goethe's travels in Italy in 1786–88 reconverted him to classical tastes, such that in 1795 his essay on Palladio reaffirms the Vitruvian principles of *firmitas, utilitas,* and *venustas.* His subsequent writings on Gothic architecture have a different tone from that of the youthful essay of 1772: more measured, analytical, knowledgeable. A passage in *Dichtung und Wahrheit* (*Poetry and Truth,* 1812) briefly revisits Strasbourg Cathedral, where this time the facade is observed in a detailed and highly ordered manner. Goethe sees the facade as a vertical, rectangular surface divided by its openings into nine fields, each of the three levels having three distinct apertures in the form of doors or windows. The point of this geometric description is to demonstrate that the agreeable impression made by the edifice is the product of its essentially classical principles of harmony and unison.

> The apertures and the solid parts of the wall, and its buttresses, each has its particular character deriving from its particular function. This character is communicated step by step to the subordinate parts, so that the decoration is harmonious throughout: everything, great and small, is in its place and can be easily taken in at a glance; and so the charming (*das Angenehme*) is made manifest in the gigantic. (Gage 116, translation revised)

The contrast between the sublime (*das Erhabene*) of 1772 and the merely agreeable (*das Angenehme*) of 1812 marks the writer's passage from the Sturm und Drang to the classical aesthetic mode, but equally striking is the contrast between the conclusions of the respective essays. Where the young Goethe imagined a Promethean figure bringing the bliss of heaven down to earth, the writer of 1812 concludes his treatment of Strasbourg Cathedral with a more worldly idea. Strasbourg had been French since the seventeenth century, while still fresh in memory was the Napoleonic army's defeat of Austria, along with several German states, at Wagram in 1809. As if in defiance of this French hegemony over the German-speaking world, Goethe chooses to recall that Strasbourg was "an old German city" when the cathedral was built. He proposes to abandon the disparaging term *Gothic* and, "so as to vindicate our nation" decides to confer on this style of building the title "German architecture."

In the turmoil created by the Napoleonic wars, the coincidence of the

Gothic revival with nationalistic feeling moved several nations to claim Gothic architecture as preeminently their own. In each case it was a question of defining an indigenous national architecture that would antedate and thus take symbolic priority over the classical models imported in the modern, that is, post-Renaissance, age. In Britain, Thomas Rickman's *An Attempt to Discriminate the Styles of English Architecture from the Conquest to the Reformation* (1817) created an enduring Anglocentric taxonomy for successive styles of the Gothic by naming them Norman, Early English, Decorated, and Perpendicular English.[5] However, Chateaubriand, in his *Génie du Christianisme* (1802), had already claimed Gothic architecture for the French by identifying the religious feeling it evoked with both the institutions and the natural landscape of France.

Les forêts des Gaules ont passé à leur tour dans les temples de nos pères, et nos bois de chênes ont ainsi maintenu leur origine sacrée. Ces voûtes ciselées en feuillages, ces jambages, qui appuient les murs et finissent brusquement comme des troncs brisés, la fraîcheur des voûtes, les ténèbres du sanctuaire, les ailes obscures, les passages secrets, les portes abaissées, tout retrace les labyrinthes des bois dans l'église gothique; tout en fait sentir la religieuse horreur, les mystères et la divinité. (300)

The forests of the Gauls passed into the temples of our fathers, and our woods of oak thus kept their sacred origin. Those vaults chiseled into foliage, those vertical supports that hold up the walls and end abruptly like broken tree trunks, the coolness of the vaults, the shadows of the sanctuary, the dark wings, the secret passages, the low doors, everything reproduces the labyrinths of the woods in the Gothic church; everything evokes religious horror, mystery, and divinity.

The English and French claims notwithstanding, Goethe's own preoccupation with the "patriotic idea" of Gothic as "German architecture" signals a shift from the appreciation of medieval religious architecture as the concrete form of a universal aesthetic to an interpretation of it in terms of Goethe's own historical moment. It is clear that by this time Goethe considers Gothic architecture to be of value not in itself but only as something of historical significance. He had written to his friend Karl Friedrich Reinhard in 1810 that the subject of the Gothic "only has value for us in its proper place, as a document of a particular stage of human culture" (quoted in Robson-Scott 177).

However, it is equally clear that his youthful impressions of Strasbourg

Cathedral have marked Goethe for life, even if his aesthetic position keeps shifting with the passing of time. He returns to the subject one last time in 1823, at the age of seventy-two, writing a new essay with the old title "Von deutscher Baukunst." Published in the periodical *Ueber Kunst und Altertum,* the 1823 version of the essay makes a return to the scene of the poet's youthful rapture but from the Olympian perspective of an aged poet who has seen the romantic movement come and go. The tone is at once elegiac and mildly ironic: "Here we may recall somewhat earlier years, when the Strasbourg Münster had such an effect on us that we could not help expressing our unsolicited delight." The effect was powerful not just for the young poet but for an entire generation that followed him: "Young and old, men and women, have been . . . overwhelmed and swept away (*übermannt und hingerissen*) by such impressions." Toward the end of the essay Goethe comes back once more to that early essay in a similarly ambivalent tone: "If there is something incoherent (*etwas Amfigurisches*) about the style of that essay, I hope it may be forgiven, where the inexpressible is to be expressed" (Gage 120–22; Sauder 13.2:160–64). Goethe's language carries overtones of violence: the overpowering feelings in the face of the Gothic have produced in the earlier essay a literally disfigured text. In describing his essay of 1772, Goethe has used a word so rare that it merits attention here. He has Germanicized an eighteenth-century word of unknown origin that appears in the *Dictionnaire de l'Académie Française* as *amphigouri* and is defined as either (1) burlesque writing or discourse, intentionally confused and incoherent, or (2) writing or discourse in which the sentences unintentionally present ideas in no particular order and lacking in rational sense: *I understood nothing of that discourse, it's an amphigouri from beginning to end.* In the intellectual and aesthetic contexts of Goethe's world, what this suggests is that Gothic architecture, through the overwhelming effects of the sublime, poses a challenge to the Enlightenment value of reason. Goethe's new essay on the same subject will attempt to bring the *Amfigurisches* under control by putting both his earlier feelings and Gothic architecture in general in a rational historical perspective.

The point of the new essay is therefore to make it clear that the proper way to recognize the value of these works of the past is the *historical* way. This historical understanding is made possible in particular by the recent publication of illustrations of Cologne Cathedral, which has its origins in the mid–thirteenth century, making it contemporary with Strasbourg, as well as similar in style. The occasion for Goethe's essay is in fact to recognize two new projects of historical documentation. The first is Georg

Moller's *Denkmähler der deutschen Baukunst,* completed in 1821, which puts "before us a series of early and recent illustrations of the [Cologne] Cathedral, in which we could easily see and understand the rise, perfection and finally the decline of this style" (Gage 121). Moller's engravings appeared at the same time as Sulpiz and Melchior Boisserée's illustrations of Cologne Cathedral (fig. 4).[6] As Nicolas Pevsner notes, lavish picture books of the classical architecture of Rome and Greece had existed for a long time, but these German publications, with engravings in large, table-sized format (87 × 63 cm), were the first to celebrate the Gothic style. They are the logical outcome of the Boisserée brothers' private collection of medieval art, which they put on public display in a sort of museum set up in the baroque palace on the Karlsplatz in Heidelberg. Goethe expresses the wish that the Boisserées' published work will reach a wide audience of amateurs, so that the tourist visiting Cologne Cathedral might "no longer be left to personal feeling" or otherwise hastily formed opinion, but will "rather observe what is there and imagine what is not there like someone who is knowledgeable, and is initiated into the secrets of the masons" (Gage 122). Here Goethe reminds us that in 1823 the cathedral still remains unfinished. The proper imaginative response to the monument therefore lies not in the incoherence of "personal feeling" or in flights of the sublime but in the imagined construction of the completed cathedral based on the knowledge of what is already there. The relative powers of observing subject and monumental object have been reversed: in 1772 the sublime aspect of the cathedral produced feelings that surpassed the poet's capacity for knowledge and expression. In 1823 it is, on the contrary, the subject's power of knowledge and imagination that must compensate for the incompleteness of the object.

This shift from the aesthetics of the sublime to the insistence on historical mastery is in keeping with Goethe's newfound interest in the documentation and publication of knowledge about "German" architecture. What began in the form of a personal communion between the young poet and a kindred spirit of the thirteenth century is no longer a private affair: German architecture has entered the modern public sphere through the means of mechanical reproduction and widespread dissemination and thus stands poised to regain its importance for the German people in an age of tourism, popularized culture, and political unification, even if the nature of this importance is to be completely different from its original religious function.

The form of Goethe's 1823 essay recalls Wordsworth's great poem

Fig. 4. Cross section of the choir at Cologne Cathedral in Sulpiz and Melchior Bois-serée's *Ansichten, Risse und einzelne Theile des Doms von Köln* (Elevations, Sections, and Details of the Cathedral of Cologne).

known as "Tintern Abbey" (1798) in the way it stages the return to a scene of youthful rapture, which only now can be fully comprehended by virtue of to the greater wisdom granted the poet by the passing of time. Although Goethe began to be translated into English as early as 1780 and was known to Wordsworth,[7] my subject here is a matter of formal and aesthetic affinity rather than direct influence. In "Tintern Abbey" the speaker, on a walking tour of the Wye River valley, revisits the banks of the river "a few miles above Tintern Abbey" after an absence of five years. The difference between his present state of mind and that of his former self is palpable. Endeavoring to recall his youthful response to the scene, he writes:

> I cannot paint
> What then I was. The sounding cataract
> Haunted me like a passion: the tall rock,
> The mountain, and the deep and gloomy wood,
> Their colours and their forms, were then to me
> An appetite: a feeling and a love,
> That had no need of a remoter charm,
> By thought supplied, or any interest
> Unborrowed from the eye.

Wordsworth's poem is in part an epitaph for this earlier self wholly absorbed in the immediate presence of natural forms, echoing perfectly the sounding cataract and mirroring the colors of rock, mountain, and wood. That self must now be put to rest and be consciously repudiated as belonging to the hour of "thoughtless youth."

> —That time is past,
> And all its aching joys are now no more,
> And all its dizzy raptures.

The "abundant recompense" for this loss, and the occasion for the solemn grandeur of the poem's conclusion, is the poet's accession to an intuitive understanding of the universal by means of purer and more elevated forms of thought. After years of absence from this scene he has learned to feel a deeper presence in the world:

> A motion and a spirit that impels
> All thinking things, and all objects of all thought,
> And rolls through all things.

The poem thus follows what de Man has identified as a recurring sequence in Wordsworth's poetry, the transformation of an "echo language" of perception and fancy into the more powerful language of an imaginative vision that claims a deeper understanding of the universe; this transformation has been made possible by the experience of temporal mutability ("Rhetoric" 54). Wordsworth's transformation is not precisely the same as Goethe's: it does not exactly subject youthful incoherence to the acquired discipline of historical reason, but the general movement from youthful rapture to mature wisdom is nonetheless analogous to Goethe's. The apparently triumphant nature of this transformation, however, is invariably accompanied by a sense of anxiety arising from the connection between the loss of the earlier mode of spontaneous joy and the experience of death (53). In "Tintern Abbey," this ambivalence is reflected in the poet's desire to behold his former self "yet a little while" in the person of his younger sister, Dorothy, and in the prayer that she will remember this moment when in future years he is gone, that is, "where I can no longer hear / Thy voice, nor catch from thy wild eyes these gleams / Of past existence."

In turning for a moment back to Goethe's 1823 essay, we note that here, too, the youthful self, overwhelmed and swept away by his impressions of Strasbourg Cathedral, is put to rest: "The impression weakened, and I could hardly remember the circumstances in which such a sight had aroused the most vivid enthusiasm in me" (Gage 120). And yet the late essay remains haunted by the early one, not only in its return to the original title but also in its conclusion, which looks forward to a new publication of the 1772 essay so as to "point up the difference between the earliest seed and the final fruit (*der letzten Frucht*)" (123). This last expression, like the conclusion to Wordsworth's poem, seems to hesitate between a claim to achievement and a sense of finality derived from the poet's awareness of irreparable loss and of his own finitude. In both cases, the Gothic serves implicitly as the architectural equivalent of this literary formulation.

This can be said in the case of Wordsworth because his title (*Lines Composed a Few Miles above Tintern Abbey, on Revisiting the Banks of the Wye during a Tour. July 13, 1798*) puts the poem under the sign of a ruined twelfth-century Cistercian abbey, even if the same title slightly displaces the scene of composition from the site of the abbey, and the landscape of the poem itself remains imprecise in its location. Numerous commentators on the poem have noted that in Wordsworth's day Tintern Abbey had become a tourist attraction in keeping with the late-eighteenth-century taste for the picturesque.[8] With its roofless gables and pointed arches overgrown with vegetation, the ruins of the abbey had been made famous by numerous pictures and engravings, including those of William Gilpin in 1782, Thomas Girtin in 1793, and J. M. W. Turner in 1794. It continued to be the subject of widely disseminated images well into the nineteenth century. Fanny Price, the modest and sensitive heroine of Jane Austen's *Mansfield Park* (1814), has a picture of Tintern Abbey in her room, "holding its station" between a cave in Italy and a moonlit lake in Cumberland (137), as in a secular, romantic version of the stations of the cross. Beginning with the publication of Gilpin's popular guidebook *Observations on the River Wye* in 1782, the published images of Tintern Abbey share certain recurring features: they offer an upward view through the pointed arches to the sky; they bring out the contrast between the brightness of the sky and the gloom cast by the ruin's shadows; and they emphasize the detail of stone carving along with the sharp outlines of the leaves and vines that overgrow it, as if to insist on the ultimate fusion of nature with human endeavor. This visual language of elevation, chiaroscuro contrast, and harmony between the natural and the human will be reproduced in the poetic language of Wordsworth's lines.

The analogical relation between architectural and poetic representation, as well as the place of Tintern Abbey in the English national imagination, suggests that it figures in Wordsworth's title for purposes that go beyond those of simply locating the landscape of the poem. The image of the ruined abbey provides a symbolic framework for the poem, setting the tone of solemnity, and lending a historical and material dimension to the motifs of return, temporality, and loss. Meanwhile, the characteristic forms of Gothic architecture as embodied in the abbey are mirrored in the landscape of the poem and in the imagery of the mind that beholds this landscape.[9] Thus, "the tall rock, / The mountain, and the deep and gloomy wood" figure as natural manifestations of the height, mass, and interior depth of Gothic religious architecture, whereas the poet's "elevated" and "lofty" thoughts transfer some of these qualities to the landscape of his mind. This architectural conception of the mind is made explicit in the poet's address to his sister, where he foresees that in his own image her mind shall be

> a mansion for all lovely forms,
> Thy memory be as a dwelling-place
> For all sweet sounds and harmonies.

The ruined choirs of the abbey cannot be far from the poet's mind, nor from his remembered perception, when he hears "the still, sad music of humanity." The nearness of the abbey as a place of worship is evoked in the poem's final section, presented as a "prayer" by "a worshipper of Nature" dedicated to a "holier love." As in the later sonnet on "Mutability," the historical memory and material remains of monastic dissolution provide an allegorical frame for the poet's personal history of spiritual loss and transformation.[10]

II. RUSKIN: THE ETHICAL TURN

Our reading of the Gothic motif in Wordsworth and Goethe has proceeded along two main axes. The first concerns the poet's sense of the place of Gothic architecture in the larger spiritual and social universe that he inhabits; the second shows how this architecture serves as a symbolic register for the poet's own changing relation to that universe through time. Both of these lines of inquiry offer us an entry into the writings of the single greatest champion of Gothic architecture in the nineteenth century, John Ruskin. However, where Gothic architecture serves the romantic poet as an object to which he continually returns in order to measure the changes in his own imaginative vision, for Ruskin it has a specific function whose importance is to the modern world at large: it stands as living testimony to what human beings can collectively achieve in conditions of social and spiritual harmony.

Ruskin wrote three major works on architecture. *The Seven Lamps of Architecture* (1848) is the result of the young writer's travels in France and northern Italy; as an analysis of architectural form it is concerned mainly with statuary, carving, and other forms of surface decoration, but it also introduces a series of "lamps,"[11] or principles, according to which the Gothic style in particular reflects the spiritual and ethical life of a people in their noblest forms: Sacrifice, Truth, Power, Beauty, Life, Memory, and Obedience. Ruskin's approach is largely religious in nature, being based on the conviction that "in this primal art of man, there is room for the marking of his relations with the mightiest, as well as the fairest, works of God" (VIII:102). While Ruskin continued with *Modern Painters* (1843–60), he also published the three volumes of his second book on architecture, *The Stones of Venice*, between 1851 and 1853. This work applies many of the ideas in the *Seven Lamps* to a single city, but it also includes a more general essay on "The Nature of Gothic." Ruskin's final work on architecture, *The Bible of Amiens*, was written late in life and was intended as the first of ten volumes on the material vestiges of Christianity in the Middle Ages. I shall concentrate on "The Nature of Gothic" and *The Bible of Amiens* as representing, respectively, Ruskin's principal theoretical statement on medieval architecture and his most extended commentary on a single Gothic edifice.

Ruskin represents an important departure from the romantic idea of the Gothic found explicitly in Goethe and Hegel and implicitly in the early Wordsworth. That idea elevated Gothic architecture to the level of an aesthetic ideal whose claim to truth had worked itself loose from its religious function. The form itself attained to the sublime and thus transcended the ritual and mythic context to which it had once been subordinated. In contrast to this aesthetic tradition, Ruskin proposed a profoundly *ethical* reading of Gothic architecture, inspired by the Evangelical Protestantism in which he had been raised and by the social and political conditions of his own time. Where Goethe and Hegel had sought to abstract the Gothic from religion on aesthetic grounds, Ruskin sought to demonstrate how, in an age of industrial exploitation, egotistic materialism, narrow-minded positivism, and general philistinism, Gothic architecture served as a lesson in spiritual truth. This project was both more radical and more wide ranging than that of Ruskin's Victorian contemporary, Augustus Welby Pugin, who as a Roman Catholic sought a return to Gothic architecture as the proper setting for Christian worship. If Pugin's work is limited by its doctrine and nostalgia, Ruskin's reading of the Gothic, at least in its original form, is both more humane and more relevant to his age; it amounts to a serious, if idiosyncratic, critique of the political economy of the modern world.

In *The Stones of Venice,* the ethical nature of Ruskin's Gothic is already evident in his definition of the "moral elements" of the style—Savageness, Changefulness, Naturalism, Grotesqueness, Rigidity, Redundance—and in its analogies with human character (10:184). Like every human being, every Gothic building is individual; it differs in some important respect from every other and is characterized by a distinction between its internal, moral nature and its external, material form. The Gothic is indeed as much a quality of the human soul as it is an architectural style; it is "this grey, shadowy, many-pinnacled image of the Gothic spirit within us" (10:182). This image has a temperamental affinity with Wordsworth's metaphor of the mind as a "mansion for all lovely forms," but the ethical character of Ruskin's Gothic extends beyond romantic metaphor to a more material consideration of architecture as a product of the time and space of human labor. Anticipating the theories of social justice later to be developed in

Unto This Last (1860) and *Fors Clavigera* (1871–84), *The Stones of Venice* connects the "savageness" of Gothic architecture to the spirit of revolution sweeping Europe in 1848–49. The very imperfection of Gothic ornament is a sign of freedom from the servile uniformity of classical architecture, a form of degradation that the machine age has once again imposed on its workers.

> It is verily this degradation of the operative into a machine, which, more than any other evil of the times, is leading the mass of the nations everywhere into vain, incoherent, destructive struggling for a freedom of which they cannot explain the nature to themselves. (10:194).

Ruskin's notion of "revolutionary ornament" (10:188) allows for the free execution of the workman's powers, in contrast to the dehumanizing precision of industrial methods, which make men into mere parts of a machine. The division of labor that characterizes modern industrial life is in fact the division of men that leads to the "universal outcry against wealth, and against nobility" (10:194). The goblins and monsters of Gothic sculpture, however savage, are "signs of the life and liberty of every workman who struck the stone" (10:193). The changefulness and variety of the Gothic likewise bear witness to the workman's freedom from the enslavement of a uniform style, as does the naturalism of the Gothic: free to represent what subjects he chooses, the workman "looks to the nature that is round him for material" (10:215). The rigidity of Gothic architecture conforms to "strength of will, independence of character, resoluteness of purpose, impatience of undue control, and that general tendency to set the individual reason against authority" (10:241). Even the redundant style of the Gothic is testimony to the workman's uncalculated bestowal of the wealth of his labor.

Ruskin's concern for the nature of labor reminds us that he is an exact contemporary of Marx, who in 1844 had conceived the notion of "alienated labor" as an estrangement from nature: "The worker can create nothing without nature, the sensuous exterior world. It is the matter in which his labour realizes itself, in which it is active, out of which and through which it produces" (79). But where Marx's theories are based on a material theory of history as the effects of class conflict, Ruskin's are based on a nineteenth-century version of English Protestant Christianity. For Ruskin, the meaning of labor in its relation to Gothic architecture is therefore significantly different not only from other nineteenth-century theories of labor, such as Marx's, but also from what that meaning would have been for those who built the cathedrals of the twelfth and thirteenth centuries. What is known of the latter suggests that the medieval stonemason considered himself as engaged in the sacred duty of building the house of God according to the geometrical model of the universe itself. As the architectural historian Hanno-Walter Kruft puts it, "[T]he cosmos was a work of architecture, God himself its architect, and mathematical ratios relating to the structure of the cosmos, music, and architecture [were] identical" (36). Although the medieval workman would have possessed a variety of skills, all thoughts of individual freedom or originality of interpretation would have been subordinated to the notion of duty, to the communal function of the cathedral, and to its symbolic import according to well-known scholastic norms. This point of view is supported by various medieval works of architectural theory, including the only surviving masons' lodge book of the Middle Ages, an early-thirteenth-century work of Villard de Honnecourt based on "the rules and precepts of geometry" as taught in the university *quadrivium* (Kruft 37).[12]

Whereas for the Middle Ages Gothic architecture bore a conventional metaphorical relation to the divine design of the universe, for Ruskin it bears an essentially metonymic relation to the spirit of the medieval artisan, whom he conceives of as a nineteenth-century Protestant. By devoting his attention to decoration rather than architectonic structure, Ruskin is able to read the sculpted forms of the Gothic as concrete evidence of a spiritual condition located in the individual. According to modern ideas of the artist as an independent creator and of the identity between artist and work, sculpted decoration becomes the trace of the artisan's hand that directly translates his imaginative power. To some degree, Ruskin follows Hegel in seeing the Gothic as the external expression of the inner life. Hegel attributes the intense variety of the Gothic, for example, to the need for the "inmost heart" to render itself manifest to contemplation by interrupting and breaking up wherever possible the inert and essentially lifeless mass of stone material (*Aesthetics* 2:696). However, in a more Christian formulation of the same relation between inner life and external form, Ruskin attributes the changefulness of the Gothic to an inner sense of imperfection: "Our building must confess that we have not reached the perfection we can imagine, and cannot rest in the condition we have attained." He adds, in a lively play on words, that "the work of the Gothic heart is fretwork still" (10:214). If we compare this to Goethe's exclamation on Strasbourg Cathedral, "how everything was fretted (*durchbrochen*), and yet fashioned for eternity!" (Gage 108), the difference is between an achieved unity of the temporal and the eternal made possible by a sense of the sublime, and a perpetual striving toward that unity, which itself remains unrealized in the consciousness of sin.

Ruskin's most explicit references to the Protestant faith come in the context of his analogies between architectural form and the spiritual character of the individual Christian. The Gothic at its best transcends both the "monkish enthusiasm" of the early period (10:238) and the excessive rudeness and rigidity analogous to extreme Puritanism, which can lose itself in "frivolity of division, or perversity of purpose" (10:242). The "utmost nobleness" of the Gothic expresses in its every line "the very temper which has been thought most averse to it, the Protestant spirit of self-dependence and inquiry" (10:242). It is a spirit that Ruskin has learned from contemporary religious figures such as Henry Melvill Gwatkin and John Charles Ryle, author of an essay on "Self-inquiry," which in *Practical Religion* (1878) inveighs against a merely formal religion in favor of an "inward Christianity" and "the paramount importance of close self-examination."[13]

Ryle, an evangelical Anglican clergyman, was among Ruskin's most admired examples of religious fervor at this time of his life. Ryle defined the distinctive nature of his faith according to the importance given to five doctrines: the supremacy of Holy Scripture as the only test of truth, the awareness of human sinfulness and corruption, the experiential knowledge of Christ, the inward work of the Holy Spirit in the heart of man, and the outward, visible work of that Spirit in the life of man (Landow, chap. 4). All of these articles of faith figure in Ruskin's appreciation of the Gothic. Taking Ryle's doctrines in reverse order, we have seen the importance for Ruskin of the outward, visible form of architecture as a reflection of the inner spirit of the individual. Ryle's insistence on the individual experience of Christ has its counterpart in Ruskin's personal testimony to the immediate power of the spiritual experience conveyed by the Gothic churches he has visited in Venice, Verona, Rouen, and elsewhere. Ruskin's awareness of human sinfulness and corruption is apparent in his analysis of the changefulness and "fretwork" of the Gothic as the confession of inherent imperfection, not to say original sin. Finally, the Gothic church itself is for Ruskin a three-dimensional rendering of the spiritual truth of Holy Scripture.

This last and most important point accounts for Ruskin's insistence on the *reading* of architectural detail; the criticism of a building is to be conducted "on the same principles as that of a book," so that its appreciation will depend on the "knowledge, feeling, and not a little on the industry and perseverance of the reader" (10:269). That is, the spectator as reader must come to an understanding of the Gothic through personal diligence, not through the passive acceptance of doctrine. Ruskin's idea of architectural history, moreover, is inspired by the history of revelation in Scripture, with an evangelistic emphasis on the New Testament. For Ruskin there are three fundamental forms in architectural history: the Greek architecture of the lintel, the Romanesque architecture of the rounded arch, and the Gothic architecture of the gable, or pointed arch. The Greek, based on the principle of the simple stone beam, is the worst of the three and is "always in some measure barbarous" (10:252). The highest glory of the Romanesque is that it has no corruption, and "perishes in giving birth to another architecture as noble as itself" (10:253). This new architecture is the Gothic, which attains to perfection in the middle of the fourteenth century, a moment Ruskin earlier celebrated as "the Lamp of Truth," when "the rudeness of the intermediate space had been finally conquered, when the light had expanded to its fullest, and yet had not lost its radiant unity, principality, and visible first causing of the whole" (8:89). The three stages of architectural history, classical, Roman, and Gothic, thus stand in an analogous relation to the three human dispensations defined by the history of revelation through Scripture: pagan, Judaic, and Christian. The pagan Greek in his barbarism remains ignorant of the God of Israel; the Old Testament, if not graced by the presence of Christ, has the merit of prophesying the coming of the Savior; and the New Testament declares the fulfillment of that prophecy in the revelation of Christ's presence in the world.

The importance Ruskin gives to the practice of reading is directly related to what he calls the spirit of inquiry, a spirit to which, he claims, England in the nineteenth century owes whatever greatness it has, that is, to the habits of "stern self-reliance, and sincere upright searching for religious truth" (10:243). In this manner Ruskin manages to transform the religious architecture of the Middle Ages into the concretization of the idealized spirit of England in his own age, a spirit of inquiry that goes beyond religion to the development of the natural sciences and medicine, to the recovery of literature and the establishment of the "necessary principles of domestic wisdom and national peace" (10:237). Ruskin is often read, not without reason, as ideologically conservative and nostalgic for a utopian past. But his profound influence on the thought and the aesthetic values of his century is the product of his reflection on the most troubling questions of that age. In *The Stones of Venice* his appreciation of medieval religious architecture is quite deliberately made relevant to the crises of the nineteenth century—those of spiritual doubt, revolutionary turmoil, and the alienating effects of an industrial economy—all experienced alongside the continuing search for knowledge and social progress as the inherited ideals of the Enlightenment. At his best, Ruskin registered these crises with feeling and sought ways to redemption with an eloquence that surpassed that of his evangelical models.

Like Goethe, Ruskin returns to the subject of Gothic architecture late in life, with the publication of *The Bible of Amiens* in 1885. In Ruskin's case, the book marks a return to religious belief, or to at least a determined will to believe, after his crisis of faith in the late 1850s. However, where Goethe's writings on the subject had progressed with the poet's age from a sense of the sublime to one of historical mastery, Ruskin moves in the reverse direction: his attempt in *The Stones of Venice* to make the Gothic relevant to his own historical moment gives way to an idealized sense of the Gothic as belonging to an irrecoverable past, an almost mythic formulation that corresponds to a more general disillusionment with the decadence of modernity. Ruskin's book on the cathedral of Amiens—the "Bible" of his title by virtue of the scenes from Scripture represented in its sculpted ornament, was intended as the first of a ten-volume series entitled *Our Fathers Have Told Us: Sketches in the History of Christendom for Boys and Girls Who Have Been Held at Its Fonts.* Each volume was intended to tell the story of Christian history by focusing on a different locality in the thirteenth century; besides Amiens, there were to be other volumes on the cathedrals of Rouen, Chartres, and Notre-Dame de Paris. Each was to follow the design of *The Bible of Amiens,* which is divided into four chapters: the first three tell the story of the arrival of Christianity in the region, the early history of the Church there, and the building of the cathedral. The fourth, "Interpretations," consists of a detailed commentary on the cathedral itself as the observer moves into and through its space.

Despite the subtitle of the series and whatever Ruskin's original intention, *The Bible of Amiens* is not particularly written for "boys and girls." Its style is little different from that of Ruskin's other works designed for the general public, except perhaps for a decline in the writer's powers brought on by age and occasional fits of madness. It demands on the part of the modern reader a certain erudition in its lengthy footnotes devoted to Gibbon and its citations of Latin and medieval French poetry. The fourth chapter is written in the form of a learned tourist guidebook, and even today serves that purpose well. One hopes that Ruskin is not addressing children when, admiring a particularly beautiful part of the cathedral, he dismisses the reader who might not share his enthusiasm by saying, "you need not travel farther in search of cathedrals, for the waiting-room of any station is a better place for you" (33:130). The book as a whole is treated as an accomplished literary work by its French translator, Marcel Proust, and that is how I propose to treat it here. That being said, it must also be observed that Ruskin's book on Amiens lacks the complexity, the nuance, and the eccentric, feverish brilliance of *The Stones of Venice*. Instead, it bears the signs of a willed return to traditional moral certainties at the end of a life marked by mental illness, mourning, spiritual crisis, disappointed love, and disillusionment with the age. In contrast to the progressiveness of Ruskin's earlier work, the orientation here is fixed exclusively on the cultural past, beginning with the series title, *Our Fathers Have Told Us,* which suggests the most traditional form of the transmission of cultural and religious value.

The symbolic economy of *The Bible of Amiens* is based on a mythology of origins and purity at the center. For Ruskin, the foundations of the Cathedral of Amiens are prepared, centuries before the first stone is laid, by the provident convergence of a natural landscape, a people, and a faith. The landscape is named in the first chapter as being "by the rivers of waters" (33:25) where the Somme fans out into streams to form a Venice of the North. "This limestone tract, with its keen fresh air, everywhere arable surface, and everywhere quarriable banks above well-watered meadow, is the real country of the French. Here only are their arts clearly developed" (33:36). The banks will be quarried for the building of the cathedral, thus bringing together the true landscape and the true architecture of France. The people who build the cathedral are direct descendants of the Franks, whom Ruskin considers the true French, as opposed to the Gauls, Romans, Burgundians, and so on. They have migrated to this country from the gloomy Rhineland "under the Drachenfels" in order to found a nation here (33:53). The word *Frank* itself signifies to Ruskin "Brave, strong, and honest above other men . . . in a most human sense Frank, outspoken, meaning what they said, and standing to it, when they had got it out" (33:67–68). It is here that Clovis was baptized by Saint Rémy and was crowned the first Christian king of the Franks in 481 in Notre-Dame des Martyrs, thereby founding the kingdom of France in the first cathedral of the French nation. In a miraculous historical conjuncture of racial character, earth, and religious devotion, everything prepares for the building of the present cathedral and its consecration by Saint Louis in 1264. Not even the Cathedral of Saint-Denis, coronation and burial place of kings, is more essentially French than Amiens, the character of whose people, "intelligently conservative and constructive," with "an element of order and crystalline edification," finds its consummation in the form of the cathedral itself (33:76).

Apart from having created this mythic context, Ruskin may be credited with having written the first systematic architectural reading of a medieval Gothic cathedral, as opposed to merely recording impressions of its most striking features. Even Viollet-le-Duc, the other great theorist of Gothic architecture in the nineteenth century, does not have a comparably detailed interpretation of a single building. In the manner of a Protestant reading of the printed Bible, Ruskin's *Bible* is both intimately personal and highly methodical, while the practice of reading is understood as bringing the subject into the presence of revealed truth, a process by which the subject is himself transformed. The rigorous modalities of this procedure, however, are tempered by the conventions of travel writing, with its conversational tone and practical navigation of time and space. Ruskin makes a casual approach to the cathedral through the winding streets of Amiens, finding himself as if by accident before the portal of the south transept, above which stands the *Vièrge dorée,* her head tilted pertly to the side. Ruskin's description of this statue is notable for its irreverence: "A Madonna in decadence she is, though for all, or rather by reason of all, her prettiness, and her gay soubrette's smile" (33:128). The "decadence" in question is that of the fourteenth century, when the pretty Madonna, looking like one of the girls of the town, replaced the sober statue of Saint Honoré and so began a downward slide toward anarchy: "And thenceforward, things went their merry way, straight on, 'ça ira, ça ira,' to the merriest days of the guillotine" (33:128–29). Ruskin's irreverence toward the Catholic Madonna is therefore in fact a form of nostalgia for the original sanctity of her honored place over the south portal.

Ruskin's itinerary takes him through the south door into the nave, where his eyes rise in awe toward the clerestory: "[I]t is not possible for imagination and mathematics together, to do anything nobler or stronger than that procession of window, with material of glass and stone—nor anything which shall look loftier, with so temperate and prudent measure of actual loftiness" (33:130). He compares the sensation to that of beholding the Staubbach falls in the Berner Oberland, made part of the iconography of romanticism by Turner's watercolors and Byron's *Manfred.* He then moves up the aisle and out the west door, pausing on his way to interpret the epitaphs of those buried under the floor, including the cathedral's builder, Robert de Luzarches. Ruskin has reversed the usual direction of passage through a cathedral, which is to enter through the west door and proceed eastward to the intersection of transept and choir, traditionally regarded as the holiest place in the cathedral, as this is where the host is raised at the altar in the Roman Catholic mass. Instead, Ruskin's pilgrimage culminates not in the heart of the sanctuary but before the biblical text inscribed in statuary form on the cathedral's western exterior. His reading begins with the central figure of Christ himself, the *Beau Dieu* over the main door, to whom Ruskin gives the words of John 14:6: "I am the Way, the truth and the life." In this figure of prosopopoeia, Ruskin effectively unites the written and spoken biblical word with its three-dimensional representation in stone, a procedure he pursues throughout his interpretation of the facade, as his reading radiates outward from the center for an exposition of fifty pages before returning to the figure of Christ, who, holding the Bible in his left hand, raises his right in what Ruskin interprets as the promise of Luke 10:28: "This do, and thou shalt live" (33:170).

The moral lesson of *The Bible of Amiens* is that the cathedral serves as an example of what can be built by faith and that it should thus serve as an inspiration to those who, if they have not faith in the manner of the thirteenth century, at least acknowledge that the things promised by faith are to be desired. The book's eloquent conclusion ("vraiment sublime," says Proust)[14] is therefore written in the optative mode: if the reader would care for eternal life supposing its promise to be true, if he would care to meet his companions after death, and would want, if it were possible, "to walk in the peace of everlasting Love," then this desire itself is declared to be the reader's love, hope, and faith, and thus to confirm the promises of "our Lord and of his Christ" (33:174). By means of this rhetorical tour de force Ruskin offers a doubting Victorian public a spiritual alternative to the secular faith in culture promoted by Matthew Arnold.[15] But unlike Arnold, Ruskin has abandoned his former interest in the real conditions of his age, so his examples of faith remain nostalgically rooted in what is for him the social and spiritual perfection of the Middle Ages. However, the most important criticism of Ruskin comes from his greatest disciple, Proust, in the preface to his 1904 translation, *La Bible d'Amiens,* where he finds "idolatry" in the following circumstance of Ruskin's writing.

Les doctrines qu'il professait étaient des doctrines morales et non des doctrines esthétiques, et pourtant il les choisissait pour leur beauté. Et comme il ne voulait pas les présenter comme belles mais comme vraies,

il était obligé de se mentir à lui-même sur la nature des raisons qui les
lui faisaient adopter. (80)

*The doctrines he professed were moral and not aesthetic doctrines, and yet
he chose them for their beauty. And as he wanted to present them not as
beautiful but as true, he was obliged to lie to himself about his reasons for
adopting them.*

This criticism could only come from a student of the finer points of aes-
theticism. It says that Ruskin's religion is a religion of beauty that mistakes
itself for a religion of pure faith; he professes the doctrines of the good and
the true not because of their goodness and truth but because of the beauty
of these doctrines. It is as if Ruskin were on some level already aware of
what Gadamer and de Man would later observe, that wherever art seeks to
impose itself only as art, that is, independent of its function within a religious or mythic context, it is already on the decline. Ruskin has attempted
to restore that religious and mythic function but has done so in a cultural
context that will not sustain it.

III. BACKWARD GLANCES: JAMES, PATER, ADAMS

Henry James, Venice, 1892. Gazing across the Grand Canal at the Ca' Foscari—a noble example of fifteenth-century Venetian Gothic—James finds
it "a masterpiece of symmetry and majesty" but notices that it is visibly
"kept up" and therefore wonders whether he is right to think so highly of
it: "We feel at such moments as if the eye of Mr. Ruskin were upon us; we
grow nervous and lose our confidence" (*Collected* 325). The confession is
from James's *Italian Hours,* published in 1909 but based on impressions
gathered seventeen years earlier. It testifies to the authority of Ruskin established by the publication of *The Stones of Venice* (1851–53), but its expression of doubt, however ironic, is also symptomatic of the fact that by
the end of the nineteenth century Gothic architecture no longer has the
power of an ideal: neither aesthetic, as in the early Goethe; religious, as in
Chateaubriand; architectonic, as in Viollet-le-Duc, nor ethical, as in
Ruskin. Instead, writing on Gothic architecture is based on more personal
and local occasions; it generates meaning as a function of the subjective experience of distinct and lived moments.

Italian Hours belongs to the series of travel writings that James began
with the publication of *A Little Tour of France* in 1884, illustrated with
drawings by Joseph Pennell. The tone of these writings is set in the intro-

duction to *A Little Tour*, where James offers his "light pages" as a demonstration that there is more to France than Paris and as "aids to amused remembrance" (18). The modesty and casualness of these remarks, however, should not allow us to forget that James's travel writings record the impressions made by some of Europe's greatest monuments on one of the finest sensibilities of the modern era. The nature of these impressions differs qualitatively from those we have documented from writers of earlier generations. It is not that the sense of the sublime is altogether lost for James. Standing before the cathedral of Chartres in 1876 and looking up at the great southwestern facade,[16] he notes "the clear, silvery tone of its surface, the way three or four magnificent features are made to occupy its serene expanse, its simplicity, majesty, and dignity—these things crowd upon one's sense with a force that makes the act of vision seem for the moment almost all of life" (679). However, what distinguishes this language from the traditional discourse of the sublime is the emphasis on "sense" rather than some nobler faculty; the location of agency in "the act of vision" rather than in some external, transcendent power; the fleeting nature of the "moment"; and the restraint registered by the strategically placed *almost* in "almost all of life." James's universe is always partial and contingent; he consciously refuses the absolute and unconditional. Returning to Venice for a moment, one senses the hint of ironic distance when he reports that many find the great middle stretch of the Grand Canal, the "long, gay, shabby, spotty perspective" between the Foscari and the Rialto, to be *dull,* but he imagines it was not dull for Lord Byron, who lived in one of the palaces there, where "the writing-table is still shown where he gave the rein to his passions" (329). It is not so much that James is unwilling to give rein to his passions but that, even before the majestic front of Chartres, what he experiences are not passions but "impressions." For Edmund Burke, the passion caused by the sublime, which includes elements of astonishment and horror, is occasioned by the incommensurability of human understanding to the object it beholds. But if James finds the harmony of Chartres inexpressible, it is not, for him, a matter of the human subject's inadequacy to the sublime object. Rather, it is a problem of aesthetic translation from one art form to another: "The impressions produced by architecture lend themselves as little to interpretation by another medium as those produced by music" (679). Having observed the Cathedral of Chartres from twenty different angles at every hour of the day, he has gained a certain sense of familiarity with it, "yet I despair of giving any coherent account of it" (678). For James, there seems to be no satisfactory way of getting a building into writing.

Faced with this radical incommensurability between writing and architecture, James's response is one of invention: rather than being the object of description and analysis, Gothic architecture becomes the setting for narrative digression and literary allusion. James's discussion of the twelfth-century Cathedral of Tours is dominated by Balzac's "terrible little story" *Le Curé de Tours* (1843), one of the French writer's truly depressing *Scènes de la vie provinciale,* in which the unsuspecting Abbé Birotteau falls victim to the rapacity of his landlady, Mlle Gamard, and his envious rival, the Abbé Troubert. James goes round the north end of the cathedral to find the real house of the fictional Mlle Gamard; in the courtyard of this house is anchored one of the flying buttresses of the church itself. "All this part of the exterior of the cathedral is very brown, ancient, Gothic, grotesque; Balzac calls the whole place 'a desert of stone'" (30). Indeed the cathedral seems more real, and acquires its true significance for James, in Balzac's novella than in its actual presence. In a way, James solves the problem of the mutual impermeability of writing and architecture through recourse to the mediating function of literary memory: he experiences the real Cathedral of Tours by entering the imaginary space it occupies in Balzac's novel. In addition to the phrase cited above by James, Balzac had evoked the house of Mlle Gamard and the adjacent Cathedral in the following terms.

> Située au nord de Saint-Gatien, cette maison se trouve continuellement dans les ombres projetées par cette grande cathédrale sur lequel le temps a jeté son manteau noir, imprimé ses rides, semé son froid humide, ses mousses et ses hautes herbes. (41)

> *Located on the north side of Saint-Gatien, this house was continually in the shadows cast by the great cathedral on which time has thrown a coat of black, printed its wrinkles, and given seed to its damp coldness, its mosses and its tall weeds.*

We may acquire a sense of the particularity of James's sensibility with respect to the Gothic by seeing what he later writes about Balzac in an essay originally written as a preface to the English translation of the *Mémoires de deux jeunes mariées* (1902) and later published in both *Notes on Novelists* (1914) and *The Art of Fiction* (1948). Even a single sentence of Balzac's materially dense prose, with its shadows, old stones, and humid mosses, provides a convincing example of what principally interests James in Balzac: his obsession with things, his local color, "thick in his pages at a time when it was to be found in his pages almost alone" (*Art* 31). Balzac has created a "terrible mess of matter" (36) that is "drenched in the smell of the past" (35), as if his estranged view of the modern world were one from out of the Middle Ages. Balzac's world is a massive labyrinth he has built around himself, which he can only attempt to bore through. The incompatibility of architecture with writing that James has claimed for his own work seems not to apply to Balzac, for whom the old stones of Tours serve as the very foundation for the construction of his fictional universe. Indeed, James regards the old Gothic cathedral as a kind of metaphor for the mass and material complexity of Balzac's world. While viewing that world with sympathy and admiration, James distinguishes his own writing from Balzac's as "working in the open" (36), which is James's way of designating the novel of consciousness as opposed to the novel of the concrete, palpable world defined by the horizon of one's birth and race, even given the latter's infinite social complexity:

> When we work in the open, as it were, our material is not classed and catalogued, so that we have at hand a hundred different ways of being loose, superficial, disingenuous, and yet passing, to our no small profit, for remarkable. (36)

James presents his own work with characteristic self-deprecation, but he nonetheless disengages it qualitatively from that of Balzac. His "ways of being loose" are ways of being free from the massive, confining world in which Balzac's imagination struggles with so much exertion. James would claim to be less weighty than Balzac, but he is also more subtle and agile, more true to the fugitive nature of consciousness itself. The particular nature of his artistic temperament is to seize on what is transitory and contingent and to find human truths there.

James's thoughts on these matters may help us to understand the studied impertinence with which, unlike Balzac, he treats the mossy old stones of the Cathedral of Tours. At those moments when, almost out of a sense of duty, James applies himself to the description of architectural detail, he cannot always resist the temptation to fanciful invention. Above the balustrade on the upper southwest facade of Chartres, extending from tower to tower, there is a row of sixteen niched statues of the kings of France.[17] The little gallery below the row of kings has for James a "peculiar charm": he imagines them, of a late afternoon, "strolling up and down their long balcony in couples, pausing with their elbows on the balustrade, resting their stony chins in their hands, and looking out, with their little blank eyes, on the great view of the French monarchy they once ruled, and which has now passed away" (*Collected* 680). They have become, in the writer's imagination, figures of the late nineteenth century: the idle, nostalgic members of the dispossessed aristocracy who inhabit the novels of Henry James.

We have seen how, at Tours, James deserts the cathedral proper to explore the deserted labyrinth of alleys behind it. At Chartres as well, he strays from the central object of touristic interest in search of fresh impressions. His article on Chartres concludes not with the cathedral itself but with a scene just outside the old city gate of washerwomen who come to dip their colored rags into the yellow stream of the ditch that flows beneath the moldering wall.

> The old patched and interrupted wall, the ditch with its weedy edges, the spots of colour, the white-capped laundresses in their little wooden cages—one lingers to look at it all. (683)

The scene is painterly rather than architectural, and it is likely that James's perception here is conditioned by the visual arts; the subject of *les lavandières,* or washerwomen, often rendered in scenes of architectural ruin, was already favored in the eighteenth century by Fragonard and Robert Hubert. The subject was attractive for the striking contrasts it afforded between the sensual forms of the women stirring the water and the imposing antiquity of their architectural surroundings. Closer to James's own time, laundresses, or *blanchisseuses,* were a subject for such artists as Louis Français, Jean-Louis-Ernest Meissonier, and Edgar Degas.[18] James's own language is visually impressionistic in its naming of colored forms— patches, edges, caps, and spots—all composed in a lingering glance; it anticipates the lyrical juxtaposition of images that modernist poetry would later explore. Moreover, it is instructive to compare this passage to one in Ruskin, who, in *Modern Painters,* recounts a similar excursion down to the banks of the Somme, where the dyers and spinners form a "picturesque" scene. Ruskin notices the unhealthy and melancholy faces of the working poor, and remarks, "I could not help feeling how many suffering persons must pay for my picturesque subject and happy walk" (6:20). In this comparison James comes out as a purer aesthete than

Ruskin, but there are other moments, inspired by the particular atmosphere of Gothic architecture, that force James to confront the question of its contemporary meaning.

As a final instance of what we might call productive distraction, let us join James at Rheims in 1877, where he has sought a moment of rest from his exploration of the thirteenth-century cathedral by sitting down on a little stool, from which he leans against one of the choir stalls. James thus finds himself at the very heart of the cathedral, at the intersection between the nave and the transept. As he gazes upward and loses himself in "the large perfection of the place," he is suddenly confronted by a beadle who stands before him, motioning him to depart "with an imperious gesture." A look of silent protest from the writer produces a distinct gesture of displeasure from the beadle, and James is obliged to retire from the "sacred precinct" (740). The anecdote is first of all remarkable for the way the writer's own body figures as an alien presence in the sacred space, while James also dramatizes, in his self-deprecating way, the contestation of that space between the traditional prerogatives of the clergy and the insistent if polite requirements of the tourist. The choir stalls are now occupied by elderly men in red capes who begin to chant, and James discovers that the impending vesper service was the reason for his expulsion. However reasonable this might be, his thoughts nonetheless turn in irritation from the architectural to the political; he finds his expulsion to be an example of the arbitrary authoritarianism of the Catholic Church and thus finds a new reason to resent the Church's support for the forces of reaction against the attempt to consolidate the political gains of France's fledgling Third Republic. James is, among his other qualities, a product of his own time and place: an American Protestant imbued with democratic feeling. However refined his aesthetic sensibility, he now feels compelled to confront the question of what the Gothic cathedral means for the modern era. On one hand, he feels called upon to recognize the generosity and hospitality of the institution responsible for erecting the magnificent structure about him. On the other hand, he has fallen out the state of mind favorable to such acknowledgment, and he asks himself to what extent that lapse is "unbecoming." Simply put, how does one feel about the magnificence of the cathedral when one realizes that the institution that built it, and is ennobled by it, is an enemy of liberty and social justice? It is a question he imagines thousands asking themselves, in the conflict "between the actively, practical liberal instinct and what one may call the historical, aesthetic sense, the sense upon which old cathedrals lay a certain palpable obligation" (742). James's solution to this conflict is characteristically modern: in his mind, the concept of the "sacred" is redefined out of its religious sense in order to define the sense of duty characterized by the anti-Catholic passion as it burns in the breasts of certain radicals, as in the "sacred duty" to resist oppression. James does not claim to be one of these radicals, but he finds this sense of the sacred congenial to the present occasion, so that he can once more appreciate in good conscience the beauty of Rheims Cathedral: "I raised my eyes again to the dusky splendour of the upper aisles and measured their enchanting perspective, and it was with a sense of doing them full justice that I gave my fictive liberal my good wishes" (742). In other words, the enchantment of medieval architectural form is now identified with the Enlightenment cause of justice, joining aesthetic response to noble sentiment in a manner particular to James's era. However, a stylistic difference between Ruskin and James is that the latter does not treat such matters with entire seriousness; he remains a slightly comical figure in his own eyes. The principal result of the little operation just described is to restore his "equanimity," making him able, in what risks being perceived as a "rather vulgar feat of gymnastics" to climb the cathedral towers, scramble over expanses of roof, and admire a series of stone eagles unaccountably sculpted with human legs. James asks of the anonymous sculptor, "Why did he indulge in this ridiculous conceit? I am unable to say, but the conceit afforded me pleasure. It seemed to tell of an imagination always at play, fond of the unexpected and delighting in its labour" (742), the imagination, in other words, of a Henry James.

James's sense of play amounts to both a gesture of refusal and a recognition of otherness. He refuses the constraints of Balzac's universe, in its confinement of experience to the objective world of things, property, and institutions, just as he refuses for more obvious reasons the authority of the Catholic Church. The sheer mass of Balzac's world represents a totalizing force that, from James' point of view, can be compared to that exercised by the Church in the Middle Ages; the Gothic cathedral stands as a concretized metaphor for this determination of the spirit within a universal institutional framework. James's resistance to both the fictional world of Balzac and the institutional world of the Church registers at the same time his freedom of consciousness—working in the open, as it were—and his profound sense of difference, his solitude and strangeness. His expulsion from the precincts of the choir in Tours Cathedral is in this sense an allegory of his condition of otherness: celibate but not priestly, a writer without the material of a national, social life descended from the Middle Ages such as provides ground for the fiction of a Balzac or Victor Hugo. In his fictional version of the life of James, Colm Tóibín imagines him as a young man reading Balzac for the first time and sensing already that "he himself would never possess a subject so richly layered and suggestive, as sharply focused and centered, as the France of Balzac's *Human Comedy*" (150). The cathedrals of Tours and Chartres are part of that France, and Balzac's novels, in their devotion to the representation of French life, make them part of the collective meaning assigned to that life. It is in the shadow of such monuments that James affirms the lonely freedom of his exile. Ultimately, then, for all their seeming formlessness, these travel notes tell a story, with James himself as his own Jamesian protagonist, an uprooted American wandering over the old stones of Europe, confronting his own weightlessness with pleasure and apprehension.

Whatever their narrative force, the formal and expressive freedom of these writings is precisely what Walter Pater claims for the essay as the literary form best adapted to the spirit of modernity. According to Pater, in an early essay on Coleridge, modern thought cultivates the relative in place of the absolute, and the essay is "the literary form necessary to a mind for which truth itself is but a possibility, realisable not as general conclusion, but rather as the elusive effect of a particular personal experience" ("Coleridge's" 48). In his book on Pater, Wolfgang Iser remarks that just as the modern, relative spirit has used the ancient absolutes in order to grasp its own otherness, "the essay is for Pater the modern form that gains its shape against the background of earlier shapes to be discerned in the history of forms" (18). The essay is distinguished from other literary forms in its openness to random and subjective experience; it is "a form which deconstructs itself in order to represent open-endedness, unrelatedness and endlessness as facts of experiential reality" (19). Viewed in this light, Pater's essays on architecture acquire a special meaning. On one hand, architecture itself becomes the experiential reality against which the essay takes form, in a dialectical manner. On the other hand, the open-endedness of the essay can serve as an analogy for certain architectural forms. The question of "translating" architecture into writing is thus put aside in favor of a more dialectical and dynamic relation between the two arts.

Pater's *Some Great Churches in France* was originally published in the form of two essays, respectively on Amiens and Vézelay, that appeared in successive issues of the periodical *Nineteenth Century* in March and June 1894 and were later reprinted in the posthumous *Miscellaneous Studies* (1895). Pater's title, as well as the travels he made in preparation for this work, allow us to suppose that had he lived longer he would have added essays on Auxerre, Autun, and Chartres. Indeed the second chapter of his unfinished novel *Gaston de Latour* (1896) includes a rich evocation of the Cathedral of Chartres, with its "gift of a unique power of impressing" (28). Had Pater completed the project we imagine him to have undertaken, it would have rivaled in scope that other unfinished work on the great French cathedrals, Ruskin's *Our Fathers Have Told Us*. However, where Ruskin's work is consciously didactic in its avowed purpose of transmitting Christian traditions, Pater's by comparison is free of doctrine, including the anti-Catholic sentiment that at moments animates James's thoughts at Chartres. In his writing on Amiens and Vézelay, Pater demonstrates how the essay embodies the modern form of subjective freedom, in dialectical relation to the material reality of archaic architectural forms.

One way to compare Pater's essay on Amiens with Ruskin's is to follow the respective movements that each makes through the space of the great cathedral. Ruskin approaches the cathedral indirectly through the winding little streets of the town, coming suddenly upon the south door. We have seen how he enters through that door and passes through the nave and out the main door, ending his visit before the great western front. Pater's movement through the same space is more conventional, passing through the west door and advancing to the heart of the sanctuary, where he pauses before the Eucharist suspended in the central bay, with "all the poor, gaudy, gilt rays converging towards it" (119). The nature of Pater's journey, however, is not one that builds toward a narrative climax but rather one of expansion and overture. His entrance into the nave is experienced as an opening out into light.

> Light and space—floods of light, space for a vast congregation, for all the people of Amiens, for their movements, with something like the height and width of heaven itself enclosed above them to breathe in. (107)

Pater's attention is naturally drawn upward, to the clear glass of the great windows of the triforium. It seems to him that the entire building is composed of its windows, as if those who built it had had for their sole purpose to enclose as large a space as possible with glass (110).

Once he has stepped through the western doorway, the entire space of the cathedral is at once visible and intelligible, from the triforium to the "realms of light which expand in the chapels beyond; the astonishing boldness of the vault; the astonishing lightness of what keeps it above one; the unity, yet the variety of perspective." Everything is "full of excitement" (109). In his enthusiasm for space and light, for the clarity and intelligibility of the space, and for the properties of large expanses of glass, Pater anticipates some of the values that, a generation later, modernist architecture would put into practice. The modern form of thought represented by the essay is thus combined with an early expression of the modernist aesthetic.

The end of Pater's essay ascends to the height of the great western towers of Amiens and from there takes in the prospect of the surrounding country—a wide architectural region to which belong

> Soissons, far beyond the woods of Compiègne, . . . with St. Quentin, and, towards the west, a too ambitious rival, Beauvais, which has stood however—what we now see of it, for six centuries. (121)

The overall movement of the essay, then, begins in the singularity of a moment and spreads outward from there into a much wider expanse of space and time. The lived moment in the individual space of consciousness is indeed at the origin of Pater's vision. His desire to know "precisely what, is this to *me*" (113) arises not out of egotism, but rather from a sense of his own temporal and temperamental difference from those who built and first worshipped in the churches of the Middle Ages. It is precisely this historical difference that grants compensation for his inability to see the cathedral with medieval eyes, "something verily worth having, and a just equivalent for something else lost, in the mere effect of time" (113). This just equivalent is provided in material ways by, for example, the fading of medieval coloring to reveal the rich texture of the stone underneath. But it also lies in the subjective freedom with which Pater responds to the Gothic, as if he were able to endow it with new meaning by virtue of his historical distance from its origins.

In contrast to Gothic revivalists working in the Catholic context, such as Pugin and Joris-Karl Huysmans, and even in some degree to Ruskin, Pater interprets the form of Gothic architecture in human and secular, rather than religious terms. He insists on the secular nature of Amiens as a "people's church" and to this principle attributes its splendor, space, and novelty. The great expanse of the nave, built all on one level, is designed to accommodate the entire population of Amiens and to make possible "the easy flow of processional torrent" (107). The pillars, with their softened angles and graceful compassing, are designed for the same purpose, "to carry a multitude conveniently round them" (108). The form, function, and materials of architecture are thus interpreted in terms of real human experience. Pater's tactile sense of the cathedral, as something made for the bodies and senses of the faithful, is fully consistent with his own sensual impressions of light, space, matter, and movement. When Pater defines Gothic construction as "consolidation of matter naturally on the move, security for settlement in a very complex system of construction" (108), one hears echoes of the conclusion to his *The Renaissance* (1868), where only a "quickened, multiplied consciousness" can do justice to the ceaseless motion of the object world and its inward counterpart of thought and feeling, as if the excitement of the movement suspended in stone had seized a form grown perfect in its own historical moment.

Returning to Hegel for a moment, it becomes possible to gauge the distance between his ideas and Pater's fin-de-siècle aesthetic. In one of his lectures on "romantic architecture," Hegel had said that art now had the dual function of producing, on one hand, a "tranquillity of the heart" released from the external world, and, on the other hand, the "impression of a majestic sublimity which aspires beyond and outsoars mathematical limitation" (2:686). Both effects take place in the subject of aesthetic experience, whereas Hegel leaves open the question of whether the "impression" (*Eindruck*) of sublimity is merely that or a real apprehension of a transcendent order, as Blake or Shelley would claim. In contrast, Pater is resolutely materialist; his aesthetic affirms immanence over transcendence and stands against abstraction, "nothing of mystery in the vision, which yet surprises, over and over again" (109). What he seeks is not the tranquillity of the heart, but rather the "excitement," the sense of being alive that art produces in the subject. Pater's emphasis on the nature of the moment, whether of subjective perception or historical existence, leads him to see in Amiens not just a certain method of construction but also something distinct in human achievement. Unlike Ruskin, he sees the surrounding country of Picardy as unfertile ground for the imagination: a flat, drab region of "cheerless rivers" (121). To have made something great and beautiful just *here* is to have intervened with immense effort in the natural course of things; Pater's metaphor is from Isaiah 52:3: "a root out of a dry ground" (122).

This idea of the cathedral is in keeping with Pater's more general theory of *expression,* which again distinguishes him from Ruskin. As Iser points out, Ruskin sees no essential difference between expression and communication in art: artistic expression is but a means to communicate the moral and natural truth of a world whose beauty is accessible to everyone. But for Pater, expression is self-expression, the objectification of an inwardness "seeking to establish superiority over the 'burdensome character' of experience" (Iser 27). According to this model, the Cathedral of Amiens expresses the inner spirit of a people in their effort to overcome the conditions of their own meager existence in an inhospitable landscape. On the level of the individual artist, Pater claims that the popular, almost secular teachings of the thirteenth century created a new spirit by means of which art became personal. The artist in such an environment makes his own way of conception and execution prevail: he "renders his own work vivid and organic" (Pater 116). Whereas for Ruskin the harmony of landscape, people, and cathedral in Amiens makes a perfect unity that can only be looked back on with admiration and regret, for Pater it is precisely the discord between a sterile landscape and the achievement of Amiens that renders the cathedral exceptional and provides an implicit analogy for the nineteenth-century artist seeking to express his inward reality amid the hostile cultural landscape of modernity, populated as it is by the barbarians and Philistines against which Matthew Arnold wrote in *Culture and Anarchy* (1869). More than the capacity to appreciate the rough texture of stone that has lost its color, this is what constitutes the "just equivalent" for what has been lost since the thirteenth century: the image, in the cathedral of Amiens, of a willed dialectic between the confusion of the object world and the expressive power of an inward spirit to impose itself on that world. It is through such expression, through its power to inscribe itself as architecture on the landscape or writing on the page, that the inner world of the artist makes use of its freedom.

"The expression concerns us; the construction concerns the Beaux Arts" (Adams 106). This is Henry Adams in *Mont Saint Michel and Chartres* (1904), a work that carries into the twentieth century the literary meditation on architectural expression and cultural memory that characterizes the work we have examined of Goethe, Ruskin, James, and Pater. In his description of the Cathedral of Chartres, Adams here is addressing the question of the use of flying buttresses, and his point is that whereas their virtue as structural supports is a matter for the École des Beaux Arts (the principal institution for the training of architects in France), what concerns him and his readers is the "expression they gave to a church" (106), whether this expression be understood as religious or as purely aesthetic. The precise nature of what is being expressed in medieval religious architecture, and to what extent the object of that expression can be understood by the modern mind, are the questions posed by Adams's essay. His approach to these questions is made under the sign, as it were, of Words-worth's "Intimations" ode (1807), quoted in the opening paragraphs of Adams's first chapter. His use of Wordsworth reminds us of the importance of the subject of personal memory in modern literature and of the ways it has been related to that of cultural memory. Indeed, the "problem" posed by the presence of medieval architecture in the modern age can be under-stood as one of cultural memory and its analogy in the personal memory of the individual subject.

Let us recall the argument of Wordsworth's ode: as mature human be-ings we have lost the memory of our heavenly origins, which can nonethe-less be recovered through an imaginative act, that of the recollection of early childhood, the age at which, freshly issued from heaven, we still lived in its divine light. Adams's device is to transpose this myth onto the his-torical dimension: the earliest manifestations of Gothic architecture, in the twelfth century, represent a childhood of the human spirit whose divine dimension has been lost but which might be recovered through a form of recollection that returns to the state of childhood: "The man who wanders into the twelfth century is lost, unless he can grow prematurely young" (7). Adams reminds us of the conditions that Wordsworth poses for the success of this endeavor: in a "season of calm weather" one can still have sight of the "immortal sea," which brought us hither from our origins, and can even travel there to see the children sporting on the shore. In other words, in the right frame of mind we can return to the twelfth century and bear witness to the spirit that alone could produce the monuments of Mont Saint Michel and Chartres: "Our sense is partially atrophied from disuse, but it is still alive"(8).

Adams's visit to Chartres is thus conducted as a quest that is at once his-torical and personal. Standing before the southwest front, he sees the Christ over the central door, flanked by a scene of the Ascension over the left door and a statue of the seated Virgin over the right door: "Here is the Church, the Way, and the Life of the twelfth century that we have under-taken to feel, if not to understand" (70). The search for this feeling will not be through the central, "royal" door where Christ figures in all his majesty but through the adjacent south door of the Virgin, who, in her qualities of mercy and intercession, belongs to the people rather than to the Church.

Stop a moment to see how she receives us, remembering, or trying to remember, that, to the priests and artists who designed the Portal, and to the generations that went on the first and second crusades, the Virgin in her shrine was at least as living, as real, as personal an empress as the Basilissa at Constantinople! (71–72)[19]

This attempt at memory and this search for feeling define the mode of Adams's first chapter ("Towers and Portals") on the cathedral proper. The transition to the next chapter ("The Virgin of Chartres"), however, is marked by the writer's actual passage into the sanctuary, where he must take ten minutes to accustom his eyes to the light. It is in this blind interval that he begins to realize that his quest is in vain; the twentieth century will never recover the feeling that built the cathedral of Chartres, for "the gothic gets away . . . it casts too many shadows" (87). Sobered by this realization, he now puts the Wordsworthian disposition at an ironic remove.

> What is curious to watch is the fanatical conviction of the gothic enthusiast, to whom the twelfth century means exuberant youth, the eternal child of Wordsworth, over whom its immortality broods like the day. (87)

Adams finds that in such a person the "youthful yearning for old thought is . . . disconcerting, like the mysterious senility of the baby that

> Deaf and silent reads the eternal deep, Haunted forever by the eternal mind." (87)

The quotation from the "Intimations" ode is inexact, but the intention is clear: Adams must distance himself from the mythic illusions of the romantic model; his response to the Gothic henceforth alternates between persistent statements of purpose—"we have set out to seek the feeling" (183)—and expressions of irremediable loss.

This sense of loss, of a failure to properly comprehend, is repeated before each of several of the cathedral's most remarkable architectural details. This is the case, for example, in the use of *grisaille* in the windows of the choir. *Grisaille* is a technique of coloring glass using only shades of gray so as to create a kind of shimmering, sculptural effect. As a technical reference on this effect, Adams cites a passage from Viollet-le-Duc that reveals, unexpectedly, an almost Paterian sensibility.

> The solid outlines then seem to waver like objects seen through a sheet of clear water. Distances change their values, and take depths in which the eye gets lost. With every hour of the day these effects are altered,

and always with new harmonies which one never tires of trying to understand. (151)

For Adams, however, a complete understanding is beyond the reach of his age. *Grisaille* is just one branch of an entire system of lighting and *fenêtrage,* which "will have to remain a closed book because the feeling and the experience which explained it once are lost, and we cannot recover either" (152). In the absence of such experience, Adams's solution to the problem of describing the cathedral takes the form of a dramatic and historical mise-en-scène based primarily on the images in the stained glass windows. Where Ruskin relies on sculpture and Pater on materials and architectonics, Adams is almost entirely devoted to the two-dimensional images offered by windows. The northwest and southeast ends of the transept, for example, place in opposition two rose windows: the Rose of France, donated in 1230 by Queen Blanche of Castille; and, facing it from the south, the Rose of Dreux, donated by Pierre de Dreux, the noble Breton warrior who revolted against Blanche in the 1230s and was later to die in the Crusades. The Rose of France shows an image of the Virgin with a scepter in her right hand and her Son seated on her knees; it is an allegory of Blanche's own rule and of the future reign of her son Louis. The Rose of Dreux opposes to this image the fierce scenes of the Apocalypse, dominated by the figure of Christ as emperor of heaven. As Adams points out, Pierre de Dreux "carries the assertion of his sex into the very presence of the Queen of Heaven" (175). This presence is most strikingly recorded in the window known as Notre-Dame de la Belle Verrière, to the right of the choir, just above the altar. It is to this image that Adams turns at the conclusion to his visit of the cathedral, finding that the Virgin and the prophets around her remain "as calm and confident in their own strength and in God's providence as they were when Saint Louis was born,[20] but looking down from a deserted heaven, into an empty church, on a dead faith" (186).

This judgment is without possibility of appeal and effectively marks Adams's break with the Wordsworthian notion of a return to origins. But Adams retains enough of the romantic sensibility to want, by means of imagination, to fill the void left by the vision of the past as empty and dead. That space will be filled by the eternal figure of the feminine.

Throughout his essay, Adams's emphasis on the figure of Mary is consistent with his contention that Chartres was built primarily as a shrine to this deity rather than as a place of public worship (97) and that Gothic architecture is essentially feminine. *Mont Saint Michel and Chartres* is in effect a kind of hymn to the feminine principle. The chapter on the three most important "queens" of the Middle Ages (Eleanor of Aquitaine, Marie de France, and Blanche of Castille) begins by declaring, against Pope, that the "the proper study of mankind is woman," followed by the suggestion that "nature regards the female as the essential, the male as the superfluity of her world" (187). For Adams, the great period of Gothic architecture is defined by a series of female reigns. It begins when Eleanor of Aquitaine becomes Queen of France in 1137, continues through the life of the poet Marie de France, and ends with the death of Blanche of Castille in 1252: "For a hundred and fifty years, the Virgin and Queens ruled French taste and thought" (193). The nature of that rule is reflected in the respective characters of the three women celebrated there. Eleanor of Aquitaine, "the greatest of all French women" (198), figures as the principle of feminine law and strength while being at the same time a woman who did what pleased herself: "While the Virgin was miraculously using the power of spiritual love to elevate and purify the people, Eleanor and her daughters were using the power of earthly love to discipline and refine the Courts" (200). Marie de France celebrated the spirit of courtly love in her lays, and under her authority the noble lesson of that ideal lasted for centuries as the standard of taste (202). Blanche of Castille, as regent of France following the death of Louis VII in 1226, successfully resisted the revolt of the barons, including Pierre de Dreux, whose rose window faces hers in the transept of Chartres. Tradition holds that she inspired the love poems of Thibaut de Champagne, and their secret love is held to be a thirteenth-century version of the story of Tristan and Isolde. Adams's argument is that the art of the twelfth and thirteenth centuries, including Gothic architecture, owes its particular grace and power to the influence of these women, and to the feminine principle in general. Commenting on Thibaut's verses to Blanche, he compares their eloquent simplicity to "the simplicity of the thirteenth-century glass,—so refined and complicated that sensible people are satisfied mainly to feel, and not to understand" (214). Adams thus brings about an association between the feminine and Gothic architecture through the mediating figure of poetry.

In his treatment of the Virgin, as well as these historical figures, a number of elements are combined in Adams's work to form the feminine principle. The cult of the Virgin, figure of mercy, emanates from the people and not from Church doctrine; she is present to them with a reality that never belonged to the Son or to the Trinity, just as women in general form a counterforce to the masculine hierarchy of the Church and to the male monastic tradition. The Virgin is so much a person of the people that even in Adams's own age she is "little to the taste of any respectable middle-class society" (244). By the same token, the "feeling" that Adams seeks vainly to recover, but of which he sees evidence everywhere in the Gothic, belongs to the province of the Virgin and the other female figures of his essay; it is implicitly opposed to the intellectual principle represented by the fathers of the Church. The various manifestations of the feminine principle in Adams give it a quality of multiplicity, as well as irregularity and even non-rationality, as implied in the very title Virgin Mother. In his chapter on the miracles of Notre Dame, Adams writes, "If the Trinity was in essence Unity, the Mother alone could represent whatever was not Unity; whatever was irregular, exceptional, outlawed; and this was the whole human race" (248). The Virgin, and by extension the eternal feminine, is outside of doctrine.

✦ ✦ ✦

So ends our excursion. This chapter began with the observation of a tension between two strains in nineteenth-century responses to Gothic architecture: the aesthetic, which celebrates architectural form independent of its originally sacred function; and the ethical, in which the writer attempts to come to terms with the significance of Gothic architecture for his own time. The first two sections have sought to show how the essential conflict between aesthetic transcendence and ethical value is manifested in three key literary figures of the early and mid–nineteenth century: Goethe, Wordsworth, and Ruskin. In all three, the tension between the aesthetic and the ethical is combined, according to the temperament of the individual writer, with the more subjective discourse of personal impression, experience, perception, and memory. It is this discourse that becomes more pronounced in the writers treated in the third section, which registers the twilight of the influence of Gothic architecture as reflected in late-century literary sensibilities: James's ironies, Pater's insistent questioning, and Adams's sense of incomprehension and of the radical otherness of the medieval world that built these monuments to a kind of faith his generation can no longer experience.

What unites the several writers studied here is the sense of spiritual, cultural, and personal loss inspired by the survival of Gothic architecture;

their works constitute, collectively, a series of negotiations with that loss that leads to a more modern accommodation of it. Adams registers that loss as definitively as it is possible to do, his sense of loss extending from personal experience to the aesthetic and historical realms. But for this loss there is something gained : "abundant recompense," as Wordsworth writes in the "Intimations" ode, or Pater's "just equivalent." Having complained that the Gothic gets away, it turns out that Adams has, after all, discovered a way to speak of the Gothic: it is for him the architectural embodiment of the feminine principle in its irregular, multiform, and fragmentary nature, its organic relation to the people, its disruption of hierarchical relations, its elusiveness, and its appeal to feeling, emotion, and the sense of the miraculous. In these ways Gothic architecture opposed the Romanesque tradition with its origins in the monasteries, just as women stood symbolically in opposition to the male institutions of the Church. In all of these qualities, combined with Adams's emphasis on the emotional effects of hard-cut images, we may discern the early signs of a modernist aesthetic, one that can come into being only with the conscious abandonment of romantic mythologies and the clear-eyed vision of a deserted heaven, an empty church, and a dead faith. Adams's treatment of the Gothic is a swan song, made at a time of waning literary interest in the subject; it seems to acknowledge that the great questions of what medieval religious architecture means to the nineteenth century have been played out if not fully answered, and that they now must give way to other, more urgent questions and ways of seeing.

With these questions in mind, the development described in this chapter's last section, "Backward Glances," should be seen as a consequence of the tension between the tendencies outlined in the first two sections. That is, the tension between sublime transcendence and ethical value that we witness variously in Goethe, Wordsworth, and Ruskin is translated, later in the century, into the language of immediate subjective experience. This kind of experience still makes claims to aesthetic and ethical value, but these claims are more modest, and more contingent on individual sensibility, than those of romanticism. I would also make the point that this translation functions as a prefigurement of modernism in both architecture and literature. The ethical and the aesthetic will remain distinct values in the twentieth century, but architectural modernism will seek to serve both of them in structures that propose a functional beauty liberated from the burden of history in favor of the sensory experience of space and light. Literary modernism, for its part, will find both aesthetic and ethical value in various forms of immediate if fragmentary experience: Proust's involuntary memory, Joyce's epiphanies, Woolf's "moments of being."[21] This is to propose a way in which the changing responses to Gothic architecture in the long nineteenth century serve as a ground for understanding the transition from romantic and Victorian sensibilities to those of both literary and architectural modernism.

4
———

Figures of Ruin and Restoration:
Ruskin and Viollet-le-Duc

The two most prominent architectural theorists of the nineteenth century—Eugène-Emmanuel Viollet-le-Duc and John Ruskin, both champi-
ons of the Gothic—held diametrically opposed ideas on the question of
architectural restoration. Viollet-le-Duc devoted a successful career to
restoring many of France's great architectural monuments of the Middle
Ages and wrote extensively in defense of his practices. Ruskin, on the
other hand, abhorred restoration of any kind, and defended the aesthetic
value of ruins. The reason for this difference in architectural doctrine has
been put down to one of temperament between the rational *architecte de
terrain* and the eccentric Oxford aesthete. However, in attempting to go
beyond these stereotypes, I have found that the question of architectural
restoration rather quickly opens out onto a wider field of inquiry that includes the relation of nineteenth-century architecture to the other arts.
My approach to these two writers will propose the notion that the opposition between an aesthetics of architectural ruin and one of restoration
bears comparison with another burning issue in nineteenth-century art:
the opposition between allegory and symbol. At the same time, I will suggest that both of these oppositions are symptomatic of a condition marking the advent of modernity: its complex and unstable relation to the historical past.

The aesthetic of ruins in the late eighteenth and early nineteenth centuries needs to be understood as part of the emerging distinction between the figures of allegory and symbol, as defined by romantic critics such as Samuel Taylor Coleridge and Georg Friedrich Creuzer. At the risk of covering some familiar territory, allow me to recall some of their formulations. Coleridge introduces the distinction between allegory and symbol in order to show that the latter concept is the proper way to read the Bible, against the "dead letter" of literalism or the "counterfeit product of mechanical understanding" (6:30). For Coleridge, "an allegory is but a translation of abstract notions into a picture-language, which is itself nothing but an abstraction from objects of the senses" (6:30). A symbol, on the other hand, unifies the material object with the metaphysical, between the phenomenon and its essence. Coleridge thus speaks of "the translucence of the Eternal in and through the Temporal" as the symbolic mode that transfuses the entire Bible, while Creuzer speaks of the instantaneousness, totality, and unfathomable origins of the symbol (cited in Benjamin, *Origin* 166). The unity of the symbol is above all temporal: eternity manifests itself in the instantaneous.

It is useful, however, to understand these theories not only in their romantic formulations but also in their redefinitions by a twentieth-century theorist such as Walter Benjamin. Coleridge sees allegory, in its purely conventional relation between the sensible and the abstract, as only an artificial and degraded form of the symbol; but it is something else entirely for Benjamin. In the *Origin of German Tragic Drama* (1925), Benjamin overturns the romantic primacy of the symbol in favor of allegory. For him, allegory is the figure that rigorously refuses the sublimation of the Fall, resists the illusory reconciliation of the temporal with the eternal, and insists on the ontological difference between the object and its meaning. Benjamin offers an emblematic image of this aesthetic of negation and difference.

Während im Symbol mit der Verklärung des Unterganges das transfigurierte Antlitz der Natur im Lichte der Erlösung flüchtig sich offenbart, liegt in der Allegorie die facies hippocratica der Geschichte als erstarrte Urlandschaft dem Betrachter vor Augen. (*Ursprung* 343)

Whereas in the symbol destruction is idealized and the transfigured face of nature is fleetingly revealed in the light of redemption, in allegory the observer is confronted with the facies hippocratica *[death face] of history as a petrified, primordial landscape. Everything about history that, from the very beginning, has been untimely, sorrowful, unsuccessful, is expressed in a face—or rather in a death's head.* (Origin *166*)

This is a powerful figuration of the two opposing rhetorical figures, and in each case there figures a face (*ein Antlitz*). In the symbol, it is the face of nature that is transfigured, its destruction idealized by the light of redemption (*Erlösung*) from the metaphysical realm. In allegory, no such redemption takes place; the face is instead that of history, and its countenance consists of the petrified features of the death's head. The death's head is, in other words, the allegory of allegory, the figure of the allegorical relation that insists on the death of the past, on the temporal distance between signifier and signified, on the ontological difference between the natural and the spiritual.

Paul de Man, who has pushed this distinction as far as seems possible, defines it quite clearly.

> Whereas the symbol postulates the possibility of an identity or identification, allegory designates primarily a distance in relation to its origin, and renouncing the nostalgia and the desire to coincide, it establishes itself in the void of this temporal difference. (*Rhetoric* 207)

De Man speaks here of the inauthentic or false nostalgia that seeks to relive the past by abstracting it from any historical reality. Allegory, on the contrary, is without illusion and inconsolable; based on the principle of disunity and discontinuity in its form of representation, it marks a permanent exile from the past and in this way acquires for the modern world a kind of authenticity that is lacking in the symbol.

For Benjamin, allegory is to the realm of thought what ruins are to the realm of things. In both cases, the rupture between the material signifier and the ideal signified appears irreconcilable. The parallel traditions of allegory and ruin come together, however, in the fragment, a figure both literary and architectural. Benjamin likens baroque writing to the process of ceaselessly piling up fragments, as opposed to a more organic model of literary creation, so that "the perfect vision of this new [literary] phenomenon was the ruin" (178). Baroque writing is "constructed" (*baut*), a quality that the writer does not attempt to conceal under the sign of genius or heavenly inspiration. "Hence the display of the craftsmanship that, in Calderón especially, shows through like the masonry in a building whose rendering (*Verputz*) has broken away" (179). The recurring image here is one of brokenness and fragmentation, both in the relation of the parts of the composition to one another and in the relation of the composition to its ostensible origin. According to Benjamin, this notion of an irreconcilable rupture lies at the heart of the cult of ruins in the baroque aesthetic of the seventeenth and eighteenth centuries, for ruins testify to the irreversible effects of time even as they mark the rupture of the object with its origins.

The aesthetic of ruins can thus be seen as an authentic nostalgia, as the melancholy cult of the past arising out of the space of rupture, and conscious of the irremediable absence of its object. Diderot writes in his *Salons de 1767:*

> Les idées que les ruines éveillent en moi sont grandes. Tout s'anéantit, tout périt, tout passe. Il n'y a que le monde qui reste. Il n'y a que le temps qui dure. Qu'il est vieux ce monde! Je marche entre deux éternités.
>
> *Great are the ideas that ruins awaken in me. Everything is annihilated, everything perishes, everything passes away. There is only the world that remains. There is only time that endures. How old this world is! I walk between two eternities. (*Quoted in Mortier *94)*

What perishes is history and its transcendental meaning; what remains are merely the physical existence and temporal phenomena of the world. The two eternities between which Diderot walks are not those of heaven and hell; they are those of the void stretching out before and after life. These reflections belong to the more general baroque cult of ruins as a cult of absence. As Jean Starobinski describes it:

> La ruine par excellence signale un culte déserté, un dieu négligé. Elle exprime l'abandon et le délaissement . . . Sa mélancolie réside dans le fait qu'elle est devenue un monument de la signification perdue. Rêver dans les ruines, c'est sentir que notre existence cesse de nous appartenir et rejoint déjà l'immense oubli. (180)
>
> *The ruin par excellence is the sign of a deserted cult, a neglected god. It expresses abandonment and desertion. . . . Its melancholy lies in the fact that it has become a monument to lost meaning. To dream in the ruins is to feel that our existence no longer belongs to us, and that it is already part of the immense oblivion.*

In speaking of the dreamlike aspect of the aesthetic of ruins, Starobinski reminds us that, even if ruins are seen as testimony to the ravages of time, the cult of ruins should not be confused with any sort of historical realism. He notes that "the sacrilege, in the eyes of those who remain attached to this feeling, is to wish to *date* that which should remain *immemorial*" (181).

There would thus appear to be a historical abstraction even in the aesthetic that sees architectural ruin as the negation of any metaphysical transcendence and as the sign of the inescapable immanence of the world in time. However, if this is one form of historical abstraction, it should not be confused with that which comes into play with the aesthetic of architectural restoration, at least as this will be put into practice by Viollet-le-Duc and his followers. Restoration implies another kind of abstraction, a different dream. Where the aesthetic of ruins fetishizes the marks of time, restoration seeks to erase them. In this respect restoration belongs to the form of nostalgia that dreams of the timeless unity of the object with its ideal origins—the unity of the *symbol*—whereas the ruin, as we have just seen, expresses the temporal disunity proper to *allegory*. In the sense that the nineteenth century gave to these terms, restoration is symbolic, whereas ruins are allegorical.

This excursion into an episode of the history of aesthetics is meant to prepare the ground for a more direct comparison between Viollet-le-Duc and Ruskin, as the two principal nineteenth-century apologists of architectural restoration and ruins, respectively. Viollet's work has come under intense criticism,[1] but we nonetheless have him to thank for the fact that many of the most important buildings of medieval France remain more or less intact today. He began his career of restoration in 1840 with the twelfth-century Basilica of Vézelay in Burgundy. In the same year, with Jean-Baptiste Lassus, he undertook the restoration of the Sainte-Chapelle in Paris. He achieved national prominence in 1844 by winning the competition to restore Notre-Dame de Paris. The projects of the basilicas of Saint-Denis and of Saint-Sernin in Toulouse also belong to this period. Following the fall of the July monarchy, the revolution of 1848, and the coup d'état of Louis-Napoléon, Viollet continued to enjoy the favor of the ruling régime. He oversaw the work of restoration at Amiens and Chartres. In the 1850s he turned to secular architecture by rebuilding the citadel and ramparts of Carcassonne and by restoring the Château de Pierrefonds at Compiègne as an imperial residence. His last major architectural restoration was the Cathedral of Lausanne in 1874. Apart from this extremely active architectural career, Viollet sought to provide a theory for his practice in several major works. We will be concerned chiefly with the *Dictionnaire raisonné de l'architecture française du XI au XVI siècle* (1854) and the two volumes of *Entretiens,* or "discussions," published respectively in 1863 and 1872. Because of the rational approach to function and structural unity taken in these works, Viollet-le-Duc has often been considered as the first modernist architect.[2] Ruskin, of course, was not an architect by profession, but through his writings and lectures he had a profound effect on Victorian ideas of art in general, and of architecture in particular. We will be concerned mainly with his two major works of architectural theory, both written from the experience of his voyages to Italy as a fairly young man in midcentury: *The Seven Lamps of Architecture* (1849); and *The Stones of Venice,* published in three volumes between 1851 and 1853.

A general comparison between Ruskin and Viollet-le-Duc has been made by Nikolaus Pevsner, who remarks on several points in common between the two figures: their celebration of the Gothic art of the thirteenth century, of course, and the importance that both of them attach to a certain notion of truth in architecture in which the appearance of a building corresponds to its actual structure and material composition. In *The Seven Lamps,* for example, Ruskin tells us that the architect must avoid the suggestion of a means of structural support other than the real one, as well as the painting of surfaces to represent a material other than that of which they are made. Likewise, Viollet-le-Duc insists in the *Entretiens* that "stone appear really as stone, iron as iron, wood as wood," and so on. (1:472). Both writers seem to agree on the role of the people in constructing Gothic architecture. For Viollet-le-Duc, it is to the common people of the thirteenth century that we owe the great monuments of that age, while for Ruskin these buildings represent the work of an entire race (Pevsner 18). In his last major work, *The Bible of Amiens* (1880–85), Ruskin several times cites Viollet-le-Duc as an authority on French medieval architecture.

The common ground ends just about there, however, and the differences between these two figures are much more significant than any points of convergence. Viollet-le-Duc, for example, privileges architectonic structure, whereas Ruskin gives greater importance to decoration. We must keep in mind that Viollet-le-Duc, as an active architect, is primarily concerned to justify the methods he has put into practice, whereas Ruskin, even more than a theorist, is above all a stylist and *connoisseur* who has little interest or experience in the practice of building. For Pevsner, however, the difference comes down to one of sensibility: in Viollet-le-Duc, he sees a French rationalism that favors the concrete and empirical and in Ruskin a supposedly English emotivity that privileges suggestion and evocation. In this rather facile analysis, however, Pevsner reduces important aesthetic and theoretical differences to a stereotypical view of national temperament. Let us attempt a deeper appreciation of these two theorists by looking more closely at their respective ideas on ruin and restoration.

In the article on restoration in Viollet-le-Duc's *Dictionnaire raisonné,* we read:

Les travaux de restauration entrepris en France . . . ont sauvé de la ruine des œuvres d'une valeur incontestable. . . . Ces édifices, une des gloires de notre pays, préservés de la ruine, resteront encore debout pendant des siècles, pour témoigner du dévouement de quelques hommes plus attachés à perpétuer cette gloire qu'à leurs intérêts particuliers. (31)

The works of restoration undertaken in France . . . have rescued from ruin a number of works of undisputed value. . . . These buildings, part of the glory of our country preserved from ruin, will remain standing for centuries as a testimony to the devotion of a few men motivated more by the perpetuation of that glory than by their private interests.

This last phrase is aimed at the architects of the École des Beaux-Arts and their supposed disdain for the practical work of restorers working in the provinces. Viollet-le-Duc was to be associated with the École only briefly; appointed controversially to a professorship in 1863, he was prevented from teaching his courses by his "classical" colleagues and students.[3] For our purposes, however, it is more important to note that for Viollet-le-Duc, in opposition to the baroque and romantic traditions, ruins have no value as such. On the contrary, the ruin of ancient buildings is to be avoided at all costs because their restoration can transform them into monuments of permanent and transcendent value. "The perpetual glory of the French nation" here should be understood as a rhetorical appeal directed at his imperial patrons in 1856 and not necessarily as an expression of Viollet's own political feeling, which was essentially republican. In any case, this idealized and transcendent notion of architecture conforms to the famous definition with which Viollet-le-Duc begins his dictionary article on restoration.

Le mot [restauration] et la chose sont modernes: restaurer un édifice, ce n'est pas l'entretenir, le réparer ou le refaire, c'est le rétablir dans un état complet qui peut n'avoir jamais existé à un moment donné. (14)

The word [restoration] and the thing itself are modern: to restore a building is not to maintain it, repair it, or rebuild it; it is to reestablish it in a complete state that might never have existed at any given moment.

For Viollet-le-Duc, architectural restoration was a new science, like those of comparative anatomy, philology, ethnology, and archaeology. Laurent

Baridon has shown how the architect's ideas incorporate the scientific concept of organicism characteristic of the mid–nineteenth century: the architectural restorer is to the medieval building what the paleontologist is to the remains of a prehistoric animal: each of them seeks to reconstitute an organism. This theory presupposes a number of qualities in the object to be reconstituted: its unity, its internal logic, its visibility. Like the paleontologist Georges Cuvier, Viollet-le-Duc saw in the object of his study a "correlation of organs" and the subordination of its different elements, so that every part could be understood in terms of its function within the overall structure. The point, however, was not merely to re-create a building by imitating medieval practices but rather to find the solutions to architectural problems that medieval artisans would have adopted had they had the technical means available to the nineteenth century (Baridon 18–20). For Viollet-le-Duc, medieval architecture is not essentially a multiple series of historical phenomena rooted in distinct and local contexts. Rather, his theory implies the existence of an ideal form of the building independent of its concrete realization at any given historical moment.

In other words, Viollet-le-Duc reached into the art of the Middle Ages for a certain number of a priori principles, an architectural grammar that guided his projects even where the work of restoration went consciously against the historical realities of a given edifice. As the studies of Viollet-le-Duc are full of examples of this controversial practice in his major projects, I shall cite a relatively minor but nonetheless instructive example from his project for the restoration of the Chapelle des Macchabées in Geneva, built in 1405 by Jean de Brogny as an annex to the twelfth-century Cathédrale de Saint-Pierre. The chapel had been converted into a storeroom by Calvin's reformers and later had been used as a lecture hall by the Académie de Genève, today the University of Geneva. Leila El Wakil has shown how Viollet-le-Duc, based on his own understanding of Gothic principles, proposed the "restoration" of several elements that in fact had never belonged to the building. Among these was the erection of a spire that Viollet-le-Duc freely admitted might never have existed. Nonetheless, he argued, it ought to have existed even if it never did, because such a spire conformed to "accepted practice in all independently built chapels" (El Wakil 52). Similarly, he proposed to create a rose window in the otherwise intact facade of the western gable, a pure invention justified on the aesthetic grounds that "an intact gable over the architecture of the ground-level story will appear overly heavy" (53). Characteristically conservative, the city of Geneva rejected these innovative features of the project, judging that "one should put aside those things which, while they might beautify the building, one cannot claim to have ever existed" (54). Although Viollet-le-Duc withdrew from this project after an administrative disagreement, the city went ahead with the restoration of the chapel on the basis of his plans but without the spire, the rose-window, and other innovative features. Viollet-le-Duc's original plans are reproduced in figures 5 and 6. Figure 7 shows the chapel as it appears today.

A few years later, in restoring the cathedral adjacent to the chapel, Geneva had to fend off pressure from a very different quarter. A sense of the intense polemic surrounding the question of restoration is given in the official report of the Association for the Restoration of Saint-Pierre, which took on the task of restoring the cathedral proper in 1891. Having caught wind of the new plans, William Morris's Society for the Protection of Ancient Buildings had made an urgent appeal to Geneva to abandon its plans to restore Saint-Pierre, on the grounds that any such work would destroy the work of time and risk betraying the ideas of the original builders. Morris's society recommended instead that the protection of the cathedral be limited to the simple reinforcement of those parts of the building that were falling into ruin. The response of the Geneva association was unambiguous.

> Donner satisfaction à des théories aussi subversives de notre raison d'être, c'était nous suicider; nous avons préféré vivre et répondre à nos correspondants que nous ne partageons pas leur manière de voir. (Fornara 104)
>
> *To give in to theories so subversive of our reason for being would be to commit suicide. We preferred to live, and answered our correspondents by saying that we did not share their point of view.*

In other words, Geneva sought a middle way between the conservative movement, which, following the principles of Ruskin, opposed restoration of any kind, and the radical restorations of Viollet-le-Duc.

Viollet-le-Duc's practice of restoring buildings from a priori principles rather than historical evidence continues to attract controversy today. One of his more severe critics finds that his theory amounts to a "delirium" founded on a fundamental tautology: "[His] observations allow the definition of a law, but the law pre-exists, so that the observations conform to the law" (Leniaud 91). Despite the often brilliant investigations that Viollet-le-Duc conducted in order to discover the history of a building, his principles tend to make an abstraction of history in two ways. First, he ide-

Fig. 5. Viollet-le-Duc's plan
for the restoration of the
Chapelle des Macchabées,
west face, 1875. (Musée d'art
et d'histoire, Geneva.)

Fig. 6. Viollet-le-Duc's plan for
the restoration of the Chapelle
des Macchabées, south face, 1875.
(Musée d'art et d'histoire,
Geneva.)

Fig. 7. The Chapelle des
Macchabées, Geneva.
(Photo by Michael
Röösli.)

alizes a given period, the Gothic era, as the privileged moment of all architectural history. Second, by consciously reconstructing a building into a
form that does not correspond to any of that building's past forms, he refuses a rigorously historical approach in favor of an aesthetic of timeless
unity. Of course, one might ask how could it be otherwise, once one has
started down the path of restoration. Given a building such as Notre-
Dame de Paris, which underwent continual transformation from the
twelfth to the seventeenth centuries, how does one decide which of its
many forms to restore it to unless one has, for example, an ideal notion of
what it might have been in the thirteenth century? The point is, however,
that for Viollet-le-Duc Gothic architectural form is not primarily historical; rather it consists of an ideal unity that is structurally analogous to the
unity of the romantic symbol, even if its content is different.

By its very nature, the romantic symbol represents the secularization of the metaphysical qualities once attributed to the sacred object. Given the declining authority of religious institutions, the symbol responds to a demand in the nineteenth century for a language that would bring material being into harmony with spiritual being in atemporal but secular terms. In Viollet-le-Duc the Gothic cathedral, like the romantic symbol, is secularized as an aesthetic object.[4] Neither his writings nor his architectural practices take seriously the status of the medieval Gothic church as an edifice designed for the ritual of worship and the administering of the holy sacraments. On the contrary, he writes in the *Entretiens* that the great Gothic cathedrals of medieval France are essentially the work of lay craftsmen organized into guilds. While employed by the bishops, these craftsmen worked independently, adopting a new system of construction and new forms in architecture and sculpture. Whereas the religious institutions of the early Middle Ages could only reproduce designs in the Romanesque and Byzantine traditions, the "lay school" of the late twelfth century made a complete break from these traditions, replacing them with principles founded on reason, that is, the principles of Gothic architecture. It is only at this point, argues Viollet-le-Duc, that there emerges "le génie propre à la nation française" (the special genius of the French nation) (*Entretiens* 1:265). From here it is a relatively short step to the national ideology that Viollet-le-Duc invokes in support of his projects of restoration. In this way the metaphysical dimension of the symbol, traditionally given the name of the infinite, the eternal, and so on, acquires an identity rather more specific but equally eternal: the glory of France. This is a rhetorical strategy that we might call the appropriation of the symbolic structure by ideology.

In order to understand Viollet-le-Duc's aesthetic, we need to see it in the context of France's Second Empire and its ideology, which, while aspiring to recover the imperial glories of the first Napoleonic era, nonetheless embraced the values of industrial progress inherited from the bourgeois monarchy of Louis-Philippe. We see both elements in the discourse of Viollet-le-Duc, who pays homage to Napoléon I while insisting on the progress made in the artisanal industries of the provinces, thanks to the works of architectural restoration under way all over France. To take up just the first of these elements, we note that for Viollet-le-Duc, restoration is above all a national project whose origins lie in the First Empire and "the will of the Emperor Napoléon I, who was ahead of his times in all things, and who understood the importance of restoration" (*Dictionnaire* 22). Viollet-le-Duc's politics, however, are not a simple matter, for they suggest a certain discrepancy between his personal convictions and his public discourse. If, after the fall of the Second Empire, he showed himself to be an ardent republican, there was little to suggest such a conviction in his close connections to the authoritarian regime of Napoléon III, connections he needed for the support of his architectural projects. By no means the least of these was his restoration of the fourteenth-century Château de Pierrefonds into an imperial residence, where his energetic direction of court entertainments earned him the nickname "the stage prompter of Compiègne" (Gout 51).

Viollet-le-Duc's discourse on art, however, is not predominantly royalist. It is instead a texture of theories and observations that reflects all of the tensions inherent in mid-nineteenth-century aesthetics. This tension is evident from the very first of the *Entretiens*. On one hand, in keeping with the emerging symbolist aesthetics of his age, Viollet-le-Duc argues for the essential unity of art and its value as independent of historical circumstances: "Art has its value independent of the milieu in which it is born and grows up." On the other hand, and in keeping with the scientific humanism of Charles-Augustin de Sainte-Beuve, Viollet-le-Duc sees the *form* if not the *essence* of art as intimately tied to the way of life of a people: "[T]he arts of the Middle Ages follow step by step the manners and customs of the people in the midst of which they develop" (*Entretiens* 1:11). This double discourse allows Viollet-le-Duc to argue both for an ideal Gothic, independent of historical specificity, and for the revival of the Gothic as an expression of national unity and character. Thus, in the seventh *Entretien*, Viollet-le-Duc claims that "l'art en France, dès les premières années du XIIIe siècle, est un instrument dont le pouvoir royal se sert pour développer ses efforts vers l'unité nationale" (art in France, from the early years of the thirteenth century, has been an instrument used by royal power in its efforts to develop national unity) (1:282). This is not offered as a critique of the instrumentalization of art for political ends. On the contrary, Viollet-le-Duc is citing the precedent of the thirteenth century as an argument for the continued support of his various projects of restoration by the imperial regime. National unity is offered as a political justification for the pursuit of an essentially aesthetic ideal.

Like Viollet-le-Duc, Ruskin defends the Gothic against architectural classicism but with a very different declared ideology. For Ruskin, the individual freedom inherent in the Gothic style stands in opposition to the authoritarian classicism of the ancien régime, while the nineteenth-century revival of the Gothic marks a parallel revival of Christian faith, in reaction to the declining authority of religious institutions in modern life.

When Ruskin first went to Oxford in 1836, the Oxford movement of John Keble and John Henry Newman had already begun. It helped to create an intellectual climate in which Ruskin could write of art and architecture in strongly ethical terms, which, in his work, resonated with the egalitarianism of the equally important political movement that produced three reform bills between 1832 and 1884.

Like Viollet-le-Duc, Ruskin also speaks of a national architecture, declaring, for example, in *The Crown of Wild Olive* (1866), that "all good architecture is the expression of national life and character; and it is produced by a prevalent and eager national taste" (*Library Edition* 18:434). But this national character is to be distinguished from Viollet-le-Duc's discourse of national unity. For Ruskin, it is a matter of the impact of architecture on public life, of the manner in which a building becomes a permanent part of the landscape, and of a certain ethical responsibility of the architect toward the people. The monumental character of the Gothic building resides in its capacity to bear witness to the history of a people, which it does through the richness of documentation contained in its ornamentation.

> Its minute and multitudinous sculptural decorations afford means of expressing, either symbolically or literally, all that need be known of national feeling or achievement. . . . Better the rudest work that tells a story or records a fact, than the richest without meaning. (8:229–30)

Already we may note two points on which Ruskin's discourse differs from Viollet-le-Duc's. First, although he speaks of feeling and national achievement, Ruskin does not privilege any nation in particular. Where Ruskin affirms the style and the moral force of what he calls the Goth (the Englishman, the Frenchman, the Dane, the German) against the supposed languor and subjection of Mediterranean peoples, his use of *nation* is essentially racial in the nineteenth-century sense and has little to do with the meaning given this word by the nationalism of the modern state. Second, Ruskin wishes to affirm the *memorial* function of the Gothic building: if poetry constitutes what a people has thought and felt, then architecture constitutes "what their hands have handled, and their strength wrought, and their eyes beheld, all the days of their life" (8:224). For Ruskin, the Gothic building has the same *aura* that Benjamin will attribute to the work of art that still bears the marks of the artist's hands, a quality lost in reproduction. In general, Ruskin's notion of the memorial function of the Gothic contrasts with Viollet-le-Duc's ideas, which are both more abstract and more pragmatic. Stephen Bayley has remarked that in the French architect the Gothic is made into "a flexible system adapted to all needs and their changing nature. The Gothic describes a language of many words" (32).

For Ruskin ruins also have a memorial function, but they are distinguished from other architectural formations by the quality of what he calls "parasitical sublimity," the sublime that derives, somewhat paradoxically, from accident or the nonessential character of the object. This particularly fortuitous form of the sublime corresponds, for Ruskin, to a certain sense of the picturesque. He finds it in the accessory details of a painting by Tintoretto or Rubens,

> in the clefts and folds of shaggy hair, or in the chasms and rents of rocks, or in the hanging of thickets or hill sides, or in the alternations of gaiety and gloom in the variegation of the shell, the plume, or the cloud. (8:240)

Here there is an echo of the baroque poetics of a seventeenth-century poet such as William D'Avenant. Defending the style of his epic poem *Gondibert* (1651), D'Avenant calls attention precisely to its ephemeral, aleatory, and indistinct qualities, "the shadowings, happy strokes, secret graces, and even the drapery, which together make the second beauty" (16–17). Similarly for Ruskin, his sense of the sublime is independent of the main lines and principal substance of the object as such. In architecture in particular this fortuitous beauty, this sublime of the supplement, takes the form of the ruin. There is, then, a sublime that resides in ruptures, fissures, stains, and moss—in everything that marks the effects of nature and of time on the architectural work.

The striking quality of such effects had been appreciated by Hugo in *Notre-Dame de Paris* (1831), where, in condemning the various attempts at architectural restoration of that cathedral—attempts to be once more taken up by Viollet-le-Duc in 1845—he notes that "le temps a rendu à l'église plus peut-être qu'il ne lui a ôté, car c'est le temps qui a répandu sur la façade cette sombre couleur des siècles qui fait de la vieillesse des monuments l'âge de leur beauté" (time has perhaps given the church more than it has taken away, as it is time that has spread over the facade that dark color of the centuries that makes the old age of monuments the age of their beauty) (191). Similarly, Ruskin holds that "it is in the golden stain of time, that we are to look for the real light, and colour, and preciousness of architecture" (8:234).

Ruskin's own rendering of Kenilworth Castle, done in 1847 (fig. 8),[5] shows the Great Hall shorn of its roof, the crumbling masonry overgrown with ivy. Stone and vegetation alike are subject to the variegated effects of light and shadow. The picture retains the strong sense of verticality belonging to the Gothic elements of the building, but these are set in stark contrast to a gray and empty sky. Just enough of Gothic tracery remains in one of the windows to recall the splendor of this edifice in the days of John of Gaunt, in the fourteenth century. From reading Walter Scott's novel *Kenilworth* (1821), Ruskin would have known the rich descriptions of this castle as it stood in Elizabethan days. His sense of the ruin's sublimity, however, would have come from the visible effects of time's ravages in the margins and interstices of the weakening stone.

According to Ruskin, Gothic architecture creates conditions that are particularly advantageous to this external or parasitical sublime, because the effects of the Gothic that depend on the play of shadow and light are enhanced by the partial wearing away of sculptural detail. Ruskin denounces architectural restoration, then, because it effaces the sublime effects of time. If Hugo attacks specific projects of restoration on the grounds of their incompetence or lack of architectural understanding, Ruskin's condemnation is more categorical and even more impassioned.

> Restoration, so called, is the worst manner of Destruction. It means the most total destruction which a building can suffer: a destruction out of which no remnants can be gathered. . . . It is *impossible,* as impossible as to raise the dead, to restore anything that has ever been great or beautiful in architecture. (8:242)

The dominant figure in this discourse is that of death. Ruskin declares the impossibility of summoning back to life the spirit of the dead artisan and commanding him to direct other hands and other thoughts. The very concept of restoration is "a lie from beginning to end."

> You may make a model of a building as you would of a corpse, and your model may have the shell of the old walls within it as your cast might have the skeleton, with what advantage I neither see nor care. (8:244)

As for those monuments that fall into ruin:

> *We have no right to touch them.* They are not ours. They belong partly to those who built them, and partly to the generations of mankind who are to follow us. The dead still have their right in them. (8:245)

Fig. 8. John Ruskin, Kenilworth Castle, 1847. (From Ruskin, *Diaries*, vol. 1, plate 31.)

It is as if ruins were still the dwelling places of the dead and that to restore them would be to destroy the eloquent means by which the dead, or death itself, make themselves understood.[6] To declare "we have no right to touch them" implies the kind of veneration for architectural ruins that is felt for mortal human remains, which, for profoundly emotional and cultural reasons, cannot be disinterred or displaced. This insistence on the presence of death in ruins recalls Benjamin's notion that the emblem of allegory is the *facies hippocratica,* the pale and shriveled aspect of the human face just before the moment of death.

Ruskin's ideas on death and ruins force us to revise the common understanding that for him the Gothic is a primarily organic art, in both its structural principles and its resemblance to vegetation. In fact, his essay "The Lamp of Power" finds that one of the elements of sublime architecture is precisely its *inorganic* character, found in the geometric form of the wall and other "wide, bold, and unbroken" surfaces (8:109). Both the organic and the inorganic principles are found in nature, "the one in her woods and thickets, the other in her plains and cliffs and waters"(8:109). If the former "gives grace to every pulse that agitates animal organisation," the latter "reproves the pillars of the earth, and builds up her barren precipices into the coldness of the clouds" (8:102).

> [T]he grey cliff loses not its nobleness when it reminds us of some Cyclopean waste of mural stone . . . even the awful cone of the far-off mountain has a melancholy mixed with that of its own solitude, which is cast from the images of nameless tumuli on white sea-shores, and of the heaps of reedy clay, into which chambered cities melt in their mortality. (8:103)

As Andrea Pinotti suggests, Ruskin expresses a nostalgia for death and mineral stillness. The language of melancholy, solitude, and mortality with which he contemplates the mountains and cliffs belongs also to the discourse of ruins. In the ruin, where climbing vegetation meets the resistance of ancient stone, we witness the same eternal struggle between the organic and the inorganic principles of nature. The stone, in its hardness and coldness, but also in its marred and worn condition, has the awesome aspect of death itself. It evokes the melancholy, "dead" relation of the allegorical sign to its object, in contrast to the living, organic nature of the symbol.

This identification of Ruskin with the aesthetics of allegory is bound to surprise those who read too literally his insistence on "naturalism" in architectural representation. There is, for example, the passage in "The Nature of the Gothic" where Ruskin contrasts the representations of purgatorial fire in two different churches. The first is in the twelfth-century mosaic of the Last Judgment in the Romanesque cathedral of Torcello, in the Venetian lagoon. Here, the fire is purely allegorical. It takes the form of a red stream that descends from the throne of Christ and extends itself to envelop the wicked. The other, in the Gothic porch of Saint-Maclou in Rouen, is strongly naturalistic: "The sculptured flames burst out of the Hades gate, and flicker up, in writhing tongues of stone, through the interstices of the niches, as if the church itself were on fire" (10:233). Ruskin offers this as a demonstration of the "love of veracity" reflected in Gothic design, by which he means a faithful imitation of natural form. As always in Ruskin, however, there is a difference between factual representation and truth. He goes on to say that, on reflection, one will perhaps find more truth in the allegorical figure, "in that blood-red stream, flowing between definite shores, and out of God's throne, and expanding, as if fed by a perpetual current, into the lake wherein the wicked are cast," than in the "torch-flickerings" of the Gothic, naturalistic figure (10:233). The point is that for Ruskin allegory represents a deeper truth than naturalistic imitation. A similar point has been made by Gary Wihl, who writes that for Ruskin, "sincerity is increasingly figured as allegory, as a writer's or sculptor's self-consciousness about the fictiveness . . . of his idealizations" (113). The allegorical figure acknowledges the gap between signifier and signified, and this implicit acknowledgment of the inadequacy of signification is itself the sign of a truth.

In general, we could say that Viollet-le-Duc's aesthetic is to Ruskin's what symbol is to allegory: on one hand, the timeless unity of the object with its ideal essence; on the other hand, rupture, disunity, and the pathos evoked by the material remains of an irrecoverable past. Here it might be useful to point out the affinity between the aesthetic of ruins and that of the monument. The monument does not claim to evoke the totality of what it commemorates. It signifies its object only allegorically, and by convention; it presents itself as the dead letter of a departed spirit, and its affective power resides precisely in this irreconcilable ontological difference.

Ruskin's implacable rejection of modern architecture for a long time caused him to be seen as an incurable nostalgic, devoted to a regressive pastoralism in the face of modernity.[7] But there is in Ruskin's particular form of nostalgia a certain resistance to nostalgia, just as, conversely, there is nostalgia in Viollet-le-Duc's particular form of modernism. To the extent that the work of each of these figures resonates in the twentieth century, Viollet-le-Duc's impact is on architectural modernism, whereas Ruskin's is on literary modernism. It is on this latter point that I would like to conclude.

The aesthetic of the ruin and the fragment will be taken up, if transformed, by poets such as T. S. Eliot and René Char in their fragmentation of the word and literary form. This textual fragmentation will be justified in terms identical to those that Benjamin uses to justify the allegorical fragment, that is, in a discourse that privileges rupture and exteriority. Thus

Maurice Blanchot writes that what he calls the *parole du fragment* (fragment word) in Char is

> un arrangement d'une sorte nouvelle, qui ne sera pas celui d'une harmonie, d'une concorde ou d'une conciliation, mais qui acceptera la disjonction ou la divergence comme le centre infini à partir duquel, par la parole, un rapport doit s'établir.

> *a new kind of arrangement, not of harmony, concord, or reconciliation, but one that accepts disjunction or divergence as the infinite center from out of which, through the word, relation is to be created. (L'Entretien 453)*

Other elements of Ruskin's work can be seen as a renewal of the baroque spirit in the modern context. There is, for example, the idea of perpetual movement that Benjamin sees as a constituent element of baroque allegory. In contrast to the romantic symbol, which remains "persistently the same," allegory, "if it is to hold its own against the tendency to absorption (*Versenkung*), must constantly unfold in new and surprising ways" (*Ursprung* 359; *Origin* 183). One can compare this remark to Ruskin's insistence on "changefulness" as one of the essential qualities of the Gothic, as well as on its "disquietude."

> It is that strange *disquietude* of the Gothic spirit that is its greatness; that restlessness of the dreaming mind, that wanders hither and thither among the niches, and flickers feverishly around the pinnacles, and frets and fades in labyrinthine knots and shadows along wall and roof, and yet is not satisfied, nor shall be satisfied. (10:214)

That is, the Gothic spirit is not satisfied in its ceaseless search for a reconciliation of body and spirit, of temporal and eternal, of signifier and signified. This dissatisfaction corresponds to the allegory rather than the symbol, the architectural ruin rather than its restoration, the fragment rather than the whole. The paradox of Ruskin is that his baroque definition of the Gothic gives rise to a certain modernism; in recovering a neglected aesthetic of the past, he looks forward to the new forms of art announced by Eliot's *The Waste Land* (1922): "These fragments I have shored against my ruin" (*Collected* 69).

5

Proust's Interior Venice

Although other novels have architects as heroes, Proust's *A la recherche du temps perdu* may be the only one whose principal character conducts research in architectural history and criticism. In the sixth published volume of Proust's work, known as *Albertine disparue,* the narrator makes his journey to Venice, where he carries notebooks "où je prendrais des notes relatives à un travail que je faisais sur Ruskin" (in which I would take notes for a work I was doing on Ruskin) (*A la recherche* 4:224). This project takes him to the baptistery of Saint Mark's Cathedral, which has a central place in Ruskin's writings on Venice. The chapter of the *Recherche* devoted to Venice represents a long-awaited moment, for the narrator's dream of visiting that city, like his passion for Gothic architecture, has been a recurring motif throughout several volumes of the novel. In *A l'ombre des jeunes filles en fleurs* (vol. 2), as "le voyageur ravi dont parle Ruskin" (2:9), the enchanted traveler of whom Ruskin speaks, he makes an excursion to the renowned church of Balbec, which disappoints his high expectations, as its Gothic front faces a tramway intersection and its famous statue of the Virgin shares the sunlight with the local branch of a commercial credit bank (2:20).

When we speak of Proust's narrator in such cases, we are of course also speaking of Proust, for whom Ruskin, Venice, and Gothic architecture were always intimately related. Proust was precisely one of those enchanted travelers who carried Ruskin's works to the Gothic cathedrals of the Middle Ages. Luc Fraisse has shown how the fictional visit to the church of Bal-

bec was based on Proust's own visit to the Cathedral of Amiens after reading Ruskin's book on that monument (87). Proust first read Ruskin in
1899, and the following year made two visits to Venice, taking a copy of *St.
Mark's Rest* to the baptistery of the cathedral (Tadié 1:623–39; Proust, *Lettres* 187).[1] Figure 9 shows him on the terrace of the Albergo Europa overlooking the Grand Canal.[2] Like his narrator, Proust also wrote on Ruskin,
publishing four articles on the English writer in 1900. These are collected
as the preface to Proust's translation (1904) of *The Bible of Amiens*. Like the
narrator's journey to Venice in the *Recherche,* the chapter of *Albertine disparue* known as the "séjour à Venise" was long in gestation and has never
been established in definitive form. Parts of it appeared in Proust's notebook entries beginning in 1908, and in 1919 an abbreviated version was
published in the review *Feuillets d'art* (no. 4). The canonical version was
published four years after the author's death in Gaston Gallimard's 1925
edition of *Albertine disparue* as volume 7 of the *Recherche.* However, the
discovery of Proust's manuscript of *Albertine disparue* in 1986 gave rise to a
number of new versions of the volume, notably those by Nathalie Mauriac
Dyer and Etienne Wolf (1987), Jean-Yves Tadié (1989), Anne Chevalier
(1990), and Jean Milly (1992), with the result that the Venice episode in
particular has been reworked and even completely transformed so many
times as to endanger its coherence. This dense and multilayered textual
history, then, has its counterpart in the form and even the thematic register of the Venice chapter, which begins under the sign of what Proust calls
"transposition." The fragmentary and elusive nature of Proust's text will
have bearing on my architectural reading of this chapter.

Although I have begun by evoking Proust's Ruskinism, there is a fundamental difference between Ruskin's conception of architecture and that
of Proust. For Ruskin, as we have seen, architecture is profoundly ethical
and even political, in the sense of being the concrete practice of an ideal
of justice; it expresses the "large principles of right" with which God has
endowed the human spirit (*Library Edition* 8:20). When Ruskin writes on
Venice, he finds in that part of it that survives from the Middle Ages an
architecture erected in opposition to the sensuality and idolatry of the
Roman Empire. The two great influences on Venetian architecture have
been the Lombard or northern, giving "hardihood and system" to the en-
ervated body of Roman Christianity, and the Arab, whose work was to
"punish idolatry, and to proclaim the spirituality of worship" (9:38).
Venice was historically the point of contact between these two opposing
movements, and before the Renaissance its vigor and purity derived from

Fig. 9. Proust in Venice. (From Cattaui, *Proust: Documents iconographiques,* plate 53.)

the manner in which these two forms of spiritual energy were held in perfect suspension. The declared purpose of *The Stones of Venice* is to recover that vanished spirit, to which the finest Venetian architecture nonetheless bears mute testimony.

Architecture comes to have a different meaning for Proust. In contrast to the ethical and social preoccupations of Ruskin's Victorianism, architecture for Proust figures as a metaphor for his own subjectivity; his devotion to the study of architecture runs parallel to and indeed intersects with what he calls the search for lost time, which is in effect the search for the ground of his own being. The architecture of Venice, like the music of Vinteuil and the paintings of Elstir, functions as what Gilles Deleuze calls, in *Proust et les signes,* the artistic sign of a concealed essence. Proust's narrator is dedicated to the reading of such signs because they give the promise of unveiling the hidden essence of his own life. My own purpose, however, is less ambitious than to follow the process of that unveiling. In a previous chapter I made the point that in Proust the structures of desire are rendered in terms of architectural space. Here I wish to extend that argument in order to show that the various architectural forms that constitute the city of Venice serve as metaphorical projections of the narrator's successive states of mind, and that the discontinuity of those forms, however splendid, matches the fragmented subjectivity that it is the object of the *Recherche* to unify.

Proust's predilection for architecture is related to the fact that he is above all a writer of interior spaces, from the little garden shed that, in *Du coté de chez Swann,* the narrator uses as a reading room, to the library of the hotel de Guermantes where, in *Le temps retrouvé,* he experiences his final revelation. Among all the arts, what is specific about architecture is that it alone combines outward form with literal interiority: the architectural work can be entered and inhabited, and as such it provides the perfect metaphor for the interiority of the subject. This is what happens in the Venice chapter of *Albertine disparue:* the narrator's subjectivity is given the architectural form inspired by various scenes of the city itself. In reading the architectural signs of Venice he is in effect reading the signs of his own "interior Venice."

> Parfois au crépuscule en rentrant à l'hôtel je sentais que l'Albertine d'autrefois, invisible à moi-même, était pourtant fermée au fond de moi comme aux "plombs" d'une Venise intérieure, dont parfois un incident faisait glisser le couvercle durci jusqu'à me donner une ouverture sur ce passé. (4:219)[3]

> *Sometimes, returning to the hotel, I felt that the Albertine of old, invisible to myself, was nonetheless locked up deep inside me as if in the* piombi *of an interior Venice,[4] where sometimes an incident shifted the lid enough to give me an opening onto that past.*

One notices here a double interiority: first there is a Venice "interior" to the narrator, and then there is an interior to that: the prison of the *piombi* concealed within this inner city, as in a set of Chinese boxes. This spatial system suggesting successively deeper levels of interiority is presented within a temporal order of successively rarer incidents of unveiling: "sometimes" returning to the hotel the narrator senses an invisible Albertine en-

166 • ARCHITECTURE AND MODERN LITERATURE

closed within him, and of those times, only "sometimes" does he catch a
glimpse of the past that she represents. In this way Venice figures as a
metaphor not just for the narrator's subjectivity but also for his notion of
involuntary memory, in which an occasional incident allows him access to
an otherwise forgotten past. However, the objective form given to the narrator's subjectivity can be deceptive, because the interior Venice of the narrator's mind is no more unified than the city itself. Just as the waterways of
the city fragment it into dozens of little islands, so the mind of the narrator is fragmented into a series of disjointed, alternating movements of enchantment and disillusion, grief and forgetfulness, desire and boredom.

The "séjour à Venise" occurs as the last in a series of episodes devoted
to what the narrator calls the progressive stages of his indifference to the
death of his lover, Albertine—what a more conventional writer would call
the gradual subsidence of his grief. Plans of earlier visits to Venice had been
put off, first by the narrator's fear that his lover would come between him
and the pleasures of the city and then, after her death, by the disappointment that she wouldn't. When he finally arrives, it is as if he had come
through his grief to the other side, and to Venice as the world transformed,
or rather "transposed."

> [J]'y goûtais des impressions analogues à celles que j'avais si souvent
> ressenties autrefois à Combray, mais transposées selon un mode en-
> tièrement différent et plus riche. (4:202)
>
> *My impressions were analogous to those I had so often felt at Combray, but*
> *transposed in a way that made them entirely different and more rich.*

The effect on the narrator's sensibility is to superimpose the structure of
Venice onto the humble village of his childhood in a systematic substitu-
tion of natural and architectural forms. From his hotel room, the first
thing he sees through his open shutters in the morning is, instead of the
slate roof of the familiar village church, the golden angel atop the bell
tower of Saint Mark's. Descending to what should be the street, he finds it
transformed into water the color of sapphire. In place of the village houses
lining the main street of Combray, here palaces of porphyry and jasper line
the splendid blue of the water. On the Piazza San Marco, the shadow that
in Combray would be cast on the pavement by a shop awning is here cast
by the sculpted relief of a Renaissance facade on sun-drenched tiles, in
shadows shaped like little blue flowers. At Venice, just as at Combray, window shades are drawn against the sun. But here they hang among the qua-

trefoils and foliations of Gothic windows. In Combray, the narrator's Aunt Léonie would look out from her room through a window asymmetrically positioned, mounted on a wooden support disproportionately high. Such things, with their "humble particularity," the narrator says, become objects of affection by allowing us to recognize where we live from afar, and they are later remembered as proof that for a time we dwelled in that house. Such things have their equivalents in Venice, but here the function of marking this individuality is performed not by simple things but by, for example, the half-Arab ogive window of a facade that happens to be re-produced everywhere in museums and books as one of the masterpieces of medieval domestic architecture (4:203–4). In Combray, the narrator would enter the house on a warm summer's day to find the cool air of a little stair-case with narrow wooden steps, but in Venice the air is cooled by the sea and the hotel staircase is formed of marble surfaces splashed with sea-green sunlight.

This series of comparisons is presented as if the forms of Combray were being transformed into the splendor of Venice, but what actually takes place in the narrator's mind is that the forms of Venice recover the mem-ory of Combray, so that the two places are combined in a single vision joining past and present: Combray transformed into the splendor of Venice, Venice made familiar as Combray, and thus already an intimate part of the narrator's being. This double vision is the condition for what the narrator calls the promise of joy. When he sees the angel of Saint Mark's shining in the morning sun, it bears "une promesse de joie plus cer-taine que celle qu'il put être jadis chargé d'annoncer aux hommes de bonne volonté" (a promise of joy more certain than that which he could once have been given to announce to men of goodwill) (4:202).[5] In other words, the angel, who in the Gospel of Luke (2:14) announced the birth of Christ held out a promise of joy less certain than the one of secular, aesthetic joy now given to the narrator who awakens to the splendors of Venice. The promise made by Luke's angel is of a coming reconciliation of heaven and earth as foreseen in the final book of the Bible. The opening section of Proust's chapter thus implicitly includes, in addition to the remembered Combray and the present Venice, a third city: the New Jerusalem to come. In the narrator's mind, to the cities of memory and immediate perception is thus added the archetypal city of visionary imagination: the stones of Proust's Venice are those of the holy city in Revelation 21 and 22. Venice's sapphire-colored canals are a watery version of the foundations of the New Jerusalem where "the first foundation was jasper; the second, sapphire"

(Rev. 21:19, King James version). The porphyry and jasper palaces lining the Grand Canal appear to have been designed by the architect of the holy city, for "the wall of it was pure jasper, and the city was pure gold, like unto clear glass" (Rev. 21:18). The central avenue of Venice is a glassy canal, that of the New Jerusalem, "a pure river of the water of life, clear as crystal, proceeding out of the throne of God and of the Lamb" (Rev. 22.1). Just as Combray has been transposed from the past, so the holy city is transposed from the future, anticipated and rendered superfluous, as it were, by a Venice that not only promises but delivers joy in the present. The opening vision of Venice is therefore a kind of dream of spiritual plenitude embodied in architectural form: the heavenly city made into the earth and water of this world, joining past and future in the present and reconciling the narrator's interior Venice with the real one at hand.

It is characteristic of Proust that this moment of consummation does not last, and that the perfect equilibrium of the narrator's aesthetic stance suddenly gives way to the less exalted pursuit of sexual pleasure. When the narrator goes out on afternoons alone, that is, without his mother, he explores the remote and obscure parts of the city in the pursuit of working-class girls from the factories where they make matches, beads, glass, and lace. The account of and setting for this ritual exploration are constructed in terms of what we might call, in contrast to the architecture of consummate splendor that opens the chapter, the architecture of desire. Where the narrator's position, in the opening passage, was mainly a static appreciation of the splendor arrayed before him, here he is always in motion, actively penetrating the back streets of a city whose hidden pleasures are more erotic than aesthetic, and where the *recherche du temps perdu* is reduced to the simpler but nonetheless exciting "recherche des Vénitiennes" (4:206). In terms of narrative form, the episode imitates the oriental tale, with its secret passageways, its mysterious genie or "magical guide," its sudden materializations of exotic scenes, and its erotic overtones. As the narrator's gondola advances ever farther into the *quartiers populaires,* the little canals seem, as if guided by the hand of a genie, to open a path between the houses with their Moorish windows. He comes by "surprise" on boys dangling their legs over the walls of the canal; a little Greek temple appears suddenly "like a surprise in a box we have just opened" (4:206).

J'avais l'impression, qu'augmentait encore mon désir, de ne pas être dehors, mais d'entrer de plus en plus au fond de quelque chose de secret, car à chaque fois je trouvais quelque chose de nouveau qui venait se

placer de l'un ou de l'autre coté de moi, petit monument ou *campo* imprévu, gardant l'air étonné des belles choses qu'on voit pour la première
fois et dont on ne comprend pas encore bien la destination et l'utilité.
(4:207)

*I had the impression, increased by my desire, of not being outdoors but of
entering farther and farther into something secret, because at every turn
something new appeared on one hand or the other, an unexpected little
building or open square, with the surprised look of beautiful things one sees
for the first time and of which one doesn't yet know their purpose or use.*

What I am calling the architecture of desire applies both to the narrative
based on this dynamic of unveiling and to the design of the architectural
space—"petit monument ou *campo* imprévu" that is, its mise-en-scène.
The libertine tales of Casanova and Vivant Denon take place in just such
settings of narrow passages, secret gardens, and hidden pavilions. In Proust
the movement into and through this kind of space, moreover, is rendered
in a language ripe with images of natural abundance and abandon, as if the
object of desire were not so much the Venetian working girls as the space
that they inhabit. Garden trellises directly overhang the water, as in a
flooded city, and a little farther, again, as if to overdetermine the image of
abundance itself, gardens divided by the canal let their leaves and their "as-
tonished" fruit overflow into the water. The peristyle of the little Greek
temple is so covered with fallen leaves and fruit that it resembles a loading
dock for market produce. In this landscape, the interpenetration of natural
and architectural elements sometimes extends to the material of architectural construction itself. The garden that negligently drags its leaves into
the water adjoins a house with an edge of sandstone so rough that it seems
freshly cut. The rough stone, neglected gardens, and leaf-littered squares
have a sensual appeal for the narrator, which corresponds to his taste for
the working girls who live in this part of the city. He knows, however, that
the *recherche des Vénitiennes* cannot assist him in the more ambitious
recherche that gives his book its title, because of what he calls the "individuality of desire" (4:207): the girls he desires now cannot be the ones he desired years ago, because the latter by now have aged to the point where they
no longer would attract him. Just as, in space, he is drawn into the city by
the pleasure of constantly new surprises, in time his sexual desire can only
be satisfied by a never-ending succession of girls, because "what I loved was
youth," and "the youth of those I used to know no longer existed but in my
burning memory" (4:207–8). In these erotic excursions into the interior of

Venice, the narrator does not return by the way he came, as if knowing that no new pleasures are to be found by simply retracing the same path. Instead, he disembarks from the gondola and returns to his hotel on foot. If, as I claim they do, these excursions provide a spatial and architectural metaphor for the narrator's desire, what this itinerary suggests is that his desire cannot return to its former object simply by retracing its ground; rather, desire is pursued as if through a city in which the streets are all one way, and the way back is never the way one came, nor is it easily to be found.

In another of these excursions, this time by night, the narrator compares himself to a character in the *Thousand and One Nights,* so much has he the impression of finding himself transported as if by magic into an enchanted city. In this case, however, the analogy between lost space and lost time is made into a kind of fable. Wandering through the maze of little *calli,* the narrator suddenly comes upon a vast and sumptuous *campo* surrounded by charming palaces and illuminated by the pale moonlight. It is the kind of place that, in another city, would be placed at the convergence of several streets. But here it seems deliberately concealed by the lack of any direct approach to it.

> Ici, [cet ensemble architectural] semblait exprès caché dans un entre-croisement de ruelles, comme ces palais des contes orientaux où on mène la nuit un personnage qui ramené chez lui avant le jour, ne doit pas pouvoir retrouver la demeure magique où il finit par croire qu'il n'est allé qu'en rêve. (4:229–30)

> *Here [this architectural ensemble] seemed deliberately hidden in a network of little streets, like those palaces in oriental tales where a person is led by night and then taken home before morning, so that he won't remember how to return to the magical place, which he finally believes he visited only in a dream.*

This is exactly what happens to the narrator. On the following day he goes out again in search of the beautiful square, only to get hopelessly lost in the labyrinth of little *calli,* then finds himself, against his will, back where he started at the Grand Canal. He never again finds the beautiful square, which remains forever exiled from him in its solitude and concealment. Like the person in the oriental tale, he begins to ask himself whether he saw it only in a dream. Indeed the very geography of Venice contributes to the city's dreamlike quality: its islands are themselves crisscrossed by innumerable little *calli,* like grooves in a piece of crystal. According to this metaphor, the open square in the midst of the little streets appears as a "distension" of the crystal, an anomalous interior space within the otherwise solid geometrical design. Later, after the narrator has given up trying to retrace his steps to the square, he wonders if in his sleep there has not perhaps occurred in his mind a similar crystallization in which a strange inner distension "presented to the moonlight's prolonged meditation a vast square bounded by romantic palaces" (4:230). This impressionistic conceit should not obscure either the elegance or lucidity of Proust's fable, which presents the urban space of Venice as a metaphor for memory. The search for the lost square is an allegory of voluntary memory—the conscious attempt to retrieve a privileged moment of the past. It cannot succeed, however systematically one searches through the labyrinth, because one is invariably sent back to the present—the Grand Canal of consciousness—before one can really recapture the past as an object of subjective experience. It is this failure that leads the narrator to doubt the objective reality of those privileged moments and spaces, and this doubt extends to the continuity of his subjective selfhood; it produces the tension, expressed in the very form of the text, between the fragmentation of experience and the constant effort to recuperate those fragments into an architectural ensemble of crystallized meaning.

Proust's search for the lost Venetian square as an allegory of an irretrievable past belongs to an ancient tradition of using architectural loci in the art of memory. In *De Oratore* (II), Cicero tells the story of the poet Simonides who, on the day of a feast, happened to leave the banquet hall just before the roof collapsed, killing all who had remained inside and maiming their bodies beyond recognition. But Simonides was able to identify the dead by recalling the order in which the guests had been seated at the table. Cicero tells this gruesome story in order to teach the lesson that memory is aided when its objects can be organized in architectural space (Carruthers 22). In Proust's story the object of memory is itself an architectural space—*la belle place exilée* (4:230)—contained within the larger architectural space of the city. When the narrator is unable to find it again he confirms Cicero's principle, albeit in a negative way, since the irretrievability of his object is the direct consequence of his failure to organize in his mind the urban space surrounding it. Proust's metaphor of the mind, however, is not simply of a faculty more or less well adapted to concrete reality; rather it is of a space of more or less solid parts. In the opening pages of *Albertine disparue* the narrator discovers that, although he had thought that he no longer loved Albertine, as soon as she leaves he discovers that he does still love her. Our intelligence, he concludes, no matter how great, cannot perceive the elements of its own composition until "de l'état volatil où ils subsistent la plupart du temps, un phénomène capable de les isoler ... leur a fait subir un commencement de solidification" (from the volatile state in which they exist most of the time, a phenomenon capable of isolating them has made them begin to solidify) (4:4). The mind, then, can only know that part of itself that has become solid and concrete, like the built environment. The rest, as volatile and formless as the abyssal origin of space in what Plato calls *chora*,[6] is that part of ourselves that remains beyond our reach: "Je m'étais trompé en croyant voir clair dans mon coeur" (I had been mistaken in believing that I knew my own heart) (4:4).

The Venetian story is an exotic retelling of another episode concerning architectural memory in the first volume of Proust's work. There, a long passage is devoted to a description of the church of Combray, which is important not for any architectural distinction but for the integral role it plays in the narrator's remembered childhood: for its homely familiarity, its uniqueness, its intimate association with the life and objects of the village. The narrator's relation to it is not one of aesthetic appreciation but rather one of profound and permanent attachment. He has indeed engraved in his memory the sight of other churches seen in later life and other places. But no matter how artfully his memory made these "engravings" (1:65), they could not restore what he lost long ago, the feeling of believing in a thing as being without any equivalent:

> aucune d'elles ne tient sous sa dépendance toute une partie profonde de ma vie, comme fait le souvenir de ces aspects du clocher de Combray dans les rues qui sont derrière l'église. (1:65)

> *none of them holds such sway over a profound part of my life as does the memory of those views of the bell tower of Combray from the streets behind the church.*

The narrator has lost the capacity to believe in the immanence of things and their intimate relation to his own being. Nonetheless, the church of Combray would be an exception to the rule except that it remains removed from him in time and space. So it is that even now, while walking in some strange city, he will sometimes be stopped by the sight of some belfry or steeple in which his memory struggles to find some point of resemblance to "la figure chère et disparue" (the cherished, lost figure) (4:66) of the church of Combray. On such occasions a passerby might be struck by the figure of the narrator himself standing there motionless, trying to remember, "sentant au fond de moi des terres reconquises sur l'oubli qui s'assèchent et se rebâtissent"(feeling deep within me the lands recaptured from forgetfulness, drained, and rebuilt) (4:66), until, recalled to the present, he once again seeks his way through the streets. The architectural figures here are layered one within the other—mises en abyme, as Peter Collier puts it in another context. In this passage from the section known as "Combray," the most immediate architectural context for the structure of layering is the provincial city or the unfamiliar quarter of Paris where the narrator, having stopped to ask the way, is given directions according to some bell tower as a landmark. Within that setting there is the work of memory, here figured as an *aménagement de territoire* in which the ground must be reclaimed from the swamps of forgetfulness and reconstructed with solid habitations. Only within this figure does there stand the elusive church of Combray, just beyond the reach of conscious memory but still felt to be there deep within the heart, "c'est dans mon coeur." (1:66) What distinguishes the "belle place exilée" of Venice from the "chère et disparue" church of Combray is the newness and strangeness of the former, as well as its literally eccentric situation with respect to the narrator's being. If the church of Combray remains somewhere deep within the narrator, the lost square of Venice stands beyond the outer limits of his existence; neither is to be wholly retrieved.

In comparing the two episodes of the *recherche des Vénitiennes* and the search for the *belle place exilée,* I have considered together two parts of the *séjour à Venise* that are in fact separated by other episodes written in different registers: there is a dinner conversation between M de Norpois and Mme de Villeparisis, two satirically drawn characters who, now superannuated, married to each other, and visiting Venice, have survived from the first volume of the *Recherche;* there is an episode in which the narrator receives a telegram the text of which has been garbled in transmission but which he reads as from the mourned Albertine, with the startling news that she still lives and wants to marry him. He finds, however, that having grown indifferent to Albertine dead, he is no longer interested in Albertine alive. I will return to this scene later. The one I wish to turn to now is that in which the narrator visits the baptistery of Saint Mark's Cathedral with his mother. It is a scene we should expect to be given special importance in the narrative: the visit to Venice has been anticipated for more than a thousand pages, given the narrator's obsession with Ruskin, and for Ruskin the baptistery of Saint Mark's figures as the geographical, architectural, and spiritual center of Venice, and thus of the world.

Ruskin writes on the baptistery most notably on two occasions. The first is book II, chapter 4, of *The Stones of Venice,* where the contrast between the original splendor of the baptistery and its decayed condition in 1853 drives home the recurring motif of Venice's progressive degradation after the fourteenth century, when the baptistery was built. Ruskin's initial attention is directed not at the font itself, nor at the celebrated mosaics depicting the life of John the Baptist, but at a tomb within the baptistery chamber, a tomb so easily overlooked that one could mistake it for a narrow stone couch set beside the window. It is the Gothic tomb of Andrea Dandolo (1306–54), the last doge to be buried in Saint Mark's and a figure who serves as a frame for Ruskin's treatment of the baptistery. On Dandolo's tomb sits a figure of the Virgin bordered by "flowers and soft leaves, growing rich and deep, as if in a field in summer" (10:86). Ruskin's evocation of Dandolo's death at the age of forty-six sets the mood for his contemplation of the walls of the baptistery, "worn and shattered, and darkly stained with age," but beautiful in their ruin (10:86). Their translucent masses are "darkened into fields of rich brown, like the colour of seaweed when the sun strikes it through deep sea" (10:86). Ruskin perceives only dimly, in the gloom, the mosaic of the baptism of Christ, but raising his eyes to the roof vaulting, he sees two circles of heavenly angels and, in an architectural metaphor for poetic language, is reminded of Milton's "single massy line": "Thrones, Dominations, Princedoms, Virtues, Powers" (Ruskin 10:86; Milton, *Paradise Lost* V:601). Returning to the wall mosaics and their scenes from the life of John the Baptist, Ruskin sees "the streams of the Jordan running down between their cloven rocks" and interprets the story put before him in terms of the choice set before all men "to be baptized with fire or to be cast therein" (10:87). "Venice has made her choice," Ruskin writes sententiously, meaning that the city has chosen perdition (10:88). He adds that Dandolo would have taught the city another choice but that "he and his counsels have long been forgotten by her, and the dust lies upon his lips" (10:88). However, the moral lesson Ruskin draws from the story of John the Baptist is more cultural and aesthetic in nature than it is religious. The Gothic sepulcher of the last doge to be buried there, with its carved stone border of soft leaves and summer flowers, marks for Ruskin a final expression of medieval purity and natural plenitude, after which the decline of Venice can be read in the corrupted architecture of the Renaissance.

Ruskin's other piece on the baptistery is a twenty-page section of *St. Mark's Rest* (1884), the history of Venice he wrote late in life. The title of this section, "Sanctus, Sanctus, Sanctus," reflects both the author's return to Christian faith and the place of the baptistery at the very center of his own spiritual and aesthetic universe. However, in place of the moralizing tone of *The Stones of Venice,* Ruskin adopts a humbler approach to his subject; he gives a simple descriptive account of the mosaics, as if trusting to their own eloquence. Two moments in this account are of particular relevance to Proust's work. The first is Ruskin's description of the mosaic in the lunette over the altarpiece, which is devoted to the Crucifixion. Saint Mark himself is shown with a book (not his Gospel) open to the words "In illo tempore Maria mater" (in that hour Mary his mother), whereas Saint John the Evangelist is shown receiving the charge to take care of the mother of Christ: "When Jesus, therefore, saw his mother, and the disciple standing by, whom he loved, he saith unto his mother, Woman, behold thy son! Then saith he to the disciple, Behold thy mother! And from that hour the disciple took her unto his own home" (John 19:26–27; Ruskin 24:311). In terms of the story told by the mosaics ranged along the walls of the baptistery, the most significant is that depicting the baptism of Christ. Ruskin tells us how Christ stands in the midst of the River Jordan, with John's hand on his head. Christ blesses the fishes, while angels watch from the riverbank. The mosaic is inscribed with the words of Matthew, who relates that when Jesus was baptized he went up out of the water into heaven, where the Spirit of God lighted upon him like a dove (Matt. 3:16–17). This scene is followed by Ruskin's descriptions of the remaining mosaics, in a chapter that ends with the citation, in Latin, of Revelation 4:8: "Holy, holy, holy, Lord God Almighty, which was, and is, and is to come" (24:334).

This brief account of Ruskin's writing on the baptistery of Saint Mark's provides a context for the manner in which Proust commemorates the same architectural space in the *séjour à Venise.* Having announced that he is taking notes for some work he is doing on Ruskin, the narrator, accompanied by his mother, goes to the baptistery to contemplate the same mosaics that his master has described in so much detail. Although much of Ruskin's language and imagery survives in Proust's account of the same space, in Proust's hands the meaning of the baptistery is transformed into something very different from what it is in Ruskin. The single concrete incident of the scene in Proust is related as follows.

Voyant que j'avais à rester *longtemps* devant les mosaïques qui représen-
tent le baptême du Christ, ma mère, sentant la fraîcheur glacée qui
tombait dans le baptistère, me jetait un châle sur les épaules. (4:225, my
emphasis)

*Seeing that I would have to remain for a long time before the mosaics rep-
resenting the baptism of Christ, my mother, feeling the icy fresh air of the
baptistery, threw a shawl over my shoulders.*

In the context of Proust's own work, this takes us back to the very beginning of the *Recherche,* where the narrator tells how *longtemps* (for a long
time) as a child he would go to bed early, and that starting in the late afternoon, *longtemps* before going to bed, his bedroom became the fixed object of his anxiety because it was there that he had to separate from his
mother for the night (1:3, 9).

While resonant of the entire history of the narrator's anxious relation
with his mother, the language of the baptistery scene is also constructed on
two other textual layers: that of the mosaics themselves, which tell a story
in images; and that of Ruskin's writing on these same images. Proust's narrator sees the mosaics through the mediation of Ruskin's text; he is in a
sense baptized in their reading, but like Jesus his understanding of the ritual will be of another order than that of his baptizer. Following Ruskin's
evocation of Christ's mother at the Crucifixion, Proust draws the theme of
the mother in mourning. Having recently lost her own mother, the narrator's mother stands beside him "drapée dans son deuil avec [une] ferveur
respectueuse et enthousiaste" (draped in her mourning with respectful and
fervent devotion) (4:225). Like Ruskin, Proust's narrator is drawn to the
aquamarine mosaics of the River Jordan, but unlike his English guide, he
juxtaposes them in his imagination, as they are in fact juxtaposed in space,
with the sapphire waters of Venice where a gondola waits for him just at
the edge of the piazza. Proust shares with Ruskin not only the sense that
the baptistery stands at the center of things as a sacred space; he also shares,
both with Ruskin and with the inscription on the baptistery wall, the notion of a single, significant moment in time. To the Latin words in the mosaic translated by Ruskin as "in that hour," Proust's narrator responds:

Une heure est venue pour moi où quand je me rappelle ce baptistère,
devant les flots du Jourdain où saint Jean immerge le Christ tandis que
la gondole nous attendait devant la Piazzetta il ne m'est pas indifférent
que dans cette fraîche pénombre, à côté de moi il y avait une femme

drapée dans son deuil . . . et que cette femme aux joues rouges, aux yeux tristes, dans ses voiles noires, et que rien ne pourra jamais faire sortir pour moi de ce sanctuaire doucement éclairé de Saint-Marc où je suis sûr de la trouver parce qu'elle y a sa place réservée et immuable comme une mosaïque, ce soit ma mère. (4:225)

An hour has come for me when, remembering this baptistery before the waves of the Jordan River where Saint John submerges the Christ while the gondola waited for us by the Piazza, it is not indifferent to me that in those cool shadows, there stood beside me a woman draped in mourning . . . and that this woman with her red cheeks, her sad eyes, in her black veils, whom for me nothing could ever remove from that softly lighted sanctuary of Saint Mark's, where I am certain to find her because her place is reserved for her there, immovable like a mosaic—this woman is my mother.

This is an exceptional moment within the history of the dynamics of memory to which the entire *Recherche* is devoted, as it seems to escape the limitations of both the voluntary and involuntary forms of memory. For Proust, the limits of voluntary memory in general are those of the intellect: the idea that it conveys of the past contains no material trace of the past itself. By contrast, the limits of involuntary memory are those of time, place, and circumstance: the past, in all its presence, is returned to us only fleetingly in the chance encounter with some material object at moments we cannot predict. However, the kind of memory enshrined in the baptistery of Saint Mark's seems to belong to another order: the narrator claims to be able to return at will to the remembered figure of his mother in that sanctuary, where she remains fully present to him, immovable in that place forever reserved for her in the sacred architecture of his own mind. He can still feel her throw the shawl over his shoulders in the chilly air of the baptistery. In this manner the *Evangile* of Saint Mark's acquires a very different meaning in Proust from what it means in Ruskin. Whereas Ruskin draws an ironic contrast between the holiness of the baptistery and the historical decline of Venice, for Proust the importance of the baptistery lies wholly in its function of permanently consecrating his mother's love in his memory, creating a place of inner pilgrimage to which he can always return. With respect to the architecture of the narrator's memory, the space of the baptistery is both metaphorical, as a figure for the inner sanctuary within memory, and metonymic, as the actual setting to which memory returns, "where I am certain to find her."[7]

In the labyrinth of Proust's interior Venice, the abiding presence of the

mother in the baptistery has a different function from the imagined imprisonment of Albertine in his own unconscious, which he has compared
to the *piombi* of the Ducal Palace. The two spaces of the baptistery and the
piombi, though separated by only a few meters' distance, represent symbolic antitheses in the architecture of Venice: the city's most sacred place
versus its most abject. In the narrator's mind, the figure of Albertine locked
up deep inside him functions as a special case of involuntary memory, just
as the figure of his mother in the baptistery constitutes an exceptional case
of voluntary memory. For him the image of Albertine has been repressed
in the "prison" of his unconscious as a defense against the suffering caused
by the flight of the real Albertine. When incidents occur that happen to
open the doors of that prison, the involuntary memory of Albertine functions not as the momentary recovery of a longed-for past but as a return of
the repressed, like the terrifying emergence of Madeline Usher, in Poe's
story, from her tomb deep within the walls of her ancestral home. In this
way, when a phrase used in a letter from the narrator's stockbroker recalls
one used by Albertine, it unlocks the door of the inner dungeon of the narrator's self in which Albertine's image is still imprisoned. But the prison
door closes again after a moment, because the narrator's suffering has now
been supplanted by indifference. This newfound indifference is again
tested when the narrator receives a garbled telegram that he mistakenly
reads as from Albertine, not dead after all, and now proposing marriage.
When he feels no joy in this "discovery" that she is still alive, his indifference is indeed confirmed, but only with the realization of another loss, that
of his former self, the young man who had loved Albertine: "J'aurais été incapable de ressusciter Albertine parce que je l'étais de me ressusciter moi-
même, de ressusciter mon moi d'alors" (I would not have been able to revive Albertine because I was incapable of reviving myself, of reviving my
past self) (4:221). This past self is not mourned, precisely because "je suis
un autre" (4:221), the narrator has become someone else, but the consciousness that the passing of time creates a succession of distinct selves
makes all the more significant a memory that seems to transcend this condition of existential fragmentation in time.

When the narrator remembers the figure of his mother in the baptistery, he does so in language that recovers a significant moment of the past
in a fulfilled moment of the present, "une heure est venue pour moi," language that recalls the sacred text inscribed on the baptistery wall: *in illo
tempore,* a familiar biblical phrase. This joining of the past and present, sacred and profane, is figured in Proust's text by the location of the remem-

bered moment in architectural space: "devant les flots du Jourdan . . . tandis que la gondole nous attendait devant la Piazzetta" (before the waves of the Jordan . . . while the gondola waited for us by the Piazza) (4:225). The sacred space of the baptistery, "ce sanctuaire doucement éclairé" (this softly lighted sanctuary) (4:225), has been reconsecrated in the inner architecture of the narrator's memory, where the image of his mother will always be found, just as those of Christ and his mother are always to be found in the real baptistery. What at first seems an understatement on the narrator's part, when he says that the ability to remember his mother in this way "is not indifferent to me," acquires greater rhetorical definition when we consider the importance that the word *indifference* has acquired by this point in *Albertine disparue.* For a writer who allows no nuance of feeling to escape his attention, *indifferent* is not an indifferent word. It is first used by Albertine herself in the letter she leaves on her escape, predicting, in order to ease the pain of his loss, that the narrator will become by degrees indifferent to her. It is then used, in the ways already shown, to define the narrator's response to the various incidents in Venice that remind him of Albertine, where his indifference to her loss is attributed to the fact that he is no longer the same person he once was. When, therefore, in the present moment of narration an hour has come for him when to remember the moment of his mother's solicitude in the baptistery is *not* indifferent, the negation carries all the force of the difference between a sanctuary and a prison cell.

What we have reviewed so far in this chapter can be summed up as a series of alternating moments in the relation between Venice and the narrator's mind, in which the status of the city as a concrete metaphor for subjective interiority moves in and out of focus, just as, according to Proust, the elements of the mind itself alternate between volatile and more solid states. On one hand, Venice crystallizes in the form of a holy city or an inner sanctuary, producing a corresponding clarity in the narrator's mind. On the other hand, and just as often, the space of the city dissolves like an oriental palace seen in a dream, just as the objects of memory are themselves subject to dissolution in the oblivion of forgetfulness. For Proust's narrator even the moment in the baptistery, which seemed to fix in the architecture of Venice an enduring sign of his mother's love, must give way to the law of this rhythm of alternating unity and fragmentation, both in his mind's relation to Venice and within the elements of his mind itself. If the opening of the *séjour à Venise* presented the city in terms of visionary promise, its conclusion is one of catastrophic disillusionment. On learning that the Baronne Putbus is due to arrive with her servants in Venice, the narrator's carnal desire is reawakened, and he suddenly wishes to extend his stay. His mother refuses this change in plans and sets off for the train station alone, while the narrator, vexed but determined to stay on, orders a drink on the terrace of the hotel facing the Grand Canal to watch the sun set. However, with his mother's departure the narrator is faced with the prospect of an "irrevocable solitude" so near that it seems already upon him. His intense loneliness causes the familiar things around him suddenly to become strange: "[T]he city before me had ceased to be Venice" (4:231). This sensation of defamiliarization extends to the very architecture of the city, which now appears stripped of meaning and beauty and reduced to a mass of inert matter.

> Les palais m'apparaissaient réduits à leurs simples parties et quantités de marbre pareil à tout autre, et l'eau comme une combinaison d'hydrogène et d'azote,[8] éternelle, aveugle, antérieure et extérieure à Venise, ignorante des doges et de Turner. (4:231)
>
> *The palaces appeared reduced to simple parts and quantities of marble like any other, and the water a combination of hydrogen and nitrogen, never ending, blind, anterior and exterior to Venice, ignorant of the doges and of Turner.*

Even the Rialto now appears mediocre, not just as an architecturally inferior bridge but as false as the kind of bad actor who in spite of his blond wig and black attire fails to convince the audience that he is Hamlet. Like the palaces and the canal, the Rialto, too, has been stripped of the idea that created its particularity and has dissolved into crude materiality. As the built environment is uncannily emptied of everything that "Venice" has come to mean, the narrator feels a like estrangement from himself, a self now reduced to a mere beating heart and a set of nerves fixed stupidly by the sound of "O sole mio," the banal Neapolitan song being sung by a musician stationed in a boat just in front of the hotel. It goes without saying that the narrator's interior Venice has likewise dissolved, for in this state of hebetude he is now as devoid of interiority as Venice is devoid of charm. Finally, aware that his mother must already be boarding the train, he is seized by an instinctive impulse to run after her and arrives to join her at the last possible moment before the train pulls out of the station.

Extraordinary as this scene is, it has not received the critical attention it deserves. Not only does it escape mention in the important works on

Proust cited elsewhere in this chapter; it does not even figure in works devoted specifically to Proust's Venice.[9] An exception to this rule of critical indifference is the American critic J. Hillis Miller, who reads the passage as an allegory for the force of habit, observing that it is only thanks to habit that the narrator sees Venice as the great historical city celebrated in the lives of the doges, in Turner's paintings, and in Ruskin's writings. It is therefore the return of habit from some place of hidden reserve that breaks the spell, reanimates the narrator, and allows him to rejoin his mother at the station: "Our sense of self and the solidity of its circumambient world, this episode implies, are sustained by a force that comes not from within the self but from beyond it, from something that is wholly other to that self, though special to that self alone" (Miller 240). This interpretation largely conforms to what Proust's narrator himself has to say of the incident, and of the "defensive force of inveterate habit" that rescues him from his paralysis. The moment is similar to the famous one in part 1 of *Le côté de Guermantes,* where the narrator, returning unexpectedly from a journey, enters the apartment of his grandmother and, finding her reading Mme de Sévigné before she catches sight of him, sees her not with his habitual affection and tenderness but as if she were a strange face in a photograph: "[J]'aperçus sur le canapé, sous la lampe, rouge, lourde et vulgaire, malade, rêvassant, promenant au-dessus d'un livre des yeux un peu fous, une vieille femme accablée que je ne connaissais pas" (I saw on the sofa, under the lamp, red, heavy and vulgar, sick, daydreaming, poring over a book with eyes a bit mad, a helpless old woman whom I did not recognize) (2:440). "Tout regard habituel est une nécromancie" (the habitual gaze is a kind of communication with the dead) (4:439), he remarks; it beholds not what is there but what is already past. Samuel Beckett writes of this scene that when the force of habit fails, we experience a kind of suffering that can, however, ultimately prove benign; by delivering us from boredom and by opening a window onto reality, this suffering is the first condition of every artistic experience (*Proust* 39).

Beckett's comment suggests another way of reading the conclusion to the Venice episode, one that sees in it an instance of what Benjamin calls allegory. Let us recall that for Benjamin the figure of allegory, as opposed to the romantic symbol, affirms the fundamental difference between the object world and its figurative meaning in language. In allegory the former is implicitly acknowledged as dead, as a ruin onto which the allegorical figure is superimposed in such a way as to register the destruction of historical meaning (*Origin* 166). For Benjamin, allegory is the figure that rigorously refuses the symbolic recompense for loss, that resists the illusory reconciliation of the temporal with the eternal, and of ruin with its sublimation in language. This refusal of sublimation is essentially what takes place at the end of the *séjour à Venise*. The personality, the allure, and the name of Venice suddenly appear to Proust's narrator as obvious fictions; he no longer has the courage to transform its stones in his imagination to conform to these fictions. In Benjamin's terms, these fictions have taken the form of allegory in that they are coldly recognized as fictions, thereby allowing the inanimate objecthood of Venice to be revealed in all its reality. Proust's narrator has had the experience of the cleared-eyed observer in Stevens's poem "The Snow Man" who, "nothing himself, beholds / Nothing that is not there and the nothing that is." But unlike Stevens's observer, he has not been cold long enough to regard the landscape without being distressed by the realization of absence, so that the song "O sole mio" seems to bear witness to his own lament for the disappearance of the Venice he has known. However, by acknowledging the banality of the song and its "vulgar romance," he also acknowledges implicitly the banality of his own lament. What he describes as a sense of Venice's "unreality" (*cette Venise . . . irréelle*) is in fact the effect of his newfound if painful perception of the Real, made possible by the derealization of the historical "Venice" (4:232). For Beckett, as we have seen, the suffering caused by the failure of habitual perception may be terrifying, but it is a necessary condition for the experience of art. When, at the conclusion of Proust's passage, the narrator flies to meet his mother at the train station, he is rescued by habit only to take refuge from the reality of experience in the comforting maternal presence. Still a student of Ruskin, he is not yet ready to assume the calling of the artist. This moment will not come until *Le temps retrouvé*, where the stones of Venice are visited one last time.

Before considering the place of Venice in the final volume of Proust's work, one further remark has to be made concerning the episode in which the narrator gazes on the suddenly banal Rialto to the sentimental tune of "O sole mio." To the extent that this episode poses the question of the relation between meaning in language and the radical materiality of being, it goes to the very heart of the project of the *Recherche*. This is Proust's version of the problem posed by Joyce, for whom even the most instinctive forms of meaning, like fatherhood and religious faith, are mystical estates "founded . . . upon the void" (*Ulysses* 9:842). Indeed, Proust's narrator seems torn between two unsatisfying alternatives: either to gaze helplessly on the void or to take refuge from it in the habitual forms of received ideas.

Elsewhere in Proust, this question of the relation between meaning and being is formulated in terms of the recovery of the past in the form of memory. In such cases the moment of the past, in its radical but absent materiality, resists conscious formulation as memory in the present, just as in the *séjour à Venise* the stones of Venice, now just stones, resist assimilation to their historical and aesthetic value. In *Le temps retrouvé,* Proust's solution to this problem will take the form of an idea of art closely related to Benjamin's concept of allegory.

In one of the famous passages of Proust's final volume, the narrator goes to a *matinée* at the home of the Princesse de Guermantes. In the courtyard of her *hôtel particulier,* he happens to set his foot on a paving stone set slightly lower in the ground than the one next to it. The sensation of the uneven paving stones occasions a sudden feeling of pure joy, which he is unable to account for until he remembers that, years before, he felt precisely the same sensation while treading the uneven tiles of the baptistery of Saint Mark's, so that the present moment brings back the feelings of happiness he felt at that moment in that place.[10] But the narrator is not content merely to register this sensation, because it seems to point the way toward a solution to the otherwise irretrievable difference between past and present, absence and presence, matter and memory, and even being and meaning. He wants to know how the "image" of the past, so fortuitously if only momentarily recovered, gives him a joy "pareille à une certitude" (akin to a certainty) and in itself enough to make him indifferent to death (4:446). Having entered the Hôtel de Guermantes, the narrator is shown into a small library to await the intermission of a musical performance before entering the reception room. It is in the space and time afforded by this deferral that he is able to unfold the implications of the sensory experience that has given him so much joy. The process by which he does so is crucial not just to the discovery of his vocation as an artist, but also to his understanding of the relation between art and the reality of material existence. Briefly, these reflections occur in the following order.

The narrator realizes, as a primary revelation, that when he experiences the same material sensation that he has experienced at some past moment, the past encroaches on the present in such a way as to make him hesitate between the two; neither precisely here nor there, now nor then, he is momentarily released from the limits of time. These "resurrections" (4:453) of the past, however, are quickly extinguished by the reassertion of the conscious present; the fragments of his existence abstracted from time are fugitive. The only way to rescue them from oblivion is to interpret them as signs, that is, to convert them into ideas or thoughts capable of being rendered in language: "Or, ce moyen qui me paraissait le seul, qu'était-ce autre chose que faire une oeuvre d'art?" (The only means of bringing this about was to make a work of art) (4:457). Such a work would translate sense impressions into language, thus making them permanent as well as universal. However, where Proust departs from the symbolist tradition is in his manner of registering what is lost in this translation. The difference lies in his formulation of the relation between the work of art and the object-world of sense impressions that it seeks to revive. For a poet like Baudelaire, the work, through its symbolic form and content, brings about an ideal and lasting resurrection of impressions otherwise lost to memory. His poem "La chevelure" is itself a means of entry into the "shadowy pavilion" of his mistress's head of blue-black hair, which in turn grants him access to the azure of an eternal heaven. The poem, its symbols, and the object-world they evoke form an ideal unity in which the past is made durably present, so that the poet drinks the wine of memory in long drafts: "Où je hume à longs traits le vin du souvenir." Proust's narrator remarks with a certain envy that poems such as this one represent a deliberate search for the analogies that will evoke the object of the poet's longing, be it the azure of an immense round heaven or a port filled with masts and flaming light (4:498–99). For the symbolist, then, the conscious choice of analogies between past and present, here and there, leads to their ideal union in the form of the poem. For Proust, by contrast, past and present are unified only in a momentary sensation, the passing of which the artwork can only commemorate in a language conscious of its radical difference from the sensation itself. Even more than this, however, Proust implicitly rejects the romantic and symbolist doctrine of the spiritual immanence of the object-world, finding instead that like the stones of Venice at the end of his stay there, "la matière est indifférente et . . . tout peut y être mis par la pensée" (matter itself is indifferent, and . . . anything can be put into it by thought) (4:489). In Proust, the lifelessness of the object-world has its temporal counterpart in the lostness of the past, which can only be "regained" in an allegorical sense, that is, one that acknowledges the essential irrevocability of the past as the condition of its representation in the work of art. This is because the work of art can only come about by means of a translation or "transposition" of the past into another language. By the same logic, Combray can only be "transposed" into the ideal form of Venice when it has been definitively relegated to the past, as a time and place to which the narrator can never return.

Given the explicit and implicit connections between the *séjour à Venise* and the theories of *Le temps retrouvé,* it is remarkable how much the latter are formulated in architectural metaphors, so that the search for lost time even at this late and relatively contemplative stage is conducted through images of a constructed spatial environment. Let us recall that these meditations take place in the library of the Prince de Guermantes, which serves as the improvised waiting room for the narrator before he is to confront the death's-head figures in the famous "bal des têtes," where his old acquaintances appear as grotesque and wizened parodies of the persons he has known in the past. The library itself, of course, represents the past in another form, that of literature, so that the narrator's reflections on the book he is to write take place literally in the privileged space of the book, what some would call the intertextual field in which his own work is destined to intervene. A kind of interlude in this space is granted him before he returns to the scene of life itself, cruelly marked as suffering the ravages of time. The library, however, is not merely the space of tranquil reflection; it is also the place of mourning for the narrator's past life. When he takes down from the shelf a volume of George Sand's *François le Champi,* one of his favorite books as a child, he finds himself close to tears. He compares the feeling to that of a young man in a mortuary chamber who is about to see the remains of his late father, a man who has served his country honorably, being lowered into the grave. Within this imagined scene, a band suddenly strikes up its music outside. At first perceiving a mockery of his grief, the young man turns in outrage toward the window, only to realize that it is the music of a regiment gathered to honor his father's memory. But what does this anecdotal metaphor have to do with the narrator's sensations on finding a familiar book in the library? He explains that when he takes down the book in a spirit of tender emotion, he suddenly feels the presence of a menacing stranger, just as the solitary meditations of the young man in the mortuary are interrupted by a noise in the street. But for the narrator this stranger turns out to be his childhood self, which the book has called forth as its only rightful reader, thus estranging the aged narrator from his former self, while causing him to mourn that self as well; the childhood self, being dead, will never again respond to the book's call. Adorno remarks that for Proust there are no human beings in themselves beyond the world of images into which they are transposed, that "the individual is an abstraction, . . . [and] its being-for-itself has as little reality as its mere being-for-us" (*Notes* 2:177). The ultimate truth, however, lies precisely in those images, which (we might add to Adorno's insight) have the

same relation to the self as allegory to its object, that is, one that constitutes the mythical and absent nature of the thing signified.

In this sustained reflection on the relation between literature and life,
Proust passes from the metaphor of the library as mortuary to that of the
book as cemetery. The narrator acknowledges that in the book he intends
to write his love for this or that person would be so disengaged from its
original object that a variety of readers could apply the same terms to persons they themselves have loved, thus profaning the narrator's own memories. But the writing itself already constitutes a profanation. In the projected book, not just Albertine or the narrator's grandmother would be
reduced to literary formulas; he would also appropriate a look or a word
from a host of other people whom he no longer remembers as individuals:
"[U]n livre est en grand cimetière où sur la plupart des tombes on ne peut
plus lire les noms effacés" (A book is a great cemetery where on most of the
tombstones the names can no longer be read) (4:482). The architectural
metaphor of the cemetery is not chosen by chance. As sequences of monumental forms, both book and cemetery are also more or less readable texts
whose elements are arranged in rows, each has its syntax and its system of
manifest signifiers and buried signifieds, and both serve the essential function of commemoration: in both cases, the inscription refers to something
or someone that no longer is. However, Proust reminds us that, like the
cemetery, the book is a sign of consolation as well as one of suffering.
Where the suffering of life walls us in (là où la vie emmure), the intelligence of art pierces through to the outside; it ranges free of the impasses,
the no-exit situations that limit the possibilities of life itself (4:484). However, if thought and imagination exercise freedom from confinement, as
the means of artistic creation they also have their own space in which to
work. This space is the "atelier . . . à l'intérieur de nous-même,"[11] the inner studio where the models of both happiness and suffering pose for the
mind of the artist, inciting it to creative action. In their essential artistic
functions for Proust's work, the architectural explorations of Combray,
Balbec, and Venice ultimately come down to this little workshop of the
spirit, where the sittings of the models, particularly those of pain, force us
to enter into closer contact with ourselves, and to discover the matter,
however dispersed, of which we are made.

Monumental Displacement in Ulysses

Joyce's *Ulysses* belongs to a literary tradition that defines modernity in terms of the tension between enduring archaic forms and unceasing forces of change, a complex relation that is concretized in the structures of urban space. We have seen in chapter 1 how Leopold Bloom, the novel's principal character, has his own meditation on the "cityful passing away, other cityful coming," as he walks down Grafton Street in search of his midday meal. His mind continues with a kind of stocktaking of the urban landscape.

> Big stones left. Round towers. Rest rubble, sprawling suburbs, jerry-
> built. Kerwan's mushroom houses built of breeze. Shelter, for the night.
> (8:490–92)[1]

If "big stones" and "round towers" refer, respectively, to the standing stones of prehistoric Ireland and the towers of pre-Norman monasteries, they also serve as synecdoches for the archipelago of architectural monuments that endures amid the sea of constantly changing urban forms, represented in Bloom's thoughts by the tracts of low-cost housing put up by the building contractor Michael Kirwan. This coexistence of the archaic and the unstable forces of commercial and industrial production is central to Joyce's vision of modernity.

This chapter starts from the premise that an important part of Joyce's vision of modernity takes the form of architectural representation. Let me recapitulate some of the issues at stake in the study of architectural representation in literature: first, the role played by architectural forms in the

188 · ARCHITECTURE AND MODERN LITERATURE

symbolic economy of the literary text; second, the existence of analogies between architectural and literary form; and third, and perhaps most important for the study of literary modernism, the analysis, implicitly performed by the text itself, of the relation between architectural form and an emerging modern subjectivity, which is itself the occasion for new forms of literature such as the one embodied in *Ulysses*. This subjectivity is conditioned by the enduring but nonetheless transformed presence of the archaic in the conditions that we otherwise know as those of modernity. What I wish to explore here is the symbolic value given to the nature of this relation between the archaic and the contemporary as it pertains to the representation of architecture in *Ulysses*. Another question will be whether Joyce's architectural mapping of this relation has consequences for our understanding of the form of *Ulysses* itself. Finally, I shall address the related question of the importance Joyce assigns to the shifting and temporary forms of habitation that are scattered about the urban landscape of Dublin.

Ulysses opens with the juxtaposition of two archaic forms, one architectural, the other liturgical. The Martello tower in which the young Stephen Dedalus lives with his companions is one of fifteen built along the Irish coast between 1805 and 1815 as protection against the threat of Napoleonic invasion. The speaker of the "Ithaca" episode (chap. 17) would have described it with technical precision: a squat cylindrical, two-story tower featuring a machicolation above the doorway on the landward (western) side and a double string course below the parapet level. The masonry work is of Leinster granite ashlar, dressed with a fine punch.[2] The tower could be called archaic not only because it has lost its original function but also because it looks much older than it is, having the cylindrical form and rough stone construction of a medieval bastion, with walls nearly two meters thick. Joyce seems to insist on the antiquity of the tower, with its "dark winding stairs" (1:6) and the slanted openings that he calls "barbacans" (1:316).

On the stone deck at the top of the tower, Stephen's housemate Buck Mulligan performs a parody of the Roman Catholic mass, intoning its opening words: *Introibo ad altare Dei* (1:5). Comparing this enunciation to the ringing of bell towers in Proust and Virginia Woolf, Jean Starobinski makes the observation that modern writers, even as they subvert traditional forms of representation and narrative order, still make room in their works for the premodern figures of temporality, such as the words of the mass or the tolling of church bells. In doing so, they show that even as they transgress the archaic order, they have not forgotten it and retain a measure of nostalgia for it (27). In Joyce's representation of modernity, the Martello tower bears the same relation to modern urban space as the Latin liturgy bears to the rhythms of daily urban life: it is a vestige of the archaic, subject to parody and reappropriation, but nonetheless materially present as a form of intervention and resistance, incongruous with "the velocity of modern life" (17:1773) yet persisting in the midst of that life.

However, even if the tower materially resists the effects of time, it does not resist the forces of readaptation and reassignment of function put into movement by the forces of contemporary social reality. There is some irony in the fact that a literal bastion of the British Empire now serves as something barely above the level of an urban squat, inhabited temporarily by young men living out a provincial version of bohemian life. As such, the Martello tower stands as an ironic counterpart to Thoor Ballylee, the Anglo-Norman tower with its own winding stair that William Butler Yeats had already restored by the time Joyce published *Ulysses,* and from the parapet of which Yeats had surveyed the civil war in lordly solitude. Yeats thought of the tower as a symbol of the permanence of his work and of its rootedness in Irish ground. On the occasion of the publication of his book of poems *The Tower* (1927), he would write to T. Sturge Moore, "I like to think of that building as a permanent symbol of my work plainly visible to the passer-by . . . all my art theories depend upon just this—rooting of mythology in the earth."[3] Yeats's tower stands at the center of his poetic universe, and, as a traditional symbol of philosophical thought and meditation, it also stands in a line of lonely poets' towers that Yeats consciously inherits from Milton and Shelley.[4] In Yeats's repertoire of images, the tower belongs to a cult of noble legacy and changeless beauty; it symbolizes "the mind looking outward on men and things" (*Essays* 87).

In contrast to this figure of mastery, centrality, and rootedness, Joyce's tower stands at the margins, both symbolically and geographically. It is situated at the periphery of Joyce's Dublin, a point from which the work begins but to which it never returns. Although Mulligan facetiously refers to the tower as the *omphalos* (1:534) of a neopagan fantasy, this view is tacitly rejected by Stephen, who associates the new paganism with the privileged fatuity of the English student from Oxford, Haines (1:176). Haines himself is closer to the mark when he compares the tower to Elsinore (1:567), given what Stephen shares with Hamlet: a sense of fatherlessness, alienation, and usurpation. Under these circumstances, it is not surprising that Stephen surrenders the key to the tower when Mulligan demands it, thereby putting into play a leitmotif that sounds throughout Joyce's work: Alexander Keyes, tea, wine and spirit merchant; the crossed keys of the Manx parliament; the forgotten latchkey to no. 7, Eccles Street; Bloom as "competent keyless citizen" (17.1019); and so on. Having given up the key, Stephen decides, "I will not stay here tonight. Home also I cannot go" (1:739–40). From this point, the tower, already reduced to a marginal form of housing in modern Dublin, is given the negative if ambiguous status of something to which Stephen cannot return. It is henceforth effectively erased from the itinerary of wanderings that constitutes Joyce's work. Even as such, however, it retains its place in the work as a point of reference, both in the historical sense of the city as an accumulation of architectural layers, each of which remains visible in the present, and in the sense of marking an outer limit to the geography of Dublin. Viewed in this way, Stephen's self-willed expulsion from the tower can only drive him back into the center of the city, toward its institutions, human relations, and commerce. And indeed, a few chapters later he arrives "In the Heart of the Hibernian Metropolis" (7:1).

Stephen's appearance at the *Evening Telegraph* office in Prince Street North nearly coincides with that of Bloom, just returned from Glasnevin Cemetery, another peripheral point but at an outer limit almost diametrically opposed to that of Sandycove and the Martello tower. The "Aeolus" episode (chap. 7), in which we now find both men, opens with the figure of Nelson's pillar, a Doric column of granite 121 feet (38.6 meters) high designed by Francis Johnston and erected in 1808 to commemorate the British naval victory at Trafalgar. However, it is immediately made clear in "Aeolus" that the importance attached to this monument now is not its commemorative function but rather its position as a central point in Dublin's mass transit system.[5]

> Before Nelson's pillar trams slowed, shunted, changed trolley, started for Blackrock, Kingstown and Dalkey, Clonskea, Rathgar and Terenure, Palmerstown Park and upper Rathmines, Sandymount Green, Rathmines, Ringsend and Sandymount Tower, Harold's Cross. (7:3–6)

Joyce names the stations on the tramlines that radiate outward from Nelson's pillar to the south and east. The rhetorical form of the catalog, which in the Homeric epic is dedicated to heroic genealogy, is here displaced onto the modern system of mechanized circulation. The timetable proves a fitter model for Joyce's writing of the city than the archaic tradition of naming lines of heroic descent, a tradition represented here by the monument to Horatio Nelson.

By reducing the function of Nelson's pillar to that of a tram stop, Joyce puts into play an opposition between two systems of signification, which Gilles Deleuze and Félix Guattari designate as respectively as *calque* and *carte,* terms that might be translated as "copy" and "map." The *calque,* or transcriptive order, is comparable to that of genetic descent: descending symbolically from a long line of imperial military heroes, Nelson belongs to the same order as the Duke of Marlborough and Lord Wellington, also objects of architectural commemoration.[6] His monument constitutes a continuation of that line in the form of official public art, as a mimetic reproduction of both the man and the heroic principle that he incarnates. In Joyce's day Thomas Kirk's thirteen-foot statue of Nelson stood atop the pillar, his left arm vigorously extended southward in the direction of his past victories, the names and dates of which were inscribed on the base of the column. As an artefact, the pillar itself belongs to the ancient monumental tradition of the freestanding column and the obelisk, designed to connect the earth with heaven. The vertical elevation of the pillar, erected in the decade following the Rebellion of 1798, stood as a symbol of imperial mastery over the provincial capital; beginning in 1849, the pillar had a taller, Corinthian counterpart in the imperial capital in the form of Nelson's column at Trafalgar Square. Nelson's pillar in Dublin was blown up by members of the Irish Republican Army in March 1966 on the fiftieth anniversary of the 1916 Easter Rising.[7]

In Joyce's work the pillar, as a figure of the mimetic succession of an imperial order, is found at the center of another system, which belongs to an entirely different order of organization and signification. The logic of the transport system is that of the map, not of the copy; its parts are connected as points in a network extended through horizontally planar space, not as temporally successive representations in a linear order descended from an origin. As Deleuze and Guattari write:

> La carte est ouverte, elle est connectable dans toutes ses dimensions, démontable, renversable, susceptible de recevoir constamment des modifications. (*Mille plateaux* 20)
>
> *The map is open, connectable in all its dimensions, collapsible, capable of being turned upside down and subject to continuous modifications.*

As a model for the city's architectural form, the historical and imperial order of the empire has already been supplanted by the social and topographical order of the metropolis, with the electric tramway system as its dominant feature. As a relic of the imperial past, Nelson's pillar is curiously displaced here, finding itself both at the heart of the Hibernian metropolis and exterior to it, at once center and margin.

The ambiguous status of Nelson's pillar is again made apparent at the end of this chapter, in the story Stephen tells to his companions from the *Evening Telegraph* as they are crossing O'Connell Street, under the pillar, on their way to Mooney's pub in Abbey Street Lower. This story, which Stephen prefaces in his mind with the single word, "Dubliners" (7:922), might have come from a comic version of the collection of stories that Joyce published under that title in 1914, some lost Joycean *Margites*. Two elderly spinsters have saved their money in order "to see the views of Dublin from the top of Nelson's pillar" (7:931). After extensive preparations, they "waddle slowly up the winding staircase" with much effort and expostulation. On reaching the top, "They see the roofs and argue about where the different churches are: Rathmines' blue dome, Adam and Eve's, saint Laurence O'Toole's. But it makes them giddy to look" (7:1010–12). Instead, they sit down under the statue of Lord Nelson while eating their plums and "spitting the plumstones slowly out between the railings" (7:1026–27).

The parodic effects of Stephen's story can be registered in terms of a widening series of contexts. Most immediately, the title Stephen gives his story, *A Pisgah Sight of Palestine* or *The Parable of the Plums,* responds to the dramatic interpretation just given by Professor MacHugh of a famous example of oratory in which the barrister John F. Taylor, defending the Irish language, compared it to ancient Hebrew as "the language of the outlaw" (7:869), which, as Taylor imagines the scene, the youthful Moses might have defended before the proud contumely of a high priest of Egypt. MacHugh's rendering of this speech prompted one of his listeners to remark regretfully of Moses, "And yet he died without having entered the land of promise" (7:872), thus recalling the scene in Deuteronomy 34 where Moses, on the heights of Pisgah, sees the promised land from afar just before his death. For Stephen to borrow from this biblical passage for a title to his comical story is, rhetorically speaking, roughly equivalent to Mulligan's sacrilegious intonation of the mass during his morning ablutions. The parodic effect of Mulligan's or Stephen's humor depends on the incongruity of an archaic discursive form—the Latin mass, the book of Deuteronomy—when it is displaced onto the banal context of modern everyday life: the morning shave, the touristic outing.

My purpose here is to establish an analogy between the displacement

inherent in the function of parody and the phenomenon in which monumental architectural forms appear dislodged from their original contexts
by the shifting configurations of urban space. Joyce's language combines
discourses of differing historical origins in a manner analogous to the juxtaposition, in modern urban space, of architectural structures originating
in different historical epochs. What I have been calling the parodic effect
in Joyce's language refers to the way a given discourse is objectified as a social form, thereby giving it a second-order concreteness, just as architectural structures exist as concrete objects that acquire different meanings in
their successive social contexts. With Joyce in mind, Adorno speaks of the
twentieth-century avant-garde artwork as a "construction [that] no longer
conceives of itself as an achievement of spontaneous subjectivity. . . . The
whole is composed in structures, put together in each case from a series of
dimensions . . . that appear autonomously, or combined, or ordered hier-
archically" (*Notes* 2:103–4). This kind of art, which organizes within its
own autonomous structure the objective material of social reality, has a social resonance that cannot be attained by works that take society as their
explicit subject matter in the hope of more immediate social effect (2:101).

In the closing pages of the "Scylla and Charybdis" episode (chap. 9) of
Ulysses, Mulligan stops Stephen in the entrance hall of the National Library to chide him about an unfavorable review Stephen has written of a
work by Lady Gregory: "Couldn't you do the Yeats touch?" (9:1159–60).[8]
Whatever Stephen's options might be, Joyce himself cannot do the Yeats
touch for several reasons, including the fact that he can no longer conceive
of the artwork as an achievement of spontaneous subjectivity. Joyce's artistic form, which involves the autonomous (re)structuring of the materials
of historical reality, rejects both the subjective idealism of late romanticism
(Yeats) and the ideology of realism (Zola), which subjects artistic form to
the instrumental rationality of mere social machinery.

Stephen's story of the Dublin matrons has another parodic dimension
with respect to the nineteenth-century convention of the panoramic urban
view. An early example is in *Notre-Dame de Paris* (1832), where Hugo devotes an entire chapter to the sights of Paris to be appreciated from the top
of the towers of the great cathedral. From this vantage point, the narrator's
eye surveys in turn the island *Cité* just below him, the university quarter to
the left, and the larger urban expanse (*la Ville*) on the right bank, noting
all the principal spires, monuments, and avenues (3:2, "Paris à vol
d'oiseau"). The surveying eye is that of an architectural connoisseur:
"Quand on sait voir, on retrouve l'esprit d'un siècle et la physionomie d'un

roi jusque dans un marteau de porte" (When one knows how to look, one finds the spirit of a century and the character of a king even in a door knock) (226). The device of the panoramic view is taken up once more in the famous conclusion to Balzac's *Père Goriot* (1834), where the young Rastignac, having buried the title character, looks down over Paris from the heights of the cemetery of Père-Lachaise: "Les yeux s'attachèrent presque avidemment entre la colonne de la place de Vendôme et le dôme des Invalides, là où vivait ce beau monde dans lequel il avait voulu pénétrer" (His eyes fixed almost greedily between the column of the Place Vendôme and the dome of the Invalides, there where lived the high society into which he had wished to penetrate) (254). In Balzac's metaphor, he seems already to draw the honey from the buzzing hive of the city, to which he addresses an intimate challenge: "A nous deux maintenant!" (Just the two of us now!) (254).

Closer to Joyce in comic spirit, as well as in his exploration of the narrative possibilities of urban space, is Dickens. Yet even here the point of view is panoramic. *Bleak House* (1852–53) begins with a sweeping view of London up and down the banks of the Thames, in which the city is imagined as seen from a balloon. *Our Mutual Friend* (1864–65) strikes a characteristic note in its view over the rooftops of the city: "The towers and steeples of the many house-encompassed churches, dark and dingy as the sky that seems descending on them, are no relief to the general gloom" (393). In everything from urban planning to the great international exhibitions of Paris, London, and Chicago, the nineteenth-century panoramic view was symptomatic of a need to render the city as a "closed and unified spatial order" (Boyer 33), thereby creating the illusion of rational mastery over the aleatory, repressed, and uncontrolled elements of urban space.

Seen in this light, Stephen Dedalus's giddy Dublin spinsters constitute the travesty of an elevated tradition; in their bewilderment and frivolity they announce Joyce's break with the visual and narrative politics of the totalizing view. Joyce's own visual politics, by contrast, are rigorously decentered, presenting a series of local views by a variety of different eyes moving through the streets, not over the rooftops. Imperial monuments thus are seen from ground level and without inspiring the awe intended by their imposing design. This is the case in the concluding lines to "Aeolus," where J. J. O'Molloy "sent a sidelong glance towards the statue," and professor Machugh "halted on Sir John Gray's pavement island and peered aloft at Nelson through the meshes of his wry smile . . .—Onehandled adulterer, he said smiling grimly" (7:1064–72). To borrow another term from Deleuze and Guattari, what Joyce registers here is a movement of *deterritorialization* in the relation between the monument and its shifting context.[9] The pillar has lost both its original context and its original signifying function in a hierarchical and commemorative order, but has been reterritorialized in another order; it has become an intersection, a point in a network whose function is to allow for transit and the possibility of movement from point to point by establishing connections. This image of the shifting network, lifted directly from the configurations of modern urban space, provides a better figure for the nature of Joyce's text than the mastery and dominance of signification inherent in the faded monumental character of the pillar.

The name given by Joyce to episode 10, "Wandering Rocks," itself provides an image for the way in which the monumental and archaic architectural forms of *Ulysses* are dislodged from their original contexts in the shifting configurations of urban space. This chapter is often considered a synecdoche for *Ulysses* as a whole by virtue of its discontinuous yet synchronic form, its function as a compendium of the novel's characters, and its spatial embrace of the city from periphery to center. Given Joyce's almost medieval attention to secret symmetries, it can hardly be an accident that precisely midway through this middle chapter, in the eighth of sixteen sections, we are introduced to "the most historic spot in all Dublin" (10:409), the chapter house of Saint Mary's Abbey on the north bank of the Liffey, founded in 1139 as a monastery of the reformed Savigniac order of the Benedictines and absorbed in 1147 into the Cistercian order.[10] The architectural historian Christine Casey notes the "subterranean grandeur" of the place, which she considers "the most evocative medieval building in the city of Dublin" (86). Among the events it evokes is that in which Thomas Fitzgerald, vice deputy governor of Ireland and known as "Silken Thomas," declared himself a rebel to King Henry VIII in 1534 and launched an unsuccessful attack on Dublin Castle with his small force of rebels. The following year Fitzgerald was captured by the English and, despite a promise of pardon by Leonard Grey, lord deputy of Ireland, was hanged, drawn, and quartered at the Tyburn gallows in London. This is the only historic event explicitly associated with the abbey in *Ulysses,* making its ruins into a symbol of failed rebellion. The quixotic nature of Silken Thomas's revolt would be a feature of later Irish uprisings, notably in 1798 and 1916, the latter being recent in memory when Joyce, then living in Zurich, composed this episode in 1918–19.

In *Ulysses,* however, the hallowed site is presented in a highly ambiguous manner. Sir Humphrey Jervis, lord mayor of Dublin in the seventeenth century, used the abbey as a source of stones for the new building, notably in 1676, of Essex (now Grattan) Bridge, named for Lord Lieutenant Arthur Capel, Earl of Essex. The stones that had served as the site of Silken Thomas's rebellion now served as monuments to British rule. By Joyce's day most of the abbey had disappeared. The chapter house, a simple vaulted chamber seven feet belowground, with Gothic windows in the west facade, served as a grain storage room for Messrs. Alexander and Company, seed merchants. In *Ulysses,* we are introduced to the place by Ned Lambert, an employee of the firm, who is giving a private tour to an Anglican clergyman, the Rev. Hugh C. Love, of Saint Michael's, Sallins. Together, tourist and guide grope in the dark, peering at vaulted arches and Gothic windows obscured by stacks of seed bags while "mouldy air closed round them" (10:404–5). It is a good example of how Joyce renders architecture not only as architectonic structure but also in terms of the subjective experience of interior space. In any case, Mr. Love seems anxious to move on to his next destination, the "Tholsel beyond the ford of hurdles" (10:930).[11] Dublin's most historic spot merits barely more than a passing reference.

If we imagine the history of Dublin as a time-space continuum, Saint Mary's Abbey is the original center outward from which the city has been built over a period of seven centuries. As the site of Silken Thomas's rebellious declaration, it is also the original scene of Irish resistance to the domination of the Crown. For both of these reasons it might have been of capital importance to a novel devoted to the city itself, and to a people in the process of reviving the sense of their own cultural and political destiny. As it is, however, it lies forgotten amid the commercial bustle of modern Dublin, just as it lies buried in the middle of Joyce's work, not to receive mention beyond this brief evocation. Its just recognition remains deferred: "O'Madden Burke is going to write something about it one of these days" (10:410), says Ned Lambert. Elsewhere in the city, at about the same moment, Mulligan remarks disparagingly of Stephen's literary ambitions, "He is going to write something in ten years" (10:1089–90). The project deferred by Stephen is that of forging the uncreated conscience of his race, whereas O'Madden's deferred project is presumably to restore to Saint Mary's Abbey its true historical significance for Dublin. This double deferral anticipates Joyce's own project, in which literary and architectural meanings are closely interrelated; that is, Joyce's work derives form and content from the concrete environment of the city, while it also reinterprets architectural structures according to the realities of contemporary experience. In the meantime, Joyce's narrative interment of the abbey reproduces on a textual level the literal burial of the historic chamber beneath the premises of a thriving business.

As this analogy between textual and architectural burial suggests, there is more at stake here than simply an ironic commentary on contemporary Dublin's indifference to its own history. Let us consider this passage in the light of what Adorno calls the mimetic function of the artwork as a negative semblance (*Schein*). That is, the artwork does not simply imitate reality but also objectifies this mimetic function, thereby disposing of the immediacy of the function and negating it in the name of an autonomous aesthetic (*Aesthetic Theory* 285). The result, in modern writers like Joyce, is a work marked by mutilation, silence, and enigma (*Rätsel*): "If the subject is no longer able to speak directly, then at least it should—in accord with a modernism that has not pledged itself to absolute construction—speak through things, through their alienated and mutilated form" (118). This is the case with *Ulysses*. In the absence of a sovereign speaking subject, it can only speak through things, or through the objectified discourses of its characters. It is for this reason that, in a book designed as the city in textual form, the forgotten origin of Dublin can figure only as an empty space, just as, at the close of the Ithaca chapter, the end of all voyaging and questioning can only figure as a black dot. From this perspective it is significant that, in contrast to the monuments discussed earlier, Saint Mary's abbey survives not above but belowground, its form being literally that of a hole seven feet below street level. By passing over it in near silence, Joyce leaves this hole in the middle of his book as the enigmatic space of Irish remembrance and forgetting. By refusing to fill this absence with historical judgment or ironic accusation, Joyce participates in a historical repression while implicitly calling attention to it, thus rendering manifest the act of forgetting that defines the symbolic order. If for once Joyce resists the temptation to fill an absence, it is because here he must do so in order to signify the absent origin and empty center, the void on which the universe of modern Dublin is constructed.

I have already noted the historical parallels between Silken Thomas's rebellion and the Easter Rebellion led by James Connolly and Patrick Pearse in 1916: both rebellions were amateurish, both were brutally repressed, both created martyrs to the cause of Ireland, and both were associated with architectural sites that became scenes of historic commemoration (the chapter house of Saint Mary's and the General Post Office). Joyce treats both sites in ways that are similarly oblique, ambiguous, and ironic, although there is a difference between these buildings in the temporality of their respective historical meanings. If the symbolic origin of the chapter house, like those of Nelson's pillar and the Martello tower, has been buried under the unceasing movement of the modern metropolis, the General Post Office in 1904 has yet to attain its symbolic importance for Ireland. Its temporal displacement is in relation to the future rather than the past or present. Although it was yet to take place in the Dublin of 1904, the rising would have been, from Joyce's perspective in 1918–19, the most symbolically powerful event of Irish history to have occurred since 1904. Public commemorations of it began in 1917 and continued annually for decades.[12] In writing *Ulysses,* Joyce thus finds himself in the peculiar position of consciously "forgetting" this event, despite its profound impact on Irish national consciousness, in the process of reconstructing a Dublin innocent of the knowledge of what is to come. However, as I shall attempt to show here, the manner of this forgetting produces paradoxical and ambiguous effects.

The General Post Office was built in the classical Georgian style by Francis Johnston in 1814 in the center of O'Connell (then Sackville) Street, adjacent to Nelson's pillar, which Johnston had also designed six years earlier. Thomas Kirk's statue of Nelson atop the pillar was now given the company of three allegorical statues by John Smyth representing Fidelity, Hibernia, and Mercury. These stand above the portico of the Post Office, representing, respectively, the institution's loyalty to the Crown, its service to Ireland, and its function as a swift messenger of intelligence. The Post Office, like the chapter house of Saint Mary's Abbey, figures only briefly and somewhat obliquely in *Ulysses.* There are only two references to it. In the "Aeolus" episode the Post Office figures under the heading "The Wearer of the Crown," an allusion to Edward VII, whose initials, E. R. (for Edward Rex), are painted on the vermilion mail cars parked in front of the building. Within the space of the building itself, however, the central figures are "shoeblacks" described as calling and polishing (7:15) on the porch of the building. One of them appears later, in the "Ithaca" episode, in the series naming the imagined lovers of Molly Bloom (17:2141). From the post-1916 perspective these bootblacks, having appropriated the space of the porch for their lowly trade, perform a double historical function: on one hand, they prefigure ironically the volunteers who, in their ill-fated occupation of the Post Office twelve years later, would, in the words of Yeats's poem, "transform utterly" the cause of Ireland, "wherever green is worn"

(*Collected* 179). On the other hand, the humble bootblacks are all that remains of that rebellion in the sense that its memory has "disappeared" from the novel by virtue of the erasure of Irish history in the eighteen-year gap between the novel's setting and its publication. This double function has the paradoxical effect of both commemorating and cancelling the memory of the Easter Rising, which appears here in a form that Derrida would call *sous rature,* or "under cancellation." What is at issue here is the pressure of recent but unnamed historical events on the act of reading. By way of analogy, it is as if the initial stages of the French Revolution had failed and a novel published in 1795 but set in the Paris of the year 1777 were to make passing mention, as part of the general decor, of street urchins capering in the Place de la Bastille. Joyce's passing, ironic reference to the Post Office pointedly avoids the temptation to dwell on the site as the future (and, from the reader's historical point of view, past) scene of Irish martyrdom, a strategy that amounts to another refusal to "do the Yeats touch." However, for readers in whom the memory of 1916 is still recent, behind the shoeblacks under the porch of the General Post Office are the spectral presences of MacDonagh and MacBride, Connolly and Pearse.[13] In the first draft of what became known as the "Mamalujo" episode of *Finnegans Wake,* published in Ford Madox Ford's *Transatlantic Review* in 1924, Joyce imagines that the early colleges of Ireland taught "history past and present and present and absent."[14] His portrayal of the General Post Office and the chapter house of Saint Mary's Abbey can be read in this spirit as lessons in absent history.

What all of the architectural structures discussed so far have in common is at least an original function of territorializing the space of the city. The Martello tower marks a boundary and establishes a fortification. Nelson's pillar marks a center and a vertical mastery of the city while regulating historical memory in its memorial function. Saint Mary's Abbey, however forgotten, marks an origin and a more ancient center than that of the pillar, having been founded on the institution of the Church rather than the empire. The General Post Office is the city's center of communication, through which passes all manner of "letters, postcards, lettercards, parcels, insured and paid, for local, provincial, British and overseas delivery" (7:18–19). Together, these structures serve as crucial points in a network of institutional power over the time and space of the city. Against the ideally stable presence of these structures, Joyce's novel opposes the forces of movement that equally define the space of the city: the flow of traffic, the bustle of commerce, the steady deterioration and reconstruction of buildings, the drift of debris, the deambulation of aimless strollers and vagrants. From this perspective, the cabman's shelter of the "Eumaeus" episode (chap. 16) occupies a unique place in the architectural logic of Joyce's Dublin: a lightly constructed, temporary building, open to the heterogeneous population of night wanderers and, like Bloom's ideal poster novelty, "reduced to its simplest and most efficient terms . . . and congruous with the velocity of modern life" (17:1771–3).

During the latter half of the nineteenth century, cabman's shelters were constructed in most of the major cities of the British Empire. They were inspired and often directly managed by temperance organizations such as the Irish Temperance League, founded in 1858 by Fr. Theobald Mathew, whose statue on O'Connell Street Blazes Boylan passes on the way to his assignation with Molly Bloom in Eccles Street (11:763). The shelters served coffee and other nonalcoholic beverages to cabmen and other travelers. They were of modular construction comprising light wooden panels, with molded wooden strapping covering the panel joints. Without foundation, they simply rested on the pavement and could be moved from one location to another. A photograph in the Keogh collection of the National Photographic Archive (fig. 10) indicates that the shelter standing under the Loop Line Bridge in Joyce's day was approximately three meters high and about four to five meters long, with a pitched roof. This photograph was taken in 1917 during a protest demonstration over the arrest of George Noble, Count Plunkett, whose son Joseph Mary had been executed for his role in the Easter Rising. The date of the photograph, together with its location, allows us to surmise that this is the shelter that figures in *Ulysses*. In this image it appears almost buoyant, seeming to float on the sea of humanity surrounding it in Beresford Place. An enhancement of the photograph has shown that the lettering along its ridgepole reads, "Branch of the Dublin Coffee Palace Hotel 6 Townsend Street."[15] Bloom has characteristically skeptical views on "the Coffee Palace and its temperance (lucrative) work." On the one hand, he believes "a world of good" is done by "shelters such as the present one . . . run on teetotal lines for vagrants at night." On the other hand, the Coffee Palace paid his wife "a very modest remuneration indeed for her pianoplaying. The idea, he was strongly inclined to believe, was to do good and net a profit, there being no competition to speak of" (16:791–801). As for the refreshment served at the shelter, Bloom finds it to be an "untastable apology for a cup of coffee" (16:1141).

What I wish to emphasize, however, is the place of the cabman's shelter in Joyce's narrative and the architectural landscape of *Ulysses*. The episode

Fig. 10. A cabman's shelter in Dublin, shown here in 1917 adjacent to the railway next to the Custom House. In its place there is now a statue of John Connolly, the hero of the 1916 Easter Rising. (National Photographic Archive, Dublin.)

in which it figures is primarily transitional, taking place on the way between the drunken excesses of "Circe" and the sober interrogations of "Ithaca." In the nocturnal wanderings of Bloom and Stephen the shelter is only a temporary destination, sought for the relief of Stephen's thirst after his altercation with the soldiers. It serves as a stopping-off point between the brothel district of Tyrone Street and Bloom's home in Eccles Street. In keeping with the nature of its place on this itinerary, everything about the cabman's shelter is temporary, beginning with its construction, described as that of an "unpretentious wooden structure" (16:321). It can be categorized as an early example of what the anthropologist Marc Augé calls a *non-lieu,* or "nonplace," that is, a space of passage whose principal characteristic is its provisional and ephemeral nature, and where human relations exist, if at all, purely by chance. Hotel chains, squats, vacation resorts, refugee camps, and shantytowns are contemporary examples (100). Among the "decidedly miscellaneous collection of waifs and strays" (16:327–29) to be found in the shelter, the one acquaintance made by Stephen and Bloom is that of the sailor D. B. Murphy, himself a transient figure of dubious veracity and provenance. Even the famous rhetorical fatigue of this episode seems to derive from a certain lack of structure and purpose, as if language itself had been torn loose from its foundations and cast adrift in a Sargasso Sea of worn-out phrases and received ideas.

Among these ideas is the affirmation by a cabman that Charles Stewart Parnell, the late hero of the Home Rule cause, is not dead but has gone into hiding after the attacks against him by church and state: "Dead he wasn't. Simply absconded somewhere. The coffin they brought over was full of stones" (16:1304–05). In this way Joyce reintroduces the motif of the coffin, to be evoked twice more in "Eumaeus" as a kind of counterpart to the "unpretentious wooden structure" in which the conversation takes place.[16] The cabman's statement echoes one made in the "Hades" episode, where Mr. Power speaks in awe before Parnell's tomb at Glasnevin cemetery: "Some say he is not in that grave at all. That the coffin was filled with stones. That one day he will come again" (6:923–24). In that episode Bloom has speculated on the insulating capacities of the casket, noting that "The Irishman's house is his coffin" (6:820), thus calling attention to the architectural nature and function of the coffin: like the cabman's shelter, it is simply constructed, movable and designed for human passage. And, in the case of both structures, the occupant's final destination is the same.

To concentrate solely on the fatigue and the endgame strategy of the Eumaeus episode, however, would be to miss the spontaneous expressions of mutual confidence that it affords, for the first time, between the two main characters of *Ulysses,* as well as the invitation proffered by Bloom to a hungry and homeless Stephen: "you just come home with me and talk things over" (16:1644–45). The unpretentious and improvised nature of the shelter, visited on an impulse in the middle of the night, is the perfect setting for the spontaneity and freedom marking the nascent friendship between the two men. In architectural terms, the cabman's shelter belongs to a modernist movement of countermonumentality opposed to the traditional model of buildings firmly rooted in the earth by deep foundations and thick walls. It has affinities with what Anthony Vidler, in *The Architectural Uncanny,* calls "vagabond architecture" (207–14) and with what Deleuze and Guattari call the architecture of "nomadic knowledge" (*Mille plateaux* 447). According to their *traité de nomadologie,* the model of the nomadic is that of becoming and heterogeneity, as opposed to the stable, the eternal, the constant, and the same. As with the model of deterritorialization, the loss of rootedness and foundations becomes, under the right circumstances, a gain in possibilities for connection, relation, and incident.

Architecturally, nomadology perfects the art of camps as against the monuments of the state and the church. It comprises a series of "sciences ambulantes, itinérantes, qui consistent à suivre un flux dans un champ de vecteurs où des singularités se répartissent comme autant d'accidents" (460), ambulant and itinerant forms of knowledge that follow a flow through a field of vectors where singularities distribute themselves like so many accidents. As an instance of the architecture of nomadology, the cab-man's shelter lends itself to a singular occurrence: for the first time in the course of the narrative both Bloom and Stephen, in exchanging their respective histories, experience a turn toward the Other, and therefore the possibility of a new relation. The rhetorical and experiential exhaustion of this episode is in fact that of the arrival at a limit, the going beyond that creates an opening for chance, for incident, for a sudden change in the nature of things, and thus of promise.[17] In their celebration of the nomadic, Deleuze and Guattari echo Maurice Blanchot's affirmation, in *L'Entretien infini* (1969) of Jewish exile and exodus as ways of being. Nomadism, says Blanchot, calls into question existing distributions of space by appealing to the initiatives of human movement. If cultural rootedness and the acceptance of things as they are do not suffice, it is because the order of reality imposed by rootedness does not hold the key to everything to which we are called to respond:

> [S]i s'enraciner dans la culture et la considération des choses ne suffit pas, c'est que l'ordre des réalités où il y a enracinement ne détient pas la clé de tous les rapports auxquels nous devons répondre. (186)

An unpretentious, rootless structure found as a way station in a night of wandering, the cabman's shelter belongs to the logic of exile and exodus, which is also a logic of promise, promise differently embodied in the persons of Bloom and Stephen.

It is in this respect that the cabman's shelter is to be distinguished on a symbolic level from the conventional architecture of state and ecclesiastical institutions. Where Joyce's novel exposes the disjunctures between monumental design and the exigencies of the actual historical moment, the cabman's shelter is entirely adaptable to the flow of the historical present, thus representing a freedom from the weightily rooted edifices of class, religion, law, and language. As an example of antimonumental nomadic architecture, the form of the cabman's shelter thus has certain affinities with the form of Joyce's book, conceived as a heterogeneous textual assemblage constructed out of the protean language of a city in motion, a form opposed to the monumental character that has been imposed on the epic from which this book takes its name.

Architecture in Frost and Stevens

In a passage made famous by Martin Heidegger, Friedrich Hölderlin proclaims:

Voll Verdienst, doch dichterisch wohnet Der Mensch auf dieser Erde.[1]

Full of merit, yet poetically, man dwells on this earth.

The lines are from a poem that makes a romantic statement of the traditional analogy between poetry and architecture, and they are cited as the occasion for one of Heidegger's essays ("Poetically Man Dwells," in *Poetry, Language, Thought*) on the nature of dwelling, another of which was discussed in the first chapter of this book. Hölderlin's lines allow Heidegger to treat poetic creation as a kind of building but also to reflect on the nature of dwelling made possible by this construction. *Dwelling,* or *das Wohnen,* as we have seen, is Heidegger's word for "man's stay on earth," a sojourn marked out in time by the limits of birth and death, and in space by the expanse between earth and heaven. As the human experience of these dimensions is formed in language, poetry is the art that is capable of taking their measure, and thereby the measure of human being in the world. For the poet, language is far from being a prison house. On the contrary, the poet constructs an authentic relation to language, and thereby to being itself, by remaining open to its inherent possibilities, its unforeseen disclosures.

In this chapter I wish to take Heidegger's citation of Hölderlin as a point of departure for a study of architectural figures in the philosopher's American contemporaries Robert Frost and Wallace Stevens. My reading of their poems takes place on two levels. One is the analysis of the architectural construction as a poetic image. A precedent for such an analysis is to be found in the work of Freud and Bachelard, both of whom explore the symbolic content of the image of the house as it occurs in dreams or poems. The architectural images that draw my attention, though, are not limited to houses: they include other constructions, such as the woodpile or the stone wall, because these, too, are part of the built environment with which the poet is concerned. The second level of my reading goes beyond the poetic image in order to show that the relation between poetry and architecture is more fundamental than that of mere representation. Both are primordial forms of making, for poetry does with the material of language what architecture does with the materials of the earth. Is the relation between poetry and architecture an especially privileged one when compared to that which exists between other art forms, such as painting and music? Heidegger would have it so, based on the notion of dwelling, which he sees as belonging especially to these arts. Frost and Stevens offer their own, modern versions of the analogy between poetry and architecture; for both poets, the poem is a construction that also serves in some sense as a place of dwelling. As I shall attempt to show, however, the difference between the two poets lies in the respective meanings they assign to this dwelling in relation to the more universal conditions of being. For Frost, the poetic, like the human habitation, serves only as a temporary refuge from the surrounding chaos. For Stevens, the construction of a dwelling place for the imagination is likewise necessary to being; but the risk is that the imposed order of such a construction will stand in the way of the poet's pursuit of discovery.

The notion of dwelling is already familiar to a certain "Heideggerian" tradition of reading American poetry. I shall cite just two examples, both from influential critics. In his book on Frost, Frank Lentricchia reads the poet according to what he refers to as the Heideggerian notion that "the world is our home, our habitat, the materialization of our subjectivity" (4).[2] Similarly, in an essay on Stevens and Heidegger, Frank Kermode writes, "The place where the poet dwells, especially if it is his place of origin, will be his *mundo,* a clarified analogy of the earth he has lived in" (262).[3] In both cases, the notion of dwelling is given a reassuring plenitude, as if a perfect synthesis were possible between the poet and his world. To my way of thinking, however, such approaches fail to take account of a tension already present within Heidegger's thought between dwelling and its impossibility, a tension also characteristic of Frost and Stevens. This is apparent, for example, in the difference between Heidegger's claim that dwelling is the "*basic character* of Being" and his assertion that the "real plight of dwelling" is that human beings "ever search anew for the nature of dwelling, that they *must ever learn to dwell*" ("Building Dwelling Thinking" 160–61, emphasis in original). To this ambiguity within the concept of dwelling itself must be added the problematic nature of this ideal under the specific conditions of modernity. According to Adorno, these conditions have effectively put an end to the myth of dwelling: "Dwelling, in the proper sense, is now impossible" (*Minima Moralia* 38). "The world is no longer habitable . . . the heavy shadow of instability bears upon built form" ("Functionalism Today" 12).

Given what I take to be an inherent instability in the concept of dwelling, my approach to the architectural imagery of Frost and Stevens is closer to that of contemporary theorists such as Mark Wigley and Jacques Soullilou, for both of whom architectural meaning is inevitably involved with loss and spectrality. Wigley writes, "A house is only a house inasmuch as it is haunted" (162), whereas for Soullilou, "Le spectral est ce qui traverse l'habiter et le non-habiter architectural, rend leur destin solitaire, et défait cette opposition aussitôt qu'elle essaie de se reconstituer" (The spectral is that which is common to architectural dwelling and nondwelling, which gives them a common destiny and which undoes the opposition between them even as this opposition attempts to reconstitute itself) (75). An illustration of this principle is to be found in Frost's early poem "Ghost House" (1913), which begins:

> I dwell in a lonely house I know
> That vanished many a summer ago.

The poem goes on to describe a place where all that remains of the house are the cellar walls, now overgrown with wild raspberries, and the gravestones bearing names rendered unreadable by layers of moss. The mute and nameless persons buried there are the poet's only human companions, "tireless folk, but slow and sad." "Ghost House" is a poem in which the notion of dwelling as a poetic and spiritual condition depends, paradoxically, on the loss of the dwelling as a physical structure—a "vanished abode"—as well as on the spectral presence of its vanished inhabitants.

If the notion of spectrality is a part of the problematics of dwelling, it also serves as a way into the reading of other images of architectural building, such as Frost's wells, chimneys, stone walls, and woodpiles. Let us consider one of Frost's best-known poems, "Mending Wall" (1914). Everyone is familiar with the argument of this poem: even a stone wall is subject to constant deterioration, and therefore the poem's speaker meets yearly with his neighbor for the purpose of mending the wall that lies between their lands. The labor of mending the wall is at first described in almost technical detail, but then, in another tone, is dismissed as "just another kind of outdoor game." In a mischievous mood, the speaker attempts to convince his old-fashioned neighbor that their labor is useless, only to receive the repeated answer, "Good fences make good neighbors."

The poem is often read as a bemused affirmation of a quaint piece of folk wisdom. But this is to miss the dimension of the poem that is devoted to the art of building. The thematics of building allow us to see the mending of the wall both as a metaphor for poetic composition and as a ritual devoted to the spectral presences for which the wall serves as a monument. Although these two aspects of the poem are closely related, for the sake of clarity I shall take each of them in turn. The poetic analogy begins to be apparent when we notice that, running between the two neighbors, the wall forms a "line" in which the gaps must be filled by putting stone on stone, in a work that demands strength, skill, and even sortilege: "We have to use a spell to make them balance." Words like *spell* and *balance,* with their connotations of poetic art, call attention to the allegorical function of this work. Rebuilding the wall is analogous to writing the poem: the stone is to the length of the wall what the word is to the poetic line: its basic unit of construction. The precarious fitting and balancing of stones serves as an allegory for the art of combining words in poetic syntax. The orderly rhythm of the mending work, as

> . . . on a day we meet to walk the line
> And set the wall between us once again

matches perfectly the regular iambic pentameter of Frost's poetic line.

The second half of the poem, in which the speaker tries unsuccessfully to make his neighbor admit the uselessness of the wall,

> There where it is we do not need the wall.
> He is all pine and I am apple orchard

serves only to reaffirm the wall's aesthetic value, its status, like that of the poem itself, as a work of art: if it is lacking in any immediate practical use, it is nonetheless the object of constant labor and care on the part of its adepts.

To say the wall is useless, however, is not to say that it is meaningless. On the contrary, Frost insists on the inscription of the wall within a world of ritual and spectral presences, beginning with the mysterious "something" that doesn't love a wall, a destructive force that inheres within the logic of its ceaseless reconstruction. This something makes "gaps" in the wall that are doubly negative: figures of lack in themselves, they lack witnesses to their origins, as "No one has seen them or heard them made," and yet there they are at spring mending time: gaping absences within the promised fullness of the new season. The wall also has a sepulchral function, as a kind of memorial to the generations from which it is inherited, just as the "saying" of the neighbor is inherited from his father, and the ritual repetition of this saying accompanies the annual rite of wall mending. In the enactment of this ritual, the neighbor himself assumes a spectral aspect. Like "an old-stone savage armed,"

He moves in darkness as it seems to me,
Not of woods only and the shade of trees.

Trapped in an endless repetition of speech and gesture, the neighbor is himself a haunted and haunting figure, already joined with the dead who built the wall. His spectrality combines with the poem's mysterious forces of destruction to cast a shadow equally over the acts of building and unbuilding, mending and coming undone. The wall stands at the threshold between the living and the dead, marking the boundary between them, yet bringing them into confused intercourse.

Frost's famous definition of poetry as "a momentary stay against confusion" ("Figure" 18) makes explicit the connection between the poem and the wall—*this* wall, in constant need of mending because of all the forces set against it: the frozen groundswell, the work of hunters, the sheer pull of gravity. Frost suggests that an equally imposing set of forces threatens to destroy the art of poetry, with its roots in incantation and communion with the dead. The work of the poet, then, is one of building an extremely fragile shelter against the constant threat of destruction.

From the same volume as "Mending Wall," "The Wood-Pile" also contemplates a built object, which, in its location, serves no apparent purpose. A good deal of this poem's effect depends on the approach to the object, in winter, across a frozen and unknown terrain. At the poem's beginning, the speaker has already reached a limit from which he wants to turn back, but then he changes his mind: "No, I will go on farther, and we shall see." He loses himself in a place he can only locate as "far from

home." Frost's poems often mark this boundary between known and unknown spaces, but, as in "Stopping by Woods on a Snowy Evening," he
usually turns back before crossing the threshold. In this case, however, the
passage into the unknown is rewarded by the strange sight of a woodpile
too far from any fireplace to be of use. Here is something familiar yet, *in
this place,* completely unforeseen. One of the strengths of Frost's poetry is
its concrete sense of the human body at work in the place and with the
things that belong to that work. His poems evoke the feel of the ax, the
saw, and the scythe: the world of things ready-to-hand that Heidegger
calls *Zuhandenheit.* The woodpile lost in the midst of the forest constitutes a radical displacement of that world, one that makes the object itself
into an enigma.

As if attempting to dispel this enigma, Frost dwells on the materiality
and architectural construction of his object with the same intensity of observation given, in the earlier poem, to the stone wall.

> It was a cord of maple, cut and split
> And piled—and measured, four by four by eight.

Signs of the skilled handiwork that went into making the woodpile, however, are seen simultaneously with signs of its decay.

> The wood was gray and the bark warping off it
> And the pile somewhat sunken.

To account for the woodpile's presence so far from any human habitation,
the poem offers the only possible explanation: that it represents the forgotten labor of "someone who lived in turning to fresh tasks." But this
does not dispel the mystery of the woodpile, which remains haunted by
the specter of its builder, the invisible agent whose body is nonetheless
evoked in the marks of his handiwork and the "labor of his axe," some
ghostly woodman "who lived" and "who spent himself." In the presence of
this absent figure, the woodpile acquires an uncanny, sepulchral monumentality, grown over with clematis like a classical temple in ruins. Yet the
woodpile itself is also a dying thing, forsaking its monumental function as
it sinks into the earth, left

> To warm the frozen swamp as best it could
> With the slow smokeless burning of decay.

By ending on these lines, the text of the poem sinks into the same decay as
the object it elegizes. Once again, the built object, like the poem, stands as

a symbol of order in the midst of the wilderness, but faced with inexorable forces of destruction, its stay against confusion is only momentary.

Curiously, the wall and the woodpile seem to have more life in them than the human habitations in Frost's poems. In spite of his homespun persona, there is an almost total absence of domesticity in Frost. His houses are invariably lonely, deserted places, like that of "The Census-Taker" (1923). In this poem, as in "The Wood-Pile," the speaker must traverse a lost and empty space before finding his object. But this one is less an object of wonder than of despair.

> . . . a slab-built, black-paper-covered house
> Of one room and one window and one door,
> The only dwelling in a waste cut over
> A hundred square miles round it in the mountains.

In contrast to the woodpile, which at least testifies to the skill of its maker, this deserted house is the very figure of absence, emptiness, and negation: the words *none* and *nothing* resound throughout the poem as if echoing across the barren scene: "An emptiness flayed to the very stone." But not content with this manifest absence, the census-taker must penetrate to the very heart of this emptiness by crossing the threshold into the house.

> No lamp was lit. Nothing was on the table.
> The stove was cold—the stove was off the chimney
> And down by one side where it lacked a leg.

The absence of human life is testified to by the lack of human light and warmth: there remain only the worn-out relics of dwelling.

In its concluding lines, the poem changes register, from the census-taker's observations to the poet's private emotion.

> This house in one year fallen to decay
> Filled me with no less sorrow than the houses
> Fallen to ruin in ten thousand years
> Where Asia wedges Africa from Europe.

The reference to the "Old World" is rare enough in Frost to call for a close examination of its place here. The sorrow occasioned by the deserted house is "no less" than that inspired by ancient ruins, but it is the same kind of sorrow? Frost does not say. The traditional mode for the contemplation of ancient ruins is elegiac: Gibbon musing on the Roman Forum,

Wordsworth communing with the spirits of Stonehenge, Byron moved by the sight of Drachenfels,

> And chiefless castles breathing stern farewells
> From gray but leafy walls, where Ruin greenly dwells.
> (*Childe Harold's Pilgrimage* III:46)

But Frost's is no romantic melancholy. His ruin is unredeemed by elegy or by any lofty sense of the spirit's elevation over the ravages of time. It is instead an image of pure negativity and relentless diminishment, "where souls grow fewer and fewer every year." If, according to Shakespeare, the poet "gives to airy nothing a local habitation and a name," then Frost seems to work in the opposite direction, giving to human habitation the name of nothingness. Readers of Jacques Lacan are familiar with the notion that lack is the necessary condition of desire, and indeed for Frost this nothingness, this emptiness at the center, is the condition for the writing of the poem, an act that, in the poem's concluding line, he consciously equates with desire: "It must be that I want life to go on living."

New Hampshire (1923), the volume in which "The Census-Taker" appears, closes with another poem on the ruin of human habitation, "The Need of Being Versed in Country Things." Here the scene is of a farmhouse that has burned down, leaving only the chimney to stand. The barn across the way has escaped the fire but remains deserted; birds fly in and out of its broken windows,

> Their murmurs more like the sigh we sigh
> From too much dwelling on what has been.

The ruins of the farm seem to support this attribution of human sorrow to the things of the object-world: the dry pump flinging up an awkward arm, the fence post still carrying a strand of wire. But the poem nonetheless seems resolved not to dwell on the loss of the dwelling that this place has been. Rather, to be versed in country things means to write verse that resigns the nostalgia for human dwelling in favor of the detachment of the natural world, represented here by the indifference of the birds: "For them there was really nothing sad."

The "verse" of the poem itself constitutes the needed compensation for the destruction of human dwelling: a more durable structure than the one forsaken here. The wisdom conveyed by the verse is the only proof against the sentimentalism of the pathetic fallacy.

One had to be versed in country things
Not to believe the phoebes wept.

Concluding his volume with these lines, Frost anticipates, in thought and even in syntactical form, the argument of Stevens's poem "The Snow Man" (1923), in which "one must have a mind of winter" to regard the frozen landscape

> . . . and not to think
> Of any misery in the sound of the wind.

That is to say, according to the privileged knowledge celebrated in Frost's poem, the phoebes do not mourn the loss of the house, just as in Stevens's poem the wind, mournful as it may sound, has nothing to do with misery. But Stevens takes the logic of this idea one step further: in a consummation of detachment, the snowman not only recognizes that there is no mourning of human loss in nature; he also recognizes the radical nothingness that is common both to the desolate landscape and to himself. He himself is nothing because the "self" is as much a fiction as the notion of mourning in nature. This nothingness is the condition for the poem, whose function is simultaneously to cover and discover the void on which it is founded.

Stevens's affinity with Frost lies in such interrogations or measurements of the conditions of being, conditions that, in Stevens as well, often figure in the form of human dwellings. In his reading of Hölderlin, Heidegger makes the point that as human beings we are human only insofar as we have the capacity to measure ourselves "with and against something heavenly" (221). Because of the nature of their materials, poetry and architecture are privileged among the arts in their capacity to make this measurement, one that takes the form of building, whether as the great cathedrals of Europe or as the monuments of poetic art. In terms of this discourse, which joins poetry and architecture to the definition of the human being in relation to the divine (or to the absence of the divine), Stevens stands squarely within the tradition that runs from Hölderlin through Nietzsche to Heidegger, even if his more obvious debts are to French symbolism.

Stevens's most direct statement of the analogy between poetry and architecture is precisely that which seeks to define the human in relation to the heavenly. In "A High-Toned Old Christian Woman" (*Harmonium*, 1923), the person named in the title is addressed in the poem, which opens with the bold claim that "Poetry is the supreme fiction, madame." The dif-

ference between poetry and the Judeo-Christian "moral law" is illustrated
in the form of architectural metaphors. On one hand, out of the moral law
one can make a nave, "And from the nave build haunted heaven." The
nave is the western extension of a Christian church, traditionally built in
the form of a Roman cross. The moral aspiration toward heaven is figured
here as a purely vertical construction, like the cathedrals of the late Middle
Ages. On the other hand, out of the "opposing law" of poetry one can
make a peristyle,

> And from the peristyle project a masque
> Beyond the planets.

The image here is of classical, pagan architecture, a peristyle being a row of
columns surrounding a temple. Its construction is not vertical but built
outward from the center, and it is by following this expansive movement
to its utmost that the "masque" of imagination is projected beyond the
planets. The two constructions have the effect of converting "conscience"
and "our bawdiness," respectively, into palms: the palms of Jerusalem with
all their history of martyrdom, and the more luxuriant palms of Florida,
the place of a new paganism in the geography of Stevens's imagination. It
is these Floridian palms that stand for the imagination liberated from the
self-flagellation of Christian conscience, and for the universe of Stevens's
poetry. Poetry is thus supreme in its superior freedom, the freedom of
"fictive things" that "wink as they will."

"A High-Toned Old Christian Woman" is a more incisive version of the
longer poem "Architecture," written in 1918 but not published in Stevens's
lifetime.[4] The initial lines of the first two stanzas of this poem pose questions that are characteristic of Stevens's conception of poetry in terms of architectural form. The first asks "What manner of building shall we build?"
and the second "In this house, what manner of utterance shall there be?"
The first question is answered four stanzas later with the image of a "building of light" with towers, "Which, like a gorgeous palm, / Shall tuft the
commonplace," and with "Our chiefest dome a demoiselle of gold." The
poem ends with the injunction that only "the lusty and the plenteous"
shall walk "The bronzed-filled plazas / And the nut-shell esplanades." But
the poem never answers the other question, that of the "manner of utterance" or "what shall the speech be" best suited to this stately pleasure
dome. In other words, Stevens conceives of his artistic project as an imaginary edifice to be inhabited by or made out of language, but he still
doesn't know what kind of language that will be. The poem's failure to ad-

equately address this question, which after all was absolutely crucial for Stevens at this point in his poetic career, may be why he never chose to publish "Architecture." In this respect "A High-Toned Old Christian Woman," written in 1922, may be considered a refinement on the earlier poem. In the later poem, Stevens preserves the analogy between poetry and architecture but reestablishes the poetic question as central, while sharpening the dialectic by setting up the contest of styles between the outward-projecting peristyle of poetry and the haunted nave of religion. The outcome of that contest, as we have seen, is both a declaration of poetry's supremacy and at least a provisional answer to the question of 1918: "what manner of utterance?" The poet's speech shall henceforth bear testimony to "Our bawdiness . . . indulged at last."

The spatial opposition between Christian verticality and pagan expansion that we find in this poem is succeeded by more ambiguous architectural forms in Stevens's next book, *Ideas of Order* (1935). The central image of "Academic Discourse at Havana" is an old casino. A casino is an ornamental summer house used for dancing and other forms of public amusement; it is a fragile, ephemeral structure, offering little resistance to the ruins of time and the elements. Like the peristyle, Stevens's casino has stood at the center of an outward-expanding universe, surrounded by fountains and lakes adorned with swans and island canopies. But now the bills of the swans lie flat upon the ground, the windows of the casino are boarded up, and "a grand decadence settles down like cold." This is Stevens's language for the degraded historical present, where "Life is an old casino in a park," no longer inspired by the myths of Jehovah, Leviathan, or the nightingale, nor even by the swans that graced the twilight of these gods.

In this burgher's world unmoved by anything greater than "Grandmother and her basketful of pears," can the old casino nonetheless signify in some subtler way, in the tradition of an *architecture parlante*?[5] The decrepit structure is, after all, Stevens's metaphor for life. However, the precise nature of the relation between the old casino and "life" can be defined only by considering the function of the poet in the spiritually impoverished world evoked in the poem. "Is the function of the poet here mere sound," like "the sooth / Of trombones floating in the trees," or does he have some more redeeming role to play? Hölderlin asked the same question in his elegy "Brod und Wein" (1801): "[W]ozu Dichter in dürftiger Zeit?" (What are poets for in a destitute time?). His answer is interpreted by Heidegger as follows: "To be a poet in a destitute time means: to attend, singing, to the trace of the fugitive gods" (94). This does not mean that the poet is merely a figure of mourning for the departed gods. Rather, it means that the destitution of the present age has made "the whole being and vocation of the poet a poetic question for him" (94). In other words, the function of the poet, and not the celebration of the divine, has become the central preoccupation of poetry.

Something like this is at stake in the haunting conclusion to Stevens's poem. On one hand Stevens says, in a formulation that combines rhetorical genre with architecture, that the poet's speech may be mere "benediction, sepulcher, and epitaph." But it may also be

> An incantation that the moon defines
> By mere example opulently clear.

As a conventional poetic image, the moon belongs to that now defunct repertoire of the nightingale and the swan. But without having lost all the luster of this faded mythology, Stevens's moon is also "part of nature," an object giving concrete definition to the poet's speech by the mere example of its reflected radiance. The poetic mode here is enchantment rather than epitaph, a spell that depends on the moon's wavering status between dead myth and present, shining thing. The poem closes with a return to the casino.

> And the old casino likewise may define
> An infinite incantation of our selves
> In the grand decadence of the perished swans.

The analogy is as follows: the moon is to the poet as the casino is to our selves. Both objects, one natural and the other architectural, give concrete form and visual definition to an incantation, that is, a speech of enchantment rather than prayer, born of a kind of reverse sublime in which the human imagination, infinite in capacity, confronts a diminished world. The old casino figures forth that diminishment, but its emptiness is not the existential black hole of Frost's deserted houses. Rather, its very shabbiness resonates in mute testimony to the permanence of human desire. Too melancholy for comedy, too insubstantial for tragedy, the old casino yet stands as an image sufficiently fitting of the present age to "reconcile us to our selves."

Stevens's *ars poetica* is "Notes toward a Supreme Fiction," from the 1947 volume *Transport to Summer*. It is a poem that traces the origins of poetry to the tension between dwelling and nondwelling, to an originary estrangement from the place of "our" (i.e., human) habitation.

From this the poem springs: that we live in a place
That is not our own and, much more, not ourselves
And hard it is in spite of blazoned days.

This is the difference between us and wild animals: the spontaneous cries of the lion, the elephant, and the bear are all at one with their natural habitats. But the person addressed in the poem cannot manage such ease of speech. From his attic window, his "mansard with a rented piano," he looks out over the neighboring rooftops and remains painfully mute, or at best manages a "bitter utterance."

The question is whether the poet can build a world as perfect for the human as the mountain is for the bear or the forests of Ceylon for the elephant.

Can we compose a castle-fortress-home,
Even with the help of Viollet-le-Duc
And set the MacCullough there as major man?

Perhaps Viollet-le-Duc figures here merely as a famous architect with an elegant name. But for those who know his career, the passage has a special resonance. As we have seen in a previous chapter, Viollet was the great nineteenth-century restorer of medieval architecture, but in the process he often altered the original structure according to his own supreme fiction of the Gothic. One of his most ambitious projects was the restoration of Pierrefonds, the twelfth-century *château-fort* that he converted into a summer residence for the bourgeois emperor Napoléon III. As it happened, the emperor did not feel wholly at ease at Pierrefonds, and never adopted it as a residence; the MacCullough never took possession of his castle-fortress-home. In Stevens as well, the question of man's accession to speech as strong and spontaneous as the "power of the wave" is left open; it is a speech only to be imagined. Toward the end of the poem, the Canon Aspirin, a figure for the poet's intellect, attempts to order his world the way a classical architect does: "He imposes order as he thinks of them" and "Next he builds capitols and in their corridors . . . He establishes statues of reasonable men." But unlike the architecture of the peristyle, this institutionalized order will not do. The problem is that "to impose is not / To discover," and for Stevens the poet must find his orders, not impose them. The possibility of such discovery is held out against the inauthenticity of dwelling in a built environment constructed as an order of imposition.

In one of his last poems, Stevens is capable of imagining a perfect form of dwelling through the figure of the threshold. "To an Old Philosopher in Rome" (1952) was written in memory of George Santayana, who chose to spend his last days in the austere lodgings of a Roman convent, the hospice of the Santo Stefano Rotondo on Monte Celio.[6] The Basilica of Santo Stefano itself, built in the fifth century as a series of concentric circles around a central peristyle, is perfectly suited to the structures of Stevens's poetic imagination. In its spirit, as well as its use of architecture, both as concrete image and as metaphor for the structures of human imagination, Stevens's poem has affinities with Heidegger's essay "The Origin of the Work of Art" ("Der Ursprung des Kunstwerkes," 1935–36), where the form of the Greek temple serves the function that, in Stevens, is served by the convent and the dome of the city around it. Heidegger writes:

> The temple-work, standing there, opens up a world and at the same time sets this world back again on earth, which itself only thus emerges as native ground. (*Poetry, Language, Thought* 42)

The temple brings the landscape and the human world around it into an "open relational context" (*offenen Bezüge*), which represents not an imposition of order but rather the conditions under which the historical meaning of a people is made possible: as a work of art it both "fits together" and "gathers around itself" the world. The temple serves as a threshold between nonbeing and being in the sense that it "opens up a *world* and keeps it abidingly in place" (44, emphasis in original).

The threshold of Stevens's poem is Rome itself as it is lived by the old philosopher, "On the threshold of heaven," which is that "more merciful Rome beyond." It is not, however, a question of passing from this world into the next but of realizing the imagined ideal in the concrete present. Stevens, in other words, reappropriates the Christian imagery of the holy city for his own vision of a human world made heavenly, not by the splendor of great cathedrals but by the consecration of the austere objects of the philosopher's room, objects that stand in their poverty for the pure joy of his spirit.

> The bed, the books, the moving nuns,
> The candle as it evades the sight, these are
> The sources of happiness in the shape of Rome,
> A shape within the ancient circles of shapes.

Without abandoning the figure of the threshold, the spatial configuration here, as in so many of Stevens's poems, takes the concentric form of a gathering around and in, simultaneous with a radiance outward from the center. Stevens works through all of the stages from center to periphery and back in again. In the absence of the theological framework supporting Dante's supernatural cosmology, this structure is best expressed through the language of architecture, that is, the world as built by human beings. The outer spheres of this world are the "bird-nest arches" and "rain-stained vaults" of Rome: heaven in ruins, certainly, but not without a certain "naked majesty." From here the poem moves inward to the space of the room and the mind.

> The sounds drift in. The buildings are remembered.
> The life of the city never lets go, nor do you
> Ever want it to. It is part of the life in your room.
> Its domes are the architecture of your bed.

Despite the setting, the poem argues against the silence and solitude of monastic existence. It endorses the mutual attachment in which the philosopher and the city will not let go of one another. Similarly, the tolling bells will not let mercy be "a mystery / Of silence," nor allow any "solitude of sense" to acquire a music other than their own. Stevens's vision is of a mind and a world that give form and substance to one another.

Stanza my stone, Stevens has uttered in the exuberance of an earlier poem ("The Man on the Dump," 1938). In the present poem, the five-line stanzas of blank verse are stacked liked carved stone blocks that build toward a heightened intensity. At the end of the poem, which prefigures the end of the philosopher's life, the respective spaces of mind, room, and city combine to form a kind of grandeur in which the simplest objects are magnified and made monumental, transformed into "the immensest theatre, the pillared porch." As the setting sun "amber[s]" the room, it and its spare furnishings become

> Total grandeur of a total edifice,
> Chosen by an inquisitor of structures
> For himself. He stops upon this threshold,
> As if the design of all his words takes form
> And frame from thinking and is realized.

As in Heidegger, thinking is identified, by means of an architectural vocabulary, with building and dwelling. For the philosopher, as well as the poet, the "form and frame" through which thinking is realized is that of language. The poem as a whole makes it clear, however, that this edifice cannot be constructed out of the mind or imagination alone. Rather, it must be discovered in an "open relational context" between the imagination and the world as it is made.

Stevens wrote this poem at the age of seventy-three, three years before his own death. It is an example of what Adorno calls, in an essay on Beethoven, "late style," one conditioned by the approach of death and the impulse of the artist to leave traces of his own negative subjectivity in the material of his art. In formal terms, the artist has effectively abandoned his earlier attempts to construct a grand synthesis out of his work. Instead, the work registers "the remains of a synthesis, the vestige of an individual human subject sorely aware of the wholeness, and consequently the survival, that has eluded it forever."[7] This would be a romantic gesture except that, as Stevens says in one of the fragments of *Adagia,* "The poet is the intermediary between people and the world in which they live . . . but not between people and some other world" (*Opus Posthumous* 189). The philosopher stops on the threshold, and in that moment is capable of imagining an ideal synthesis of the design of his words and the architecture of his existence, but he is also, in that movement, passing on to some other space, perhaps to nothingness. The "as if" of the poem's conclusion remains a tentative gesture, returning us to Heidegger's assertion that dwelling must ever be sought anew, ever relearned and reinvented. Stevens's urge toward a totalizing structure of the imagination is tempered by the paradox of its impossibility in a world of time. His supreme fiction remains, as he often reminds us, a fiction, a grand design of words constructed out of the desire for an elusive reconciliation.

This is, finally, the fundamental difference between Frost and Stevens in their respective relations to architecture. Frost is essentially a poet of ruins: his houses are empty relics of some happier, more meaningful time. His woodpile, abandoned by its maker, sinks into the earth. His stone wall is a crumbling relic of an age when it made sense, the ritual of its repair a perpetual repetition of the same. The poem as "momentary stay against confusion" registers its function as a formal barrier erected against the darkness to which it testifies, so that as a poet Frost is always, in a sense, "mending wall." His poems, however, are authentic in their refusal to make any higher claim, in their implicit rejection of a consoling mythology, whether inherited or of the poet's own making.

If Frost's poems are constructed against the void, Stevens's are constructed *on* the void—acquiring their resonance, as does the sound chamber of a violin, from the emptiness within. This general difference of orientation accounts for Stevens's particular relation to architectural ruin, which only *appears* to be romantic. The romantics saw in ruins either the fragility of human existence or the sublimity of a timeless grandeur. Stevens's ruins are romantic, however, only in the sense given that adjective by his poem "Sailing after Lunch" (1935): as a figure of ourselves, both in our decadence and in our will to construct a meaning from that decadence. This is the sense in which life is an old casino in a park, and in which an old philosopher finds solace in the rain-stained vaults of Rome.

8

Annals of Junkspace: Architectural Disaffection in Contemporary Literature

The title of this chapter is adapted from a 2002 essay by the architect Rem Koolhaas, who, in the tradition of the architectural manifesto, unleashes a polemic against the constructed environment of the new twenty-first century. "Junkspace" is Koolhaas's name for the modular, temporary, and cumulative architectural forms produced by the adaptation of building technology to the imperatives of mass consumption and globalization. We see it in airports, highway systems, shopping centers, office buildings, and apartment blocks. Its materials are concrete, sheetrock, stucco, tape, glue, and staples. Its surfaces are smooth, mirrored and polished, its interiors air-conditioned, its formal logic one of addition, proliferation, successive transformation, and spatial continuity, opposing it to an architectural tradition of hierarchy, composition, permanence, and definition. According to Koolhaas, this is in fact not architecture at all; it is what fills the absence left by the disappearance of architecture at the end of the twentieth century. Nor can junkspace be considered as purely functional in the modernist sense: for Koolhaas, infrastructures of the past such as the parking garage and the filling station had a rawly functional monumentality that was the essence of modernism. Junkspace, on the contrary, corrupts its function with the bland lyricism of atriums, fountains, and "the search for a Corporate Sublime" (185). The economic model to which this kind of construction conforms is the constant expansion and mutation of corporate capitalism; the political model is one of "latent fascism" (182), with its modes of surveillance, strong lighting, and insistent signage. How does the human body survive in such space? Comfort and pleasure are proffered in abundance: the VIP lounge, the minibar, soft music, waterfalls. Everything invites disorientation and the suspension of the critical faculty. "Comfort is the new justice" (182).

In this satirical vision, Koolhaas provides an architect's perspective on a phenomenon earlier analyzed in cultural theory and anthropology. In 1991 Fredric Jameson introduced the term *hyperspace* to designate the architectural order of postmodern buildings such as the Westin Bonaventure hotel in Los Angeles. He noted, above all, the sense of disorientation engendered by the interior spaces of the hotel, whose volumes were difficult to comprehend and gave the sense of immersion without the perception of distance and perspective. This absence of reliable points of reference constituted the most local and immediate manifestation of a more general characteristic of late capitalism: the individual's inability to seize the scope and the structure of the global network of information that determines, however indirectly, the conditions of his or her existence (*Postmodernism* 43–44).

Jameson's discovery of hyperspace was followed in 1992 by Marc Augé's anthropological study of *non-lieux*: if a "place" has meaning in terms of history, human relations, or personal and collective identity, then a "nonplace" is characterized by the absence of these. Nonplaces are primarily spaces of transit and transitory consumption: airports, railway stations, highway rest areas, supermarkets, and so on. They constitute the space of the traveler and often are so organized as to spare the traveler from having to visit actual places. The highway sign announcing that you are entering the land of Beaujolais or passing by a fortified medieval village will also provide ideograms in guidebook code to give you the sense of having visited a place without having to pause on your journey. In response to Jameson's "postmodern," Augé proposes the term *surmoderne* to designate the contemporary acceleration of events, the multiplication of spaces, and the superabundance of products, which, paradoxically, create homogeneity of consumption while seeming to promote individuation through a vast range of consumer choices. For Augé the ultimate nonplace is the duty-free space of the international airport, in which the traveler is liberated from every obligation except that imposed by his or her status as a consumer. In terms of their analyses of the constructed environment, what Jameson, Augé, and Koolhaas have in common are notions of excess, of subjective disorientation, and, despite these conditions, of system: of space organized so as to maximize the functioning of an order in which the various forms of capital, information, and human desire are connected as points in an ever-proliferating global network.

In the first decade of the twenty-first century, this critical interest in what we might call architecture as absence has been accompanied by a related interest in urban space as absence. Here it is a question not so much of the built environment as of the blank spaces on the map of any large city, which nonetheless exist as a function of the built environment. These are absent spaces in the sense that they are overlooked or unacknowledged in the politics and economy of urban space. In *Un livre blanc* (2007), Philippe Vasset sets out quite literally to explore all the spaces that are left blank on the official map of Paris published by the Institut Géographique National. These are spaces that fail to fulfill a single criterion for cartographic documentation and therefore appear on the map as simply white. What Vasset often finds, in the landscape that corresponds to these cartographic voids, are abandoned factories and vacant lots surrounded by tall fences or walls with signs warning against trespassing. But there is always some breach in the barrier that allows entrance; the walls are covered with the bright colors of graffiti artists, and the spaces themselves are often inhabited by gypsies and otherwise homeless persons. In other words, there is a world off the map. There are lives that leave no official trace. In J. G. Ballard's *Concrete Island* (1974), a motorist is stranded in one of these spaces: an abandoned traffic island bounded by high concrete barriers in the midst of a network of motorways, from which he cannot escape and where he cannot be seen from the road. He resigns himself to surviving there, living a kind of Robinson Crusoe existence deep within the labyrinth of the highway infrastructure. In William Boyd's more recent novel, *Ordinary Thunderstorms* (2009), a man in London called Adam Kindred risks being convicted of a murder he did not commit. To escape almost certain imprisonment, he decides to go underground, to abandon his respectable name, profession, and way of life in order to become anonymous and therefore untraceable. He rightly reasons:

> If you made no calls, paid no bills, had no address, never voted, walked everywhere, made no credit card transactions or used cash-point machines, never fell ill or asked for state support, then you slipped beneath

the modern world's cognizance. You became invisible or at least transparent, your anonymity so secure you could move through the city . . . like an urban ghost. (55)

There are thousands of such people in every big city. Adam's new dwelling place consists of a triangle of waste ground formed by Chelsea Bridge, the edge of the Thames, and the four lanes of the Embankment Road to the north of the river. His abandonment of personal identity has led him to inhabit one of the blank spaces on the map: there is now no official trace either of him or of the place where he lives.

In these instances, the absence of personal identity on the one hand and of geographical representation on the other bears a certain relation to the ceaselessly shifting and impermanent nature of junkspace, which abandons the logic of the monument, leaving no architectural structure of lasting value. It is where individuals are made transparent, as it were, by being systematically redefined in terms of consumer transactions, transportation objectives, or security risks. As conceived in such terms, the contemporary constructed environment poses a special problem for imaginative literature, and in particular narrative fiction. Architectural forms of the past are more conducive to narrative form, partly because of the richness of their symbolic associations and partly because each of these forms, as well as each concrete instance of it, has a history of its own. The building mediates between the present and the past, and this mediation itself serves as a kind of larger narrative to the narrative proper of a novel or short story. In the case of junkspace or the *non-lieu*, however, there is no mediation, no history to which the fictional narrative can adhere.

Strictly speaking, the style of fiction that corresponds most directly to the cultural form of junkspace is the novel written as entertainment and sold at airport newsstands, such as Arthur Hailey's best-selling *Airport* (1968). The vision of the airport in *Airport* is one conditioned by the suspension of the critical faculty, which the space seems to impose. Hailey's airport is a monumental space of complex but expertly orchestrated movements of ground and air traffic. The airport general manager is a heroic figure, "lean, rangy, and a powerhouse of energy" (5), engaged in a classic struggle against the elements, which here take the form of a midwestern snowstorm. *Airport* was written in the 1960s, at a time when air travel and its characteristic architecture could still be seen as triumphs of the industrial age. The "Lincoln International" airport of Hailey's novel bears a resemblance not only to Chicago's O'Hare Airport (expanded in 1962 to accommodate ten million passengers annually) but also to Ireland's Shannon Airport. In Michel Houellebecq's recent novel *La Carte et le territoire* (2010), the principal character, an artist, marvels at the clean rectangular forms and the surprising dimensions of Shannon, which for him evokes that period of enthusiasm in the 1950s and 1960s when air transport was among the most "innovative and prestigious developments" of modern technology (134). One writer of the 1960s who did not share that vision was Thomas Pynchon. In *The Crying of Lot 49* (1965) he presents a California landscape covered with "a vast sprawl of houses which had grown up all together," a formation that reminds the novel's protagonist of the printed circuit inside a transistor radio: both patterns suggest "a hieroglyphic sense of concealed meaning, . . . an attempt to communicate" (13).[1] Pynchon's work reminds us that along with an enthusiasm for technological innovation, the sense of a conspiratorial relation between architecture and advanced technology was also symptomatic of the 1960s. This latter sense points toward the larger question of how literature can give narrative expression to the lived relation between the human subject and the built environment of a postmodern, globalized world. The literature that matters here is truly contemporary in the sense defined by Giorgio Agamben as that which is contemporaneous with but "out of phase" with the present, which does not have the same aspirations as the world of the present, and which is therefore capable of holding that world at a critical distance (24). It is in this light that I want to examine further the work of Ballard and Houellebecq, both of them contemporary writers known for their willed estrangement from the constructed environment of the present.

Ballard's fiction is distinguished by the way it imagines radical transformations in the social fabric that are driven by specifically contemporary architectural structures: the urban high-rise apartment building, the corporate office park, the suburban shopping mall, the traffic island in a highway interchange.[2] These transformations are violent and socially regressive, as if intended to put an end to the utopian dreams of early modernist architecture. One of the best-known early attempts to realize those dreams is Le Corbusier's "vertical village," the Cité Radieuse in Marseille. This *unité d'habitation* consists of 337 two-story residential apartments distributed throughout an eighteen-story building raised off the ground and supported on concrete pillars, or *pilotis*. It also houses a primary school, a hotel, retail businesses, offices, and a gymnasium. In planning this project Le Corbusier sought to redesign the concept of residential dwelling in a number of ways: the building was constructed in an urban environment but as an "island" distinct from its surroundings; the construction put into practice the architect's concept of the "Modulor," the standardized human form that served as a guide to the spatial dimensions of habitation; it favored new construction materials designed for modular construction; and it sought a form of dwelling based on new uses of space and the control of sound, light, and ventilation (Sbriglio). Inaugurating the building in 1952, Le Corbusier sought to demonstrate how advances in building technology such as raw concrete could serve the traditional values of family, hearth, privacy, and individual freedom traditionally associated with the single-family home.

> Dans ce village vertical de 2000 habitants, on ne voit pas son voisin, on n'entend pas son voisin, on est une famille placée "dans les conditions de nature"—soleil, espace, verdure. C'est la liberté acquise sur le plan de la cellule, l'individu, le groupe familial, le foyer. Au plan du groupe social, c'est un bénéfice des services communs confirmant la liberté individuelle. (*Œuvres* 5:189)

> *In this vertical village of two thousand inhabitants, you don't see your neighbor, you don't hear your neighbor. You are part of a family "in a natural state"—sun, space, greenery. Freedom is attained on the cellular level of the individual, the family group, the hearth. On the social level, the benefits of shared services confirm individual freedom.*

Le Corbusier's modernism should not be confused with the postmodern structures that Koolhaas defines as junkspace. The Cité Radieuse has dwelling and not consumerism as its object. There is real respect for the form and texture of concrete, and above all, of light. Philip Johnson writes in admiration of the Cité, "One is bathed in light from the floor, from the narrow walls, from the ceiling"; the building is a kind of "pure prism" in the blue Mediterranean air (202).

Ballard's *High-Rise* (1975), the final work of his "concrete" trilogy (after *Crash* and *Concrete Island*), is written as if to announce the failure of the promise inherent in the projects of classical modernism like the Cité Radieuse. Amid the proliferation of increasingly uniform residential high-rises in the 1970s, Ballard offers a nightmare scenario of precisely what could go wrong in the physical and social functioning of a "vertical city." The novel is set in the formerly abandoned dockland and warehouse district of London on the north bank of the Thames—precisely the site where in the 1980s the London Dockland Development Corporation would build the massive high-rise business and residential complex known as Canary Wharf. Ballard's high-rise is one of five identical towers, each forty stories tall. It has a supermarket, bank, hairdressing salon, school, and swimming pool on the tenth floor, another swimming pool on the thirty-fifth, and a children's playground on the roof, near the architect's penthouse. From the outset Ballard sets forth the three levels on which his narrative will unfold: the psychological effects of high-rise construction, the building's social organization, and the functioning of its physical plant: the electrical, sanitary, heating and air-conditioning systems, and especially the elevators, which serve as the primary means of movement within the structure.

The psychological effect of living at a considerable height from the ground is initially described as one of mere instability. Robert Laing, the single resident of a studio apartment on the twenty-fifth floor, feels his head reel as he peers upward from his balcony, looking for the origin of a bottle of sparkling wine that has just hurtled past him from a boisterous party taking place somewhere above. The dimensions of the building block itself, as well as the immense volume of open space before him, unsettles his balance: "[H]e felt that he was living in the gondola of a ferris wheel permanently suspended three hundred feet above the ground"(8). The building itself seems less than stable: sometimes, on returning home from his work at a medical school, Laing is convinced that the tower is taller than when he left it, that it had "somehow managed to extend itself during the day" (19). Beyond these purely sensory effects, more serious things are going wrong in the psyche of the high-rise dweller. A resident of the second floor has developed a powerful phobia about the building. He is "constantly aware of the immense weight of concrete stacked above him" (48), with the sense that the lines of forces created by this weight are focused on his body. He lies awake at night, as if conscious of the building pressing on him and forcing the air from his chest. His insomnia is shared by many other residents, for whom the sleep disorder, along with flaws in the building design, is a favorite conversation topic.

At the Cité Radieuse, Le Corbusier designed an environment "fait pour les hommes, fait à l'échelle humaine" (*Œuvres* 5:189), made for human beings on a human scale. But when Robert Laing looks out over the concrete landscape of curving roadways and rectilinear curtain walls, he finds that part of its appeal lies in the fact that it is an environment built "not for man, but for man's absence" (25). It appeals to him in particular, because, newly divorced, he has come to the high-rise in order to escape all relationships. In fact those who survive best in this environment belong to a new social and psychological type created by the building itself; cool, unemotional, and without the burden of lasting personal involvement with others, they thrive like "an advanced species of machine" (35).

There is a paradox implicit in Ballard's analysis of the social effects of high-rise living. If, on one hand, these conditions favor a new, socially disconnected form of human being, on the other hand the architectural order of the building reinforces certain aspects of the traditional class system in a very literal way: residents establish precedence over one another based on floor height. Architects and developers know that there are differences in the distance of view and the amount of natural light available from one level to the next, and these differences can be reflected in market values. In Ballard's high-rise, the first nine floors are occupied by a relatively inferior class of airline pilots and hostesses, technicians, and families with children. The middle floors, those above the tenth-floor commercial concourse, are a "better neighborhood" of doctors, lawyers, and tax specialists. A further dividing line is constituted by the thirty-fifth-floor swimming pool. The residents of the top five floors are an oligarchy of minor tycoons and entrepreneurs, including the building's megalomaniac architect, a caricature of the type with his long white hair, white suit, and ornamental walking stick.

Ballard's narrative, however, goes beyond observations of class difference to constitute a kind of experiment designed to test the limits of psychological and social cohesion in the artificial environment created by the high-rise. The experimental model he proposes is one in which, through its very efficiency, the building takes over the task of maintaining the social structure, thereby liberating its inhabitants from the need to repress their antisocial and deviant impulses. "The high-rise was a model of all that technology had done to make possible the expression of a truly 'free' psychopathology" (36). To borrow a formula from Slavoj Žižek, what we have here is an architectural version of the totalitarian system that implicitly tells its subjects, "Yes, you may!"—in effect freeing them to indulge their violent impulses insofar as they do so without challenging the system ("You May!" 6).

The dominant narrative movement of the novel therefore consists of a progressive breakdown of the social order of the high-rise, a breakdown made possible by the very architectural features that seemed at first to reinforce that order. In an atmosphere of parties marked by gossip, paranoia, and heavy drinking, a series of minor hostilities breaks out. Residents of the lower floors who venture toward the top are jostled and insulted. The cars of wealthier residents, parked closest to the building, are vandalized. Rubbish and graffiti litter the hallways. Children from the lower floors are banned from the tenth-floor swimming pool. In the same pool, an Afghan hound is found drowned, suggesting an act of retaliation against its owner on the thirty-fifth floor. Steadily, the level of violence escalates: stairwells are barricaded and elevators blocked to prevent access from below. Apartments are vandalized by marauding bands from within the building. Sexual assaults are committed during electrical blackouts. A man from one of the higher floors plunges to his death under mysterious circumstances. As the traditional class system is replaced by a kind of clan structure, a "renascent barbarism" (79) emerges, which only increases the violence of the atmosphere. As the material conditions of the building deteriorate, its residents have to go in search of food and water, and life is reduced to a kind of exhilarated struggle for survival. The people who once lost sleep over matters of social prestige and professional advancement are now driven by the more basic needs of physical security, food, and sex. The clan structure breaks down into a series of smaller enclaves, and eventually even this order collapses to the point where there is no social organization at all, only solitary hunters and small groups of killers. Ballard suggests that this is a more authentic order of life, as the mind and body are freed from the anxieties of repression in order to pursue their more basic instincts. At an advanced point in the regression of the social order, Laing finds himself camped out in a ruined apartment with his sister and a female neighbor, whom he protects from violence as he forages for food. Both women satisfy his sexual urges: even the incest taboo is transgressed. He feels happier than ever before, despite knowing that at any moment he could die from hunger or assault. He is satisfied with his self-reliance and pleased at having "given rein to those impulses that involved him with Eleanor and his sister, perversities created by the limitless possibilities of the high-rise" (154).

Against the general survey of social devolution in the novel, there emerges the more particular narrative of a person who will later be recognizable as characteristic of Ballard's fiction: the lonely, rebellious figure who refuses to accept the system. Richard Wilder, a television producer working on a documentary about prison unrest, abandons this subject when he realizes that what is going on in the high-rise is more interesting. A resident of the lowly second floor, he turns his camera on his own surroundings as he begins a long climb toward the top. His journey toward the upper stories becomes a sort of high-rise odyssey, as he encounters modern versions of the cyclops, the sirens, and the lotus eaters, in the form of murderous adversaries, seductive women, and other inducements to abandon his quest. As he draws nearer to the summit, however, Wilder's mind and body are progressively marked by the disintegration of the order he set out to conquer: By the time he reaches the top, his naked body is savagely decorated with streaks of blood, and his mind has become child-like. Only dimly aware of what he is doing, he kills the architect, thus, at the novel's end, making possible the first signs of a return to normalcy.

In *High-Rise* there is an implied ideology of romantic anarchism in keeping with the historical moment in which it was written. In the midst of Germany's postwar building boom, Alexander Mitscherlich's *Die Un-wirtlichkeit unserer Städte* (The Inhospitability of Our Cities, 1965) had warned, from a psychoanalytic perspective, against the effects of high-den-sity, high-rise urban planning. Ballard also has an affinity with Deleuze and Guattari's *Anti-Oedipe* (1973) in its affirmation of the savage and the barbaric as representing the liberation of libidinal impulses against a re-pressive industrial society. Given the signs of social revolt in Ballard's fiction, it is not surprising that he became something of an icon for punk rock bands in the 1970s. In *England's Dreaming,* Jon Savage's history of the Sex Pistols, Ballard figures prominently: "After Ballard's *High-Rise* and *Crash,* it was possible to see high-rises as both appalling and vertiginously exciting" (270). In 1977, the first album cover for the Clash shows them in such an environment. Savage writes that the clean, brutal silhouettes of the high-rise were "a perfect theatre for the frenetic hypermodernism" of the musical group.

In the importance given to the building's infrastructure, particularly in the battle for control of the elevator system, *High-Rise* is a novel about the final stage of the modern machine age. Ballard's more recent work is writ-ten in the later context of a fully globalized system of capital, where tech-nology is electronic and digital rather than mechanical and the architec-tural environment is designed to fully integrate the traditionally distinct functions of the private residence, workspace, and space of leisure. For Bal-lard, the social and psychological effects of such an environment are even more perverse than those of *High-Rise.*

Ballard's *Super-Cannes* (2000) is set in the "intelligent city" (5) of Eden-Olympia, its name suggesting both an idyllic garden and the seat of godly power. Eden-Olympia is a business and research park dotted with villas overlooking the Bay of Cannes. These are residences of the staff of the multinational corporations located there: Mitsui, Siemens, Unilever, Rhône-Poulenc, Elf-Aquitaine, and so on. As a design concept, Eden-

Olympia represents a synthesis of three forms of built environment that began to proliferate in North America and Western Europe in the 1980s. The first of these is the *office park* or corporate business park, a campuslike setting of low-rise office buildings located near a major roadway. The advantages to businesses of such settings include large amounts of space on cheap land, distance from the distractions and dangers of the urban environment, and the ability to restrict access to the property. The architectural historian Dion Kooijman points out that such parks "undermine the existence of public space" in that, as in the case of nineteenth-century company towns, businesses control both the economy and the politics of the space (834). One prototype is Stockley Park, north of London's Heathrow Airport at the intersection of the M4 and M25 motorways. This four-hundred-acre site was reclaimed from a contaminated waste dump in 1986. Here, the UK headquarters of such corporations as Glaxo Smith Kline and Fujitsu are surrounded by artificial lakes and footpaths adjoining an eighteen-hole golf course. The official Stockley Park website does not mention the waste dump but cites archaeological evidence of nomadic hunters and gatherers who once roamed the land now occupied by the business park, and who, by learning to use flint tools, "became more efficient at feeding, clothing and sheltering themselves."[3] There is an uncanny echo of Ballard here, as if the spirit of savage man still haunts the precincts of global economic power and at any moment might take over again.

The second model for Eden-Olympia is called in French the *technopole* (technology park). Whereas the business park is a single, enclosed property, the *technopole* is a concentration of high-tech industries and research centers in a given geographic area, like Silicon Valley. The fictional Eden-Olympia is located near the real Sophia-Antipolis, which includes a number of European corporate headquarters (ITT, Hewlett-Packard, Bayer, France Télécom) and a campus of the University of Nice, all housed in pavilions of glass and steel among the Mediterranean pines. The final model is the *gated community*, an enclosed and secured residential area in which the public spaces (streets, parks, etc.) are privatized. In *Fortress America: Gated Communities in the United States* (1999), Edward Blakely and Mary Snyder distinguish between those designed, respectively, for prestige, lifestyle, and security. However, it is the security apparatuses that really set gated communities apart from other exclusive neighborhoods. These include physical barriers such as gates, walls, and fences but also guard posts, entrance codes, and surveillance cameras. Blakely and Snyder call these communities "enclaves of fear," adding, "The fortress mentality is perhaps clearest here, where groups of people band together to shut out their neighbors" (99).

Ballard's Eden-Olympia draws on the elements of utopia and paranoia found in these various models. Beyond the gatehouse manned by armed guards is "a vision of glass and titanium straight from the drawing boards of Richard Neutra and Frank Gehry, but softened by landscaped parks and artificial lakes" (5), and by villas with swimming pools behind high walls and bougainvilleas. As always in Ballard, the design of the environment is accompanied by a certain state of mind: "Over the immaculate gardens hung the air of well-bred catatonia that only money can buy" (20). The corporate philosophy behind Eden-Olympia is comprehensive and designed to minister not just to the professional needs of its employees but to their physical and mental needs as well. A combined business and residential park, it includes facilities for yachting, tennis, and bodybuilding. Despite these amenities, it is the spirit of work that prevails, even to the point of architectural design that exposes the inner workings of its infrastructure. Ventilation shafts and cable conduits are carried on external walls, as if to signify a visceral dedication to profit and share price. There is nonetheless an active if tacit encouragement of sexual promiscuity as a release from the pressures of corporate life. The human body becomes "an obedient coolie, to be fed and hosed down, and given just enough freedom to sedate itself" (17). In the atmosphere of intense surveillance that characterizes Eden-Olympia, sexual license is granted to the employees in exchange for the relinquishment of every other kind of freedom. The architecture of the complex is designed to both encourage sexuality and ensure surveillance.

The novel's protagonist is a retired aviator named Paul Sinclair: a man from a bygone age, with a taste for antique Jaguars and Saint-Exupéry. He and his young wife Jane have left grimy London so that she can take up her duties as the staff pediatrician for Eden-Olympia. On the drive down from London they have spent the night in Hauterives, site of the Palais Idéal, the fantasy palace built pebble by pebble over the lifetime of the postman known as the Facteur Cheval. The image of the palace, with its baroque, dreamlike accretions fashioned by the hand of a single man, serves to remind the reader of all that has been lost in the corporate architecture of the business park. What Ballard suggests in *Super-Cannes,* however, is that the cost of Eden-Olympia has been much greater than whatever is symbolized by the nostalgic image of Cheval's Palais Idéal. In this novel, the design and organization of the business park literally drives people mad.

Jane is replacing another physician, named David Greenwood, a once promising, idealistic young man who went on a murderous rampage, gunning down seven senior executives before being shot dead himself under circumstances that remain obscure. The narrative thus takes the form of a murder mystery, with Paul Sinclair as an amateur sleuth investigating not so much how Greenwood died as what made him crack. In the process, Sinclair discovers the dark underside of the high-tech paradise. At first he witnesses, on an inner level of the parking structure, the savage beating by security guards of a Senegalese trinket salesman as corporate executives watch approvingly from inside their black limousines. Later he sees the same executives dressed in leather jackets in the back streets of Cannes, where they arrive in Range Rovers like a raiding party. Armed with truncheons, they wreak havoc on the local population, raining blows on the streetwalkers, small-time thugs, and North African immigrants. These *ratissages* turn out to be a regular practice among the elite of Eden-Olympia. What is more, they are part of a therapeutic program designed by the staff psychiatrist, a man named Wilder Penrose.

As Penrose explains it to Sinclair, the pressures of work in the highly controlled environment of the business park are producing a new race of highly intelligent but deracinated individuals. The glass floors and bare white walls have created individuals on whom there is similarly little trace of human experience. Of relevance here is Deleuze and Guattari's notion, in *Anti-Oedipe,* of the *surface lisse* (smooth surface), which invites swift movement, free of the moorings and attachments imposed by the *surface strié* (streaked or grooved surface). The mode of relation to the object-world on the smooth surface is one of enforced *dérive,* of "going with the flow," rather than the more adhesive, frictional mode of representation; the kind of human subject implied here does not transcend space but is rather engendered by it. In keeping with this model, the individuals of Eden-Olympia are lacking in human ties and emotions, but they possess enormous power. "It's this new class that runs our planet" (256), Penrose remarks. The members of this class have no need for personal morality, to make decisions of right and wrong: "The moral order is engineered into their lives along with the speed limits and the security systems" (255). The consequences of this engineered existence, however, are a decline in creativity among employees who have worked at Eden-Olympia for more than a year. In Penrose's diagnosis, a deep despair is imprisoned within the bars of "the corporate cage" (258). His prescription is the controlled madness of the raiding parties; racist violence has its health benefits for the corporate executive: "Bandaged fists and plastered shins on Monday mornings, but clear, confident heads" (260). For the reader, the conditions that led to David Greenwood's shooting rampage begin to take shape.

Super-Cannes shares with *High-Rise* the notion that certain forms of contemporary architecture, with the kinds of social organization they entail, produce pathologies among their inhabitants. The difference lies not just in the economic and cultural contexts of the respective built environments that figure in these novels but also in the nature of the relation between those environments and the violence they produce. The violence of the earlier novel is defined by two conditions. First, it has elements of a natural response to an unnatural environment, so that social disintegration is experienced as a joyful destruction of the class system and the architectural infrastructure by means of which that system is embodied. Second, the violence is contained entirely within the space of the high-rise; there is a tacit agreement among the residents to keep things to themselves. In this way the social regression that takes place inside the building has the character of a game. The rules may evolve, but, as in a game, whatever happens inside the well-defined boundaries of the action has no consequences for the world at large, and a return to normalcy becomes possible when the game has played itself out. In contrast to this, the business park of *Super-Cannes* is more clearly symptomatic of the conditions of power that exist in the new world order of the twenty-first century, and the pathologies it engenders are more complex. On one hand, the violence of Eden-Olympia is not self-contained; it spills out onto the streets, where European corporate executives beat up African immigrants and East European prostitutes. Ballard implies that this is merely the playing out on the local level of the inherent violence of the global economic order. Those who perpetrate the beatings are members of the new class that runs the planet. On the other hand, this violence is represented as something other than the immediate effect of the environment imposed by the business park. Although Eden-Olympia is marked by a kind of structural paranoia, the disorders from which its employees suffer are those of lack: lack of affect, lack of emotional relationships with other human beings, the blunting of the creative edge. Violence is therefore artificially introduced as an imagined corrective to these deficiencies. But this violence is not one of carnivalesque resistance to the system, as is the case in *High-Rise*. Rather, this is the violence *of* the system, carefully dosed in order to channel its energy back into the system's functioning. Ballard thus provides a metaphor for a global capitalism so resourceful that it thrives even on the violence that would otherwise threaten the conditions of its proper functioning.

If *Super-Cannes* explores the lived reality of corporate capitalism at the highest level of power, Ballard's last novel takes us to the other end of the economy, where the system is constantly regenerated by the mania of consumer spending. *Kingdom Come* (2006) is an apocalyptic novel about shopping that fixes as its ground zero a colossal shopping mall called the Metro-Centre. Ballard's Metro-Centre is the apotheosis of an architectural concept that took hold in the United States in the 1950s, the fully enclosed suburban retail shopping center. Jeffrey Hardwick's biography *Mall Maker* (2004) tells the story of the Viennese immigrant Victor Gruen, who invented the modern formula for the shopping center in his design for Southdale in Minnesota. In addition to being fully enclosed and air-conditioned, Southdale was anchored at either end of the mall by two department-store tenants. In order to reduce walking distances, shops were put on two levels connected by escalators. The building was "introverted," meaning that external walls were left bare and display windows faced only the interior space, thus concentrating shoppers inside. The shops were arranged around a garden court illuminated by a skylight, in a configuration that came to be known as the atrium, after the Roman design of an open-roofed court. The idea of the shopping center was to bring retailing away from the city centers to where the middle class lived and to serve a consumer population that favored the automobile over other forms of transportation. Like office parks, shopping centers were thus located near major roadways and offered an abundance of free parking. The common roofed enclosure, like the commercial arcades of the nineteenth century, not only protected shoppers from the elements but also provided optimal conditions for surveillance and security.[4] If at the power centers of the capitalist system corporate office buildings can be designed by star architects like Richard Neutra and Frank Gehry, the shopping mall is, by contrast, purely a product of junkspace: prefabricated and modular materials of taped sheetrock, floor tiles, and plate glass. The continual transformation of the space is not only driven by changes in the retail market, but in the United States it has also been driven by laws allowing for tax deductions on the depreciation of "nonresidential real property" for forty years after construction. Such laws created the initial boom in shopping malls in the 1950s, but they did not favor construction of lasting quality, since the profits from tax write-offs diminished each year. As Thomas Hanchett shows in an important essay, by the 1970s entire shopping centers were abandoned while new, larger centers were built nearby (1103).

There is in fact a real MetroCentre, near Newcastle upon Tyne in the north of England. At 1.8 million square feet of retail space it is Europe's largest shopping mall, although it does not come close to the 4.2 million square feet of Minnesota's Mall of America. MetroCentre's slogan is "If we don't have it you don't want it," not just a promise of abundance but a reminder that consumer desire, being continually created by the retail industry, does not exist independent of this context. In *The Ethical Foundation of Architecture* (1997), Karsten Harries cites the suburban shopping center as an example of a structure built to serve the demands of a certain way of life but which then gives a new shape and development to that way of life (147). Ballard's novel is a nightmare vision of the second stage of this process, where the shopping center has given form to a totalitarian consumer society. His fictional Metro-Centre is described as the largest in the Greater London area, and, like the real Stockley Park, it is located in one of the nondescript motorway towns spread out along the M25 north of Heathrow Airport. In Ballard's description, this is a region where "a filling station beside a dual carriageway enshrine[s] a deeper sense of community than any church or chapel" and where parking is the greatest spiritual need (7). The Metro-Centre is the focal point of this suburban sprawl, serving as a kind of cathedral for the religion of consumerism. With millions of square feet, it meets the gargantuan standards of the Mall of America. It has six cineplexes, forty cafés, and three hotels. One of these is the Holiday Inn, which overlooks a swimming pool with machine-produced waves and a crescent of sandy beach. At the center of the Metro-Centre rises the central atrium, a vast, circular, scented space of diffused light surrounded by galleries of the upper retail floors. Richard Pearson, the novel's first-person narrator, remarks, "The enclosed geometry of the Metro-Centre focused an intense self-awareness on every shopper, as if we were extras in a music drama that had become the world" (41).

The narrative of *Kingdom Come* is structured similarly to that of *Super-Cannes*, beginning as an amateur investigation of a murderous shooting rampage. Pearson, a recently fired London advertising executive, has come to the scene of the crime following the death of his father, one of several people killed or injured when a mental patient on day release opened fire into the crowd of shoppers in the Metro-Centre atrium. In fictionalizing such an incident, Ballard pays literary homage to the by now familiar social phenomenon of the shopping mall murder spree, a deadly cousin of the shopping spree. The genre seems to have been inaugurated in 1985 when a paranoid schizophrenic woman opened fire with an automatic weapon in the Springfield Mall in Pennsylvania, killing three persons and injuring seven others. Since the publication of *Kingdom Come,* similar rampages have taken place at the Trolley Square Mall in Salt Lake City (2007, five dead), the Westroads Mall in Omaha (2007, nine dead), the Sello Mall in Espoo, Finland (2009, six dead), and the Ridderhof Mall in Alphen aan den Rijn, Netherlands (2011, seven dead). Something about the shopping mall seems to invite mass murder.

The towns surrounding the Metro-Centre, however, are witnessing another phenomenon, the emergence of a culture of "soft fascism" represented by bands of vigilantes wreaking havoc on the local immigrant population. The members of these bands resemble football hooligans in their white T-shirts bearing the red Saint George's cross for England. But their violence spills over from the sporting matches and systematically targets anyone with dark skin or a foreign accent. Asian shops are ransacked, Poles are beaten up in the street, and a mosque is trashed. In a related incident Pearson's car, a low-slung Jensen, is bombed on the upper level of the basement parking garage, the last of a series of scenes of violence in concrete structures that figure throughout Ballard's fictional oeuvre.

The gathering place for the vigilantes is the Metro-Centre, where Pearson discovers a strange alliance among the men in the Saint George's shirts, the shopping mall management, and local authorities such as a prominent high school teacher named Richard Sangster. Sangster is the ideologue of the "fascism lite" (191) that constitutes the new form of consumerism. Sangster is an antimodernist, considering the modernist movement to have been driven by neuroses and alienation: "Look at its art and architecture. There's something deeply cold about them" (85). Postmodern consumerism, however, is a redemptive ideology: "It celebrates coming together. Shared dreams and values, shared hopes and pleasures" (85). It is driven by emotion, not reason, and for that reason needs emotional stimulation: "What we need now is a kind of delirious consumerism, the sort you see at motor shows. People long for authority, and only consumerism can provide it" (86). The latent fascism that Koolhaas associates with the architecture of junkspace here becomes manifest. As for Pearson, he remains enough of an adman to be inspired by these thoughts to conceive of a new marketing campaign that would both boost flagging sales at the Metro-Centre and creatively channel the racist violence of the Saint George's thugs. The campaign is one of "willed madness" in which, for example, the local television pitchman for the mall, ordinarily a benign if slick personage, would suddenly turn nasty with his guests in the manner of hosts on "shock radio." Metro-Centre shoppers are deemed to have a "suppressed need for the bizarre and the unpredictable" (155). The "bad is good" concept is intended as "the ultimate in ironic soft-sells" (187). The marketing campaign works too well. Shoppers throng to the Metro-Centre, along with marching bands and sports supporters clubs, but the mall's public relations official dons a military-style uniform and forms the Saint George's men into a disciplined organization with disturbing resemblances to a *Sturmabteilung;* outbreaks of burning and looting strike the Asian and immigrant housing estates. As police and army troops from outside the area respond to what appears to be a civil insurrection, the Saint George's men take refuge in the Metro-Centre, taking hundreds of shoppers as hostages. The novels of Ballard I have treated here all elaborate on the perceived relation between architecture and violence, but *Kingdom Come,* as the title implies, represents the apocalypse of that relation. The novel ends in a general conflagration that spreads throughout the motorway towns, the flames devouring not just the Metro-Centre but also streets of modest bungalows, executive estates and community centres, football stadiums and car showrooms, "the last bonfire of the consumer gods" (280).

Michel Houellebecq is the most controversial of the literary personalities now writing in French, a misanthrope in the consciously insolent tradition of Céline. As the daily *Libération* points out, "[H]e cares nothing for the rights of man, knows nothing of the rights of women, and doesn't like children, to say nothing of family life."[5] He has been prosecuted under French law for stating in an interview in September 2001 that Islam is "the dumbest religion in the world."[6] None of this, however, prevents him from being one of the most interesting and original writers of his generation. In an essay published in 2002, Houellebecq names J. G. Ballard as one of the writers of the previous generation who elevated the genre of "science fiction" to the level of a philosophical literature, one capable of an authentic examination of human life, of going beyond the study of custom, knowledge, and value to consider the nature of existence itself (*Interventions* II: 224). It is clear that Houellebecq regards Ballard as one of the figures who has made his own work possible. This is not, however, to underestimate the differences between the two writers. For all the desolation of his dystopias, Ballard's fictions retain a certain nostalgia for Enlightenment values. When, in *Kingdom Come,* Richard Pearson asks what has happened to "liberalism, liberty, reason" in the onset of consumer fascism, he is simply told that they have failed; they are no longer what people want (86). Ballard's novels are about what happens when these values are abandoned as metaphysical ideals. In contrast to such this idealism, Houelle-becq lays claim to an "ontological modesty" (*Interventions* II: 247) inherited from the positivism of Comte, which regards metaphysical value purely as a pragmatic means of creating order in the human world. Nonetheless, Houllebecq's work finds common ground with Ballard's in their evocation of a contemporary world where the absence of metaphysical value has given place to a kind of ontological drift, a "monstruous and global lack" in contemporary existence (*Interventions* II 156). In both writers, the built environment figures prominently as the terrain that channels this drift and figures forth this lack.

We have seen how, in the machinery of Ballard's novels, narrative pursues the imagined social transformations generated by architectural forms. In Houellebecq these elements are more loosely organized, but the built environment remains symptomatic of a more general existential condition. His depiction of this environment amounts to a practical demonstration of Augé's *non-lieux*. An article on the city of Calais, 95 percent of which was destroyed in World War II, offers an example. On Saturday afternoons, when there is no one around:

> On longe des immeubles abandonnés, d'immenses parkings déserts. . . . Le samedi soir est un peu plus gai, mais d'une gaieté particulière: presque tout le monde est saoul. Au milieu des troquets il y a un casino, avec des rangées de machines à sous où les Calaisiens viennent claquer leur RMI. Le lieu de promenade du dimanche après-midi est l'entrée du tunnel sous la Manche. Derrière les grilles . . . les gens regardent passer l'Eurostar. Ils font un signe de main au conducteur, qui klaxonne en réponse avant de s'engouffrer dans la mer. (*Interventions* II 106–7)

> *You pass abandoned buildings and huge deserted parking lots. . . . Saturday night is a little more lively, but with a particular kind of liveliness: almost everyone is drunk. Among the bars is a casino where the locals come to blow their government aid money. Sunday afternoon walks are taken by the entrance to the Channel tunnel. From behind the barriers . . . people watch the Eurostar pass. They wave to the engineer, who sounds his horn in answer before plunging under the sea.*

There are important stylistic differences between this sort of writing and Ballard's. Where the tautness and energy of Ballard's style gives off the tension of a barely suppressed outrage, Houellebecq's prose, in its flatness and lack of affect, forms a seamless continuity with the slick but lifeless environment that constitutes his object. In this scene, the parking lots, casino, train tracks, and tunnel all belong to the network of spaces of transit and transitory exchange that Augé identifies. Where Augé puts them in the context of a superabundant *surmodernité*, Houllebecq prefers to stress the absence and emptiness that haunts these spaces and the lives of the people who inhabit them.

The importance of the built environment for Houellebecq is most clearly stated in a 1997 essay entitled "Contemporary Architecture as a Vector of Accelerated Movement." At stake here are two forms of acceleration. The first is organic and refers to the accelerated bodily secretions that occur in cases of anxiety induced by the contemporary architectural environment under certain conditions, for example, late at night, against a background of police sirens (*Interventions* 59). The second form of acceleration is that of the efficient and rational displacement of human beings and may be witnessed in the transparent, readable architecture of the Gare de Montparnasse, with its redundant signage, its information conveyed by strategically placed video screens, its placement of electronic reservation points, and so on. For Houllebecq the purest form of this architecture is, as it is for Augé, the highway interchange. At the other extreme from the highway interchange is the medieval core of a European city. Among tourists put down in the cathedral quarter of a city one witnesses a sudden *deceleration,* as they are confronted with visual objects not readily decipherable; they resume their customary pace only when oriented by informational and directional signs put in place by the tourism industry (60). The image gives rise to an analogy: the speed of rational and efficient displacement is to the arrested state of contemplation as information is to the reading of books; the book as an object becomes a formidable means of disconnection from the accelerated information order. Houellebecq's project as a novelist is to write books that make this disconnection while maintaining a heightened awareness of the economic and social conditions that make the disconnection necessary.

Contemporary architecture's relation to these conditions is evoked in the figure of the enlarged supermarket: the function of such architecture is to construct the shelves of the social *hypermarché* (63), which it does in part through use of the same smooth materials of glass, metal, and synthetic composites found in commercial spaces. Houellebecq's example here is La Défense, the mammoth business quarter built west of Paris in the 1980s and 1990s. Here living and working spaces are all designed with the same modular materials and white walls, as if to affirm the transitory, commodified nature of the lives of their inhabitants. Apartments and offices serve as shelf space for their human contents. Freed from emotional attachment and the constraints of individual character, "the modern individual is ready to take his place in a system of generalized transactions in which it becomes possible to assign him, univocally and unambiguously, an *exchange value*" (65). Like an item on the supermarket shelf, he is ready to be removed, leaving no traces behind, and this mobility enhances his value on the employment market.

In the middle of his first novel, *Extension du domaine de la lutte* (1994, translated as *Whatever*), Houellebecq pauses to consider the difficulty of writing narrative fiction about people whose lives are characterized by the gradual disappearance of human relations. This was a problem rarely faced by writers of the nineteenth century; it seems that the novelistic form is not really made to represent indifferentiation and nothingness: "il faudrait inventer une articulation plus plate, plus concise et plus morne" (42). One would have to invent a flatter, more concise, and colorless articulation, a form of literary expression, that is, that corresponds in texture and uniformity to what Houellebecq takes to be the qualities of the contemporary architecture of the global order of exchange. *Extension du domaine de la lutte* is his first attempt at such an exercise. The title alludes to the fact that what was thought to be sexual liberation has turned out to be merely an extension of the competitive field already defined by the "free market" of economic liberalism, where individuals are differentiated purely as a function of their exchange value. Just as the human body is reduced to a fleeting form of capital, human relations are reduced to the exchange of information, even when this exchange includes an affective dimension (43).

In keeping with this stark view of things, Houellebecq's narrative traces the modest daily life of a middle-level program analyst at the French Ministry of Agriculture, where the author himself has worked. In the autobiographical mode assumed here, Houellebecq proposes a succession of anecdotes, apologizing for not being able to give the reader "an entire life to read" (14). The implication is that such a "life," in the literary sense of the word, would have nothing to do with the writer's experience as actually lived, no more so than the kind of novel that impresses the reader with its subtle psychological analyses, its delicate delineation of character, its accumulation of realistic detail, and so on. On the contrary, Houellebecq's narrator maintains a studied lack of feeling tempered by occasional moments of confession—"Je n'aime pas ce monde" (I don't like this world) (82)— and by ironic observations on the way in which the speech and mannerisms of those who inhabit his world seem copied from advertisements or television soap operas. As for novelistic details, Houellebecq proposes to eradicate them one by one in keeping with a contemporary historical movement toward uniformity. In this process, as the means of telecommunication advance, domestic interiors are increasingly better equipped with technology and human relations become progressively more impossible (16).

In keeping with this flattening out of the cultural landscape, not much happens in the novel. The narrator attends meetings at work, his car is stolen, he takes a business trips to Rouen, he has memories of an unhappy childhood and a botched suicide attempt, he takes another business trip to the Vendée, falls into a depression, spends time in a psychiatric clinic, goes on holiday in the Ardèche, and so on. This solitary existence is lived out in the socially institutionalized and commercialized spaces of office buildings, apartment blocks, department stores, nightclubs, vacation residences, train stations, police stations, hospitals, and clinics. At the seaside resort of Les Sables d'Olonne, the narrator sees a row of modern, white, multistory vacation residences built on an esplanade of several levels, the lowest reserved for parking. The buildings capture his interest enough for him to observe the various architectural stratagems that make it possible for most of the apartments to have a sea view. But now it is off-season, the buildings are deserted, and the gusts of cold wind buffeting the concrete structures give them a sinister air (107). The thought of the philistine vacationers who stay at the "Résidence des Boucaniers" in summer is no more comforting. There is something sinister about it in any season.

As for the narrator's work environment, it is a world acoustically cushioned by the hum of air-conditioning, where office managers speak of the "distribution of spaces" (58). When he can no longer stand it, he leaves a note on his desk with a brief message printed in large letters: "JE SUIS MALADE" (I am ill) (129). This happens to be the opening statement of Dostoevsky's *Notes from Underground* (1864), another first-person narrative of a functionary who abandons his post and who, like Houellebecq's narrator, believes that he has to be essentially devoid of "character" to escape the general mediocrity of his age. Both are paranoid figures, but whereas the paranoia of Dostoevsky's narrator manifests itself in a fury of malevolence, what we find in Houellebecq is rather a fear of mess, of the organic. He is not the first to find these qualities in Gothic architecture. In a dream, he flies over the towers of the Cathedral of Chartres.

Ces tours sont immenses, noires, maléfiques, elles sont faites de marbre noir qui renvoie des éclats durs, le marbre est incrusté de figurines violemment coloriées où éclatent les horreurs de la vie organique. (142)

The towers are huge, black, malevolent, made of black marble that gives off a splintered glare; the marble is encrusted with harshly colored figurines that reflect the horrors of organic life.

Unlike Ballard's heroes, who find an anarchic pleasure in decomposition, in the mess of bodily substance and human contact, this narrator is wedded, however unhappily, to his own solitude in the sterile environment of glossy floors and white walls. In the psychiatric clinic, a psychologist waves aside his sociological auto-analyses and demands a more personal discourse, "recentered on himself." "But I've had about enough of myself," the narrator objects (145). In other words, he refuses complicity with the clinic's system of intimate surveillance, but he lacks the resources to create for himself another kind of life. Leaving the clinic on the day of his release, he finds himself in the sunlight and feels the air of freedom in the streets: "It was intolerable" (150).

Houllebecq's second novel, *Les particules élémentaires* (1998) is more ambitious in chronicling the search for a utopian solution to what for him is the profound void of contemporary existence. On the philosophical level, he returns to the positivism of Comte and to the theory that, on one hand, social evolution is driven by scientific and technological evolution, but, on the other hand, society until recently was held together and regulated by religious practice. What happens, then, when the latter term drops out of the equation? Houllebecq's world is one in which the absence of religion has led to the collapse of any meaningful social cohesion and human relations are defined by forms of economic competition accelerated by progress in technology. The built environment of this world is important in that economic competition is a "metaphor for the mastery of space" (199). The architectural spaces of *Les particules élémentaires* represent the nature of a fiercely competitive consumer society operating in a metaphysical void.

An example is Crécy-la-Chapelle, the town east of Paris where Houellebecq himself lived as a child. The hero of *Les particules élémentaires*, a physicist named Michel Djerzinski, is also from there and has to return after years of absence in order to oversee the removal of his grandmother's grave to make room for a bus stop. Exurban sprawl spares not even the dead. The village itself has changed since Michel's childhood due to its proximity both to Paris and to Eurodisney. The former provincial village with its thirteenth-century collegial church is now dominated by a huge Casino *hypermarché*, new apartment buildings, and villas occupied by Parisian commuters. Having contemplated the unearthed remains of his grandmother, Michel seeks solace in a glass of pastis at the Bar des Sports amid video games and a television set tuned to MTV. Such spaces, along with the absence of affect attached to them, exist as points of exchange within the continuous infrastructure of parking lots, autoroutes, and Monoprix discount department stores that constitutes Michel's world. Houellebecq himself has confessed, with a degree of irony difficult to measure, "Je suis vraiment bien dans un Monoprix" (I feel very much at home in a Monoprix).[7]

This surprising sentiment finds an echo in Houellebecq's *La carte et le territoire,* where an artist named Jed Martin has become a loyal customer of commercial retail chains such as Casino, Franprix, and the Shell service stations where Pringles and mineral water can be found at any hour. Far from being *non-lieux,* for Jed these are "lieux de vie" (places of life). Jed imagines a utopia of the future in which all the retail chains would be fused into a total *hypermarché* designed to serve every human need. In the novel, Jed has befriended Michel Houellebecq, who figures here as a fictional character and shares Jed's enthusiasm for such places. Thinking of Houellebecq, Jed muses:

> Comme il aurait été bon de visiter ensemble cet hypermarché Casino refait à neuf, de se pousser du coude en signalant l'un à l'autre l'apparition de segments de produits inédits, ou un nouvel étiquetage nutritionnel particulièrement exhaustif et clair! (196)
>
> *How fine it would have been for us to visit together this newly remodeled Casino supermarket, to nudge each other in pointing out the appearance of new product categories or a particularly clear and detailed example of nutritional labeling!*

If the irony here is pushed to the point of farce, it is no doubt to camouflage a nostalgia for a more traditional economy and the architecture through which that economy once took form.

In *La carte et le territoire,* this nostalgia is not expressed by the narrator, who for formal reasons has to maintain the cool detachment characteristic of Houellebecq's style. Instead, it is assigned to Jed's father Jean-Pierre, an architect who has abandoned his youthful ideals in order to make a fortune building vacation resorts. As he puts it, "As an architect I had hoped for something other than to build stupid holiday homes for moronic tourists, under the control of basically dishonest and incredibly vulgar promoters; but that's what it means to work, to fall into habits" (215). The account of his career given by Martin *père* amounts to an essay embedded within the narrative of the novel defending the revival of figurative art in the 1980s as represented by painters like Robert Combas and Hervé di Rosa, and as it might have been represented by architects interested in a return to the values of ornamentation had they been given a chance. The fictional Jean-Pierre Martin is one of those who joined an antimodernist countercurrent among certain French architects trained at the École des Beaux-Arts in the 1960s and 1970s. For them, Le Corbusier's *machine à habiter* was a fundamentally misguided idea, not because of its functionalism but because it conceived of a human habitation completely cut off from the natural environment, "a terrifying regression with respect to any rural landscape, which is a subtle mixture of fields, meadows, forests, villages" (220). Jean-Pierre Martin goes on to recall that "Le Corbusier appeared to us as brutal and totalitarian, motivated by a decided taste for ugliness" (220). The Beaux-Arts students also attacked Mies van der Rohe, who produced the "empty, modulable structures" that would later serve as models for the panoptic "open space" of modern office space, but above all Le Corbusier, "who tirelessly built concentrated spaces divided into identical cells ideal . . . for a model prison" (223). Against these powerful figures of high modernism, Jean-Pierre Martin and his young comrades looked back to the nineteenth century, to Charles Fourier, philosopher of social and domestic happiness, and, somewhat surprisingly, to the English designer William Morris, the leading figure of the Arts and Crafts movement. What interested them in Morris was that he did away with the distinction between art and artisanry and between the conception and execution of a work: "[H]e wanted nothing less than an end to the system of industrial production" (227). Morris's example freed the young architects from Le Corbusier's strictures against ornamentation and inspired them to adapt the principles of *figuration libre* to architectural form.

In fact such ideas were to be realized in buildings like the neobaroque Harold Washington Library in Chicago (1991), designed by the architectural firm of Hammond, Beebe, and Babka. In Houellebecq's novel, however, architectural figuration is a lost, if noble, cause. Several episodes after Jean-Pierre Martin's story of his youthful rebellion against modernism, the subject of William Morris is taken up anew by the fictional Houellebecq; he turns out to be another admirer of the visionary who designed and built the elegant Red House, near London, in 1860. This Houellebecq, however, finally admits the impracticality of Morris's utopianism. Morris's eccentricity, hyperactivity, and unfailing candor made him an extraordinary figure but not one on whom a future society could be modeled: "[T]he society envisioned by William Morris would have nothing utopian about it in a world where everyone was like William Morris" (267). A similar judgment is made concerning the unrealized architectural projects of Jean-Pierre Martin. These projects exist in the form of drawings, which Jed Martin discovers after his father's death.

> Des escaliers en spirale montaient vertigineusement jusqu'aux cieux, rejoignant des passerelles ténues, translucides, qui unissaient des bâtiments irréguliers, lancéolés, d'une blancheur éblouissante, dont les formes rappelaient celles de certains cirrus. (406)
>
> *Spiral staircases mounted vertiginously toward the heavens, joining narrow, translucent catwalks strung between irregular buildings with pointed spires and of a blinding whiteness, whose forms recalled certain kind of cirrus clouds.*

For Jed there is nothing about these drawings that suggests the possibility of human dwelling.

For Houellebecq the author, however, the act of imagining these phantasmic drawings at the end of *La carte et le territoire* comes as a curious conclusion to the polemic the novel has repeatedly deployed against architectural modernism. Houellebecq grants the commercial and institutional success of modernism while condemning its human failure. At the same time, he regrets the failure of an antimodernist movement while acknowledging that it never stood a chance. As an architectural critic, his position is thus that of a resignedly ironic embrace of modernism in its degraded form as junkspace: "I feel very much at home in a Monoprix." The tone of detachment and resignation extends beyond the treatment of architectural forms to Houellebecq's entire writerly universe.

This is not to say that Houellebecq is without a certain feeling for the dwelling spaces of the present, which provide a kind of solace in the absence of affective or aesthetic demands made on those who inhabit them. In the closing chapters of *Les particules élémentaires* Michel moves to an isolated house in Ireland in order (such is the premise of the story) to conceive the brave new world of human reincarnation through cloning. It is a rented house decorated with antique objects of the kind that tourists are supposed to delight in, but this doesn't bother Michel, whose feeling is one of relief: "In this house, in life in general, he now knew that he would feel as if he were in a hotel" (364). The sentiment is akin to that of a 2003 interview in which Ballard identifies the Heathrow Hilton, designed by Michael Manser in 1986, as his favorite building in London (fig. 11).

> Most hotels are residential structures, but rightly, the Heathrow Hilton plays down this role, accepting the total transience that is its essence, and instead turns itself into a huge departure lounge, as befits an airport annex. Sitting in its atrium one becomes, briefly, a more advanced kind of human being. Within this remarkable building, one feels no emotions and could never fall in love, or need to. (Obrist 60)

If we take this feeling seriously for once, what presumably distinguishes a hotel of this kind is its status not exactly as junkspace but as a nonplace, and the life Ballard imagines there is one of the freedom granted by a series of absences: the absence of the burden of the past and of the confining sense of place; the absence of a sense of the uniqueness of one's surroundings and even of oneself; the lack of a *necessary* connection between oneself and the constructed environment. There is a freedom in rootlessness. Harries notes that what Europeans have traditionally found exciting about the American landscape is the "openness in which a democratic ethos finds expression." This is true even of the suburban landscape with its jumble of supermarkets, hamburger joints, crisscrossing highways, and cars, which would seem to provide almost the perfect illustration of "loss of place" (170).

There is something here that recalls the question posed by Heidegger in his 1951 Darmstadt lecture: how to dwell in a world where dwelling is something that must always be learned anew. Heidegger was aware that life in the Black Forest farmhouse was no longer possible; his lesson is not one of nostalgia for that life but of the search for a form of dwelling willing to abandon the ideals of fullness and presence that dominate our cultural memory of that life, and prepared to find consolation in the freedom granted by the displacements of the contemporary world. Heidegger called for an awareness of the essential homelessness of the modern, industrialized world in order to relieve the misery of that condition. Harries takes up this theme half a century later by renouncing the idea of dwelling as a figure of centeredness in favor of its eccentricity, displacement, and mobil-

Fig. 11. The Heathrow Hilton, designed by Michael Manser. (Photo by Tim Chapman.)

ity. The attempt to "come home" in the sense of returning to the true center is to deny that essential eccentricity, one that "needs to be thought in relation to a center, but a center that withdraws whenever we seek to seize it"(200). In their respective, idiosyncratic ways, Ballard and Houellebecq, as well as many other contemporary writers, return to the modern philosophical questions concerning the nature of dwelling and therefore the nature of existence in the contemporary built environment. They do not answer these questions. Rather, where philosophy seeks meaning and understanding, works of imaginative literature such as the ones studied here seek to express the lived reality of a world where meaning is elusive and comprehension fails. But if only through this expression, imaginative literature makes the connection between the concrete structures of dwelling and the complexities of human subjectivity.

Postface: Covered Ground

How to live? This is the question that modern literature implicitly poses in its interpretation of architectural form, in its testimony to the effects of that form on human relations and the mind, and in its imagination of alternate kinds of constructed space. It is also the question that modern architecture has put to itself with increasing urgency, both in the form of architectural theory and in actual construction, as the realization of architectural design. We witness in works of both literature and architecture an ongoing interrogation of the nature of the built environment as a design for living. What is specifically modern in this interrogation is the notion that the built environment must be continually reinvented. Peter Eisenman writes, "What defines architecture is the continuous dislocation of dwelling" ("Architecture" 177). Eisenman is warning against the dangers of the institutionalization of a certain way of living imposed by the way architecture occupies and organizes space. He is also speaking from within the philosophical tradition that defines dwelling not as a state of rest or habituation but as perpetual construction: dwelling and building, according to Heidegger, are bound within the same dynamic ("Building" 151). This is also to think of architecture as an art form, like imaginative literature, which must forever renew itself in order to retain its vitality. T. S. Eliot makes a similar point about literature when he says that a work designed to conform to existing standards would not really conform at all, for "it would not be new, and would therefore not be a work of art" (*Selected* 39). The nature of dwelling and its continuing redefinition has been a preoccupation of the present work in its exploration of the various modes of relation between architecture and literature. Closely related to the question of dwelling has been that of the modern world's relation to the historical past, particularly as manifested in the built environment. Finally, both of these questions have been examined in the light of a third: that of modern subjectivity, including the manner in which architecture is rendered, in literature, in terms of memory, invention, and desire. With these questions in mind, let us cast one final glance over the ground that has been covered.

In one of the lectures he gave at the National Gallery of Art in Washington in 1967, Mario Praz claimed that by the end of the eighteenth century architecture had lost its leading role in European culture. It could now seek only to borrow ideas, like those of the beautiful and the sublime, that were better expressed in philosophy and literature. Of William Beckford's extravagant project of Gothic revival, Praz says, "Fonthill Abbey tries to translate the poetic emotion of sublimity into stone" (153). This judgment resonates with Manfredo Tafuri's designation of the same historical moment as one of "semantic crisis" in architecture, as well as with Derrida's reading of architecture as a multiply layered text. However, this assimilation of the architectural to the textual has the effect of destabilizing two attributes traditionally regarded as essential to architecture: its organization around a myth of origin, and its tie to a "teleology of habitus" (*Psyché* 481). Put simply, there came a moment when architecture lost its sense of where it had come from, where it was going, and what it meant beyond its most basic functions. It is a defining moment of modernity, and one that we continue to inhabit.

The first chapter of this work documents a number of ways in which literary and philosophical works interpret this loss in terms of the human experience of dwelling. Victorian writers like Ruskin and Dickens give expression to a traditional myth of dwelling only to prepare the ground for this myth to be deconstructed. The high modernists—Proust, Joyce, and Woolf—recast the notion of dwelling as a continual process of displacement, while many of their formal procedures are analogous to contemporary developments in architectural modernism that also seek to redefine the notion of dwelling. The end of modernism marked by Beckett's purity of negation is contemporary with an architecture of nihilism that cultivates absence as a kind of clearing in the midst of modern world that is too much with us. In general, what we witness in both literature and architecture is the search for a new sense of dwelling generated by the experience of uprooting and displacement without seeking to escape from the truth of that experience.

In keeping with the idea of an ethical dimension to the built environment, the "demonic spaces" of the second chapter belong to a series of critical responses to modernity as the product of Enlightenment reason. In Sade, the Enlightenment ideals of reason and the pursuit of happiness are pursued to their terminal points of absolute subjection, in hidden chambers that represent the secret space of the demonic at the center of the rational, modern world. In Dickens this space is literally that of industrial production itself, at the heart of modern capitalism. If the respective fictional worlds of Sade and Dickens both oppose innocence to the demonic, Kafka's more radical demolition of value takes place among architectural spaces that defy the surveyor's measure; they correspond to Lacan's notion of the real as what doesn't add up, what can't be made to fit the order of language. To do this without mystification, and without reference to a transcendent order beyond language, is a modern gesture in itself.

The two chapters on Gothic architecture in the nineteenth century are naturally concerned with defining the relation between modernity and the historical past, but the material under study there also prepares the ground for the modernist movements in both literature and architecture. In the various "allegories of the Gothic" from Goethe to Henry Adams, we witness a certain confusion in the face of the great architectural monuments to what Adams calls "an empty church" and a "dead faith" (186): on one hand, a sense of wonder and a willing effort toward the sublime; and on the other, a sense of exhausted possibilities giving way to expressions of the nonrational, ironic, fragmentary, and transgressive, with privilege finally given to the materiality of immediate experience over doctrine, reason, and ideas of metaphysical transcendence. The figures of Ruskin and Viollet-le-Duc are both symptomatic of this divided response to Gothic architecture, even if they oppose one another in philosophy and temperament. Ruskin's evangelical spirit is at odds with his insistence on the irrevocable state of ruin, on the deadness of what is dead, without being able to imagine a new life for architecture. Viollet has an idealized vision of the past but one that, paradoxically, anticipates modernism in its adaptation to new materials and its readiness to put things together in new ways. Together, Ruskin's sense of an absolute rupture with the past and Viollet's pragmatic and functional designs prefigure the modernist movements in literature and architecture, respectively.

In both Proust and Joyce we see the formal elaboration of a tendency already present in nineteenth-century writing on architecture: the objectivity of subjective experience. Proust's "interior" Venice figures as an introjection of the external built environment that structures the nature of the subject. The implications of this vision are that the subject exists only insofar as his or her consciousness is assimilated to the experience of objects in space and time. To the extent that these are built objects, Proust suggests, the subject is structured architecturally, complete with visible surfaces, passages from chamber to chamber, and places hidden even from consciousness itself. Joyce's vision is even more radical than this, for in his work the subject and the object-world do not exist in opposition but are rather made coterminous: the content of Bloom's musings is that of the city flowing past him; the content of Stephen Dedalus's mind is not simply analogous to, but rather consists of, the historical forms layered within modern civilization but exposed to view like the layers of an archaeological dig.

In Frost and Stevens, the return to the problem of dwelling is made through a series of analogies between language and architecture. The works of these poets are ethical in the sense that they seek to define a way of inhabiting a modern world in which, to borrow Heidegger's words, "the divine radiance has become extinguished in the world's history" (*Poetry* 91). We have seen how both poets attempt to solve this problem through language, that is, through the forms of construction constituted by poetry as making. For these poets, language is not the medium through which the world is lived; language is what we inhabit. However, their modes of habitation are distinct from one another. Frost makes of his poetic construction a shelter from the surrounding chaos; Stevens, while acknowledging the extinction of divine radiance, seeks a solar language that will take its place. The nature of both of these projects is continually defined in terms of architectural metaphors.

The final chapter surveys the great wasteland of the contemporary built environment, along with the rueful reflections on this scene by two widely read writers of the past two decades. Ballard's vision, as implied by the title of his last work, *Kingdom Come,* makes him an heir to the literary traditions of apocalyptic ruin in poets like Blake and Eliot: the shopping center replaces Jerusalem and Margate Sands. But Houellebecq's fiction consciously evokes something closer in texture to the material of junkspace itself and is suggested in the English translation of the title of his first novel, *Whatever.* No agony, no lament, just disconnection—from any coherent sense of self, as well as from the junkspace that is the world. In its annihilation of subjective value along with everything else, this is one more move toward the ultimate tabula rasa foreseen in Loos's war on ornament and Beckett's bare stage: the clearing of an empty space as the necessary condition for some other, as yet unapprehended way of writing and building.

Notes

INTRODUCTION

1. Translations throughout this book are mine unless otherwise noted.

2. See "Type," in Quatremère de Quincey, *Encyclopédie méthodologique.*

3. I follow Frampton in using the Greek.

4. Bonaventure, *Commenataria in Quatuor Librio Sententiarum,* Book III, distinction 9, article 1, question 2.

5. The *ordo ad benedicandam ecclesiam* (ceremony for the consecration of the church building) dates from 840.

6. References to Ruskin's works are to the *Library Edition of the Complete Works,* in 39 volumes.

7. This is Sinclair's translation in Dante, *The Divine Comedy.*

8. Other examples of the genre are Jonson's "Sir Robert Wroth" (1616), Thomas Carew's "To Saxham" (1640), Robert Herrick's "A Country-Life: To His Brother Mr. Thomas Herrick" (1610), and Andrew Marvell's "Upon Appleton House" (1652). Not included in this admittedly limited definition are modernist transformations of the genre such as Yeats's "Coole Park and Ballylee, 1931" and Eliot's "Burnt Norton" (1935).

9. See, for example, Mortimer, "The Feigned Commonwealth in the Poetry of Ben Jonson"; Wayne, *Penshurst: The Semiotics of Place and the Poetics of History;* Evans, *Ben Jonson and the Poetics of Patronage;* and Riggs, *Ben Jonson, a Life.*

10. The king did in fact visit Penshurst in 1612, an event duly celebrated in Jonson's poem.

11. "Penshurst Palace and Gardens," tourist brochure produced by Penshurst Place, Tonbridge, Kent.

12. See Luigi Ficacci, "Introduction." In Ficacci, *Giovanni Battista Piranesi: The Etchings.*

13. Robin Evans 63, quoting the 1755 Leoni translation.

14. The *Invenzioni cappriciose di carceri all'acquaforte date in luce da Giovani Buzard in Roman Mercante al Corso* were published in two series; that of 1749–50 was revised in 1761.

15. Jennifer Bloomer, in a provocative work that compares Piranesi's work to *Finnegans Wake,* cites this passage as quoted in an essay by Sergei Eisenstein, "Piranesi, or the Fluidity of Forms."

16. *Inderlighed* is Kierkegaard's word, which Martin Leer translates for me as "innerness." The latter word better conveys the lived interiority of *Inderlighed* than "inwardness," which implies a dynamic movement from outside to inside. Adorno, however, was working with the German translation of Kierkegaard, in which *Inderlighed* is rendered as *Innerlichheit* (inwardness).

17. Cited in Kruft, 44.

18. This work was published in Venice in 1499. It has been attributed, with some hesitation, to the Dominican friar Francesco Colonna, who served at the Basilica of Saint Mark's. A French translation appeared in 1546, and an English translation, possibly by Sir Robert Dallington, appeared in 1592 with a dedication to Sir Philip Sidney.

19. See the International Classification of Diseases online at http://www.who .int/classifications/apps/icd/icd10online/.

20. Frampton, *L'Architecture moderne,* 30.

21. See Hilde Heynen's treatment of this movement, and of Ernst Bloch's response to it, in her *Architecture and Modernity: A Critique.*

22. In Hugo's novel the fifteenth-century archdeacon of Notre-Dame, Claude Frollo, points to a printed book and then to the cathedral with the words "Ceci tuera cela" (This will kill that).

23. Quoted in Jameson, *Marxism and Form,* 172.

CHAPTER I

1. "Esprit d'ordre, unité d'intention." Translations are mine unless otherwise indicated.

2. As in the Introduction, all references to Ruskin are to the *Library Edition of the Complete Works* (see the Bibliography). Individual volumes such as *The Seven Lamps* are part of this multivolume work.

3. Cf. Harries 162; and David Simpson's *9/11: The Culture of Commemoration,* which reads Heidegger's lecture in the light of the reconstruction of the World Trade Center site in New York.

4. Dickens shared with Ruskin a taste for Swiss architecture based on his visits to Switzerland in the 1840s. In 1865 he had a Valais-style chalet built in the garden of his house at Gad's Hill, and he used it as a study until his death in 1870.

5. Citations of *Ulysses* and other works by Joyce conform to the conventions of Joyce scholarship, with the chapter number (here 8) followed by the line numbers from that chapter in the Gabler edition (here 484–86).

CHAPTER 2

1. See Westerhoff, "A World of Signs: Baroque Pansemioticism, the Polyhistor, and the Early Modern Wunderkammer."

2. Cited in Calasso 32.

3. Citations from Kafka are given first in the original from the Fischer edition, then in English from the Muir translation. The posthumous supplements to *Das Schloss* (240–98) in the Vintage translation are by Eithne Wilkins and Ernst Kaiser.

4. Cf. the discussion of Derrida's essay in chapter 6, "Doing the Twist," of Wigley's *The Architecture of Deconstruction*.

5. For a study of agoraphobia in modern culture, see the second chapter of Vidler's *Warped Space*.

6. In German-speaking Switzerland, every village tavern has a *Stammtisch,* a table reserved for the locals, which nonetheless bears no outward sign that designates it as such. A stranger ignorant of this practice who innocently seats himself at such a table will draw hostile glances without being told the nature of his or her offense.

7. As in Husserl's *Logische Untersuchungen* (Logical Investigations), 1901.

CHAPTER 3

1. The original version of Hegel's lectures on aesthetics is to be found in Hegel, *Werke,* band 14: Vorlesungen über die Aesthetik, 2:332.

2. *Gelehrte Anzeigen,* 4 December 1772.

3. Munich edition of Goethe's *Sämtliche Werke,* ed. Gerhard Sauder, 2:835.

4. As a student at Leipzig, Goethe had read Laugier's *Essai sur l'architecture* (1753–55).

5. See also Frew, "Gothic Is English: John Carter and the Revival of the Gothic as England's National Style."

6. The Boisserée brothers had published *Ansichten, Risse und enzelne Teile des Doms zu Köln, mit Ergänzungen nach dem Entwurf des Meisters* in 1821. This was followed by their *Geschichte und Beschreibung des Domes zu Köln,* 1823–31.

7. See, for example, Schier, "The Experience of the Noumenal in Goethe and Wordsworth." The first English edition of *The Sorrows of Werter* [*sic*], translated from the French by Daniel Malthus, was published in Dublin in 1780.

8. See Levinson, "Insight and Oversight: Reading "Tintern Abbey." See also Jonathan Wordsworth et al., *William Wordsworth and the Age of English Romanticism.*

9. For other scenes of Gothic ruins in Wordsworth's poetry, see in *The Prelude*

(1805) the evocations of Furness Abbey (2:107–15) and Penrith Castle (4:218–30). My thanks to Patrick Vincent for pointing out these passages to me.

10. Between 1538 and 1541 King Henry VIII dissolved the institutions of the Roman Catholic monasteries and confiscated their property. In 1798 the land on which Tintern Abbey stands was the property of the Duke of Beaufort.

11. Ruskin refers us to two biblical sources: "The Law is light" (Prov. vi:23) and "Thy Word is a lamp unto my feet" (Ps. cxix.105), cited in *Works,* 8:22.

12. See also the excellent website on Villard de Honnecourt produced by the Bibliothèque Nationale de France: http://classes.bnf.fr/villard.

13. Ryle, *Practical Religion,* chap. 1.

14. Preface to Proust, *La Bible d'Amiens,* 84.

15. See, for example, Arnold's *Culture and Anarchy.*

16. Chartres departs from convention by being aligned northeast-southwest rather than east-west. At the summer solstice, traditionally the day of the renewal of life, the sun rises in the northeast.

17. James, without the aid of photographs taken with a telescopic camera lens, counts only fifteen kings.

18. Examples include Jean-Honoré Fragonard, *Les lavandières* (ca. 1760); Robert Hubert, *Les lavandières à la fontaine* (ca. 1760) and *Les lavandières parmi les ruines* (ca. 1760); Louis Français, *Les lavandières dans le sous-bois* (1867); Jean-Louis-Ernest Meissonier, *Les blanchisseuses à Antibes* (1869); and Edgar Degas, *Deux blanchisseuses* (1874).

19. The Byzantine empress (*basilissa*) Irene reigned in Constantinople from 797 to 802 and revived the adoration of images in Orthodox churches.

20. Louis was born on 25 April 1214 in Poissy.

21. The notion of "moments of being" is defined in Woolf's autobiographical writings, including her essay "A Sketch of the Past."

CHAPTER 4

1. See, for example, the work of Jean-Michel Leniaud, *Viollet-le-Duc ou les délires du système.*

2. See, for example, Revel, "Viollet-le-Duc, précurseur de l'architecture moderne"; and Damisch, "Du Structuralisme au fonctionalisme."

3. Among Viollet's supporters in this controversy was the American student H. H. Richardson. See James O'Gorman's *Living Architecture: A Biography of H. H. Richardson.* O'Gorman reproduces a story according to which Richardson and the poet Théophile Gautier were jailed after a demonstration in support of Viollet.

4. The analogy proposed here between Viollet-le-Duc's ideal Gothic cathedral and the romantic symbol carries a risk of oversimplification. In particular, the rationalism of Viollet-le-Duc's approach has little in common with the romantic symbol as it is found in literature. It also contrasts with that strain of romanticism

that, rather than "collapsing" the metaphysical dimension of transcendence into the material object, instead insists on the indefinite deferral of transcendental value. The proposed analogy should therefore be understood as limited to the qualities of atemporality and secularity that the symbol has in common with the work of Viollet-le-Duc.

5. Plate 31 in Ruskin, *Diaries,* vol. 1.

6. Ruskin's active opposition to architectural restoration lasted well into his mature years. In 1877, for example, he wrote letters to the editors of provincial English newspapers to oppose projects of restoration then being undertaken. His letter of 9 June to the *Liverpool Daily Post* opens with the words, "My Dear Sir: It is impossible for any one to know the horror and contempt with which I regard modern restoration—but it is so great that it simply paralyzes me in despair."

7. For a recent revision of this view, see the collection of essays in Cianci and Nicholls, eds., *Ruskin and Modernism.* Also of interest is Toni Cerutti's edited volume *Ruskin and the Twentieth Century.*

CHAPTER 5

1. See also Bizub, *La Venise intérieure: Proust et la poétique de la traduction,* 9.

2. Proust's hotel was not on the Lido, as reported in Cattaui, nor was it the Danieli, as reported by George Painter. See Tadié, 1:625, n.4.

3. Tadié gives as a manuscript variant "les ouvertures durcies" (the hardened openings), whereas Chevalier, choosing another variant, has "les parois durcis" (the hardened partition walls).

4. The *piombi* of Venice are the prison quarters in the attic of the Pallazzo Ducale, so named for the sheets of lead that line the ceiling. In 1756, Giacomo Casanova famously escaped from them in an episode famously recounted in his memoirs. Anne Chevalier, in her notes to the Folio Classique edition of *A la recherché du temps perdu,* conjectures that in his metaphor of depth Proust has confused the *piombi* with the *pozzi,* the dungeons of the same palace.

5. The original angelic promise of Luke 2:14 is evoked on the final page of Ruskin's *The Bible of Amiens:* "[I]f, preparing yourselves to lie down beneath the grass in silence and loneliness, seeing no more beauty, and feeling no more gladness—you would care for the promise to you of a time when you should see God's light again, and know the things you have longed to know, and walk in the peace of everlasting Love—*then* the Hope of these things to you is religion, the Substance of them in your life is Faith" (255–56). In the preface to his translation Proust calls these lines "truly sublime" (84).

6. *Timaeus* 49.

7. In *Glas,* Derrida remarks on the mosaic nature of the passage that Proust devotes to the mosaic on the wall of the baptistery: "the mosaic of the baptism 'in relation to the site,' where the Jordan represents a second baptistery *en abyme* inside the first one; the waves of the Jordan answered by those of the lagoon by the

piazetta, the ice-cold air in which the visitors are plunged as in baptismal water, the woman in mourning like the one in the nearby painting by Carpaccio, itself an image *en abyme* of Venice within Venice, the solemn immobility of the mother's image in the memory of the 'sanctuary' like one of the images before [the narrator] and, by means of this, the suggested analogy between the narrator's mother and the mother of Christ" (209).

8. Critical opinion differs as to why Proust describes the composition of water as hydrogen and nitrogen rather than oxygen. Marcel Muller rather valiantly attempts to defend Proust from the charge of ignorance in chemistry, or of a simple lapse in attention, by seeing in the use of *azote* a possible allusion to the pharmacist Homais in Flaubert's *Madame Bovary,* who speaks of how the prairies give off nitrogen in summer.

9. Examples include Bizub's *La Venise intérieure* and Collier's *Proust and Venice.*

10. The uneven paving stones of the baptistery are not mentioned in the *séjour à Venise*; the reader learns of them here for the first time. In other words, the chapter on Venice has not recorded all of the narrator's sensations of Venice. Some of them have been held in reserve, only to be discovered later in the form of memory.

11. This passage, printed in Pierre Clarac and André Ferré's 1954 Gallimard edition of *A la recherche du temps perdu* (15:76), is suppressed in the 1989 Tadié edition. It also appears in the 1954 Gallimard folio edition of *Le Temps retrouvé* on pages 273–74.

CHAPTER 6

1. As in previous chapters, citations of *Ulysses* and other works by Joyce conform to the conventions of Joyce scholarship, with the chapter number (here 8) followed by the line numbers from that chapter in the Gabler edition (here 490–92).

2. See the description of the nearby Seapoint Martello Tower in Pavia and Bolton, *Stone Monuments Decay Study.*

3. Yeats, *W. B. Yeats and T. Sturge Moore: Their Correspondence* (114), quoted in Bornstein, 65.

4. See Yeats's "*Il Penseroso's* Platonist," in "Meditations in Time of Civil War" (*Collected Poems* 199), and his discussion of the tower as symbol in "The Philosophy of Shelley's Poetry" (*Essays and Introductions*).

5. In Joyce's story "Clay," Maria changes trams at the pillar on her journey from Ballsbridge to Drumcondra, giving her the chance to shop for plum cake in the city's commercial center.

6. The Wellington Monument in Phoenix Park, Dublin, is an obelisk completed in 1861 by Sir Robert Smirke. Blenheim Palace in Oxfordshire was built by

Parliament, in gratitude to John Churchill, the first Duke of Marlborough, for his vistory over the French at Blenheim in 1704.

7. Adrian Hardiman, justice of the Supreme Court of Ireland, tells me that he was a student at Belvedere College on the day Nelson's statue was blown up. According to Justice Hardiman, the school's teacher of the Irish language thought it miraculous that, whereas the explosion had not been technically controlled, it had caused no damage to anything except the monument itself; he said to his students in Irish, "The hand of God was in that act." The statue's head, considerably damaged, is currently on display at the Dublin City Library in Pearse Street.

8. Joyce had reviewed Lady Gregory's *Poets and Dreamers* in 1903, writing, "In her new book she has left legends and heroic youth far behind, and has explored in a land almost fabulous in its sorrow and senility" (*Critical Writings* 103).

9. See Deleuze and Guattari, *Mille plateaux,* 164ff.

10. Casey, *Dublin,* 87.

11. The Tholsel is the Norse word, literally "toll-gatherer's stall," for the Guildhall of the Dublin Corporation, built in the early fourteenth century on the south bank of the Liffey, near Christ Church Cathedral. Dublin is known in Irish as Baile Átha Cliath, the town of the hurdle ford, after the place where the roads of ancient Ireland converged to cross the river over a ford of wicker hurdles.

12. See Moran, *Staging the Easter Rising.*

13. Of the sixteen men executed for their part in the rising, the only one whose name appears in *Ulysses* (12:1545) is Roger Casement, in the context of his *Report on the Administration of the Congo Free State,* 1904.

14. "Literary Supplement: From Work in Progress by James Joyce."

15. Personal communication from Robert Nicholson, Curator, James Joyce Museum, Sandymount, Dublin, 28 October 2005. I am grateful to Ian Gunn of Edinburgh University for calling my attention to this photograph, and to the National Photographic Archive of Ireland for granting permission to print it here.

16. I am grateful to Professor Luke Gibbons for pointing this out to me during a discussion at the International James Joyce Symposium in Budapest, June 2006.

17. Cf. Badiou, *Beckett: L'increvable désir,* 39.

CHAPTER 7

1. From the poem "In lieblicher Blaue . . ." cited in Heidegger, *Poetry.*

2. In Lentricchia's text the quoted words are attributed to van Den Berg, *The Phenomenological Approach to Psychiatry,* 32. For additional critical works on Heidegger and American poetry, see Bové and Hines.

3. As Kermode points out, the relation between Stevens and Heidegger is one of affinity rather than influence. Stevens was primarily interested in the figure of Heidegger as Hölderlin's interpreter, but he was not familiar with the philoso-

pher's work. His letters to his bookseller, Paule Vidal (29 July 1952) and his friend Peter Lee (30 June 1954) show that Stevens thought Heidegger to be a Swiss philosopher lecturing at the University of Fribourg (Freiburg), Switzerland, an institution he had confused with the German university at Freiburg-im-Breisgau. (*Letters* 758, 839, 846).

4. See Stevens's *Opus Posthumous,* revised edition by Milton J. Bates, 37.

5. The phrase *architecture parlante* was first used ironically by romantic critics to characterize some of the works of Claude-Nicolas Ledoux that constituted a three-dimensional picture language, such as his design for the salt works of Arc-et-Senans or of the cart maker's house in the form of a huge wheel. Here I use the phrase, in its more recent and general sense, to refer to the symbolic content of architecture, which is comparable to linguistic signification.

6. See Thomas G. Henderson, "Santayana Awaiting Death."

7. Adorno's "Spätstil Beethovens" (1937) is quoted in Edward Said's "Thoughts on Late Style."

CHAPTER 8

1. Quoted in Jameson, *The Geopolitical Aesthetic,* 17.

2. In 2010 an exhibit dedicated to Ballard was organized at the Gagosian gallery in London. Among the works shown were Adam McEwen's giant photograph of a Boeing 747 undercarriage and two photographs by Dan Holdsworth entitled "Untitled (Autopia)." The photographs show, from the right and left lanes, respectively, a highway gleaming under electric lights as it swerves into darkness.

3. The website is http://www.stockleypark.co.uk.

4. The authoritarian ideology of shopping mall management is documented by Mark Gottdiener, who points out that malls, being located on what is legally private property, can exclude political and union assemblies. In the United States, this includes the legal right to prevent picket lines of workers engaged in a job action against one of the shops (298).

5. "Houellebecq: La qualité du produit," *Libération,* 2 September 2010, http://www.liberation.fr/livres/0101655356-houellebecq-la-qualite-du-produit.

6. "La religion la plus con, c'est quand même l'islam." In "Entretien: Michel Houellebecq," *Lire,* 1 September 2001, http://www.lexpress.fr/culture/livre/michel-houellebecq_804761.html.

7. *Les Inrockuptibles,* April 2005, quoted in Emilie Valentin, "L'Impassible nihiliste: Portrait de Michel Houellebecq," http://www.evene.fr/livres/actualite/portrait-de-michel-houellebecq-179.php.

Bibliography

Adams, Henry. *Mont Saint-Michel and Chartres.* New York: Penguin, 1986.

Adorno, Theodor. *Aesthetic Theory.* Trans. Robert Hullot-Kentor. Minneapolis: University of Minnesota Press, 1977.

Adorno, Theodor. "Aufzeichnungen zu Kafka." In *Gesammelte Schriften,* 10:1. Frankfurt am Main: Suhrkamp, 1977, 254–87. Translated as "Notes on Kafka." In *Can One Live after Auschwitz? A Philosophical Reader.* Ed. Rolf Tiedemann. Trans. Rodney Livingstone et al. Palo Alto: Stanford University Press, 2003. 211–39.

Adorno, Theodor. "Functionalism Today." Trans. Jane Newman and John Smith. *Oppositions* 17 (1979), 30–41. Reprinted in *Rethinking Architecture: A Reader in Cultural Theory.* Ed. Neil Leach. London: Routledge, 1997, 6–20.

Adorno, Theodor. *Kierkegaard: Construction of the Aesthetic.* Trans. Robert Hullot-Kentor. Minneapolis: University of Minnesota Press, 1989.

Adorno, Theodor. *Minima Moralia: Reflections from Damaged Life.* Trans. E. F. N. Jephcott. London: Verso, 1978.

Adorno, Theodor. *Negative Dialectics.* Trans. E. B. Ashton. London: Routledge, 1990.

Adorno, Theodor. *Notes to Literature.* Trans. Sherry Weber Nicholson. 2 vols. New York: Columbia University Press, 1991.

Adorno, Theodor. "Spätstil Beethovens." Translated as "Le Style tardif de Beethoven." In *Moments musicaux.* Trans. Martin Kaltenecker. Geneva: Contrechamps, 2003, 9–12. Also translated as "Beethoven's Late Style." In *Beethoven: The Philosophy of Music.* Ed. Rolf Tiedemann. Trans. Edmund Jephcott. Palo Alto: Stanford University Press, 2002, 123–37.

Agamben, Giorgio. *Nudités.* Trans. Martin Rueff. Paris: Rivages, 2009.

Alberti, Leon Battista. *The Ten Books of Architecture.* Translation of *De re aedificatoria,* by James Leoni, 1755. Reprint; London: Dover, 1987.

Alighieri, Dante. *The Divine Comedy.* 3 vols. Trans. John D. Sinclair. New York: Oxford University Press, 1961.

Alter, Robert. *Imagined Cities: Urban Experience and the Language of the Novel.* New Haven: Yale University Press, 2005.

Althusser, Louis. "Idéologie et appareils idéologiques d'État." *La pensée* 151 (1970): 6–60.

Arnold, Matthew. *Culture and Anarchy.* London: Smith Elder, 1869.

Atherton, James. *The Books at the Wake: A Study of Literary Allusions in James Joyce's Finnegans Wake.* Carbondale: Southern Illinois University Press, 1959.

Augé, Marc. *Non-lieux: Introduction à une anthropologie de la surmodernité.* Paris: Seuil, 1992.

Austen, Jane. *Mansfield Park.* Oxford: World's Classics, 1990.

Badiou, Alain. *Beckett: L'increvable désir.* Paris: Hachette, Collection Pluriel, 2006.

Bachelard, Gaston. *La poétique de l'espace.* Paris: Presses universitaires de France, 1994.

Ballard, J. G. *Concrete Island.* London: Cape, 1974.

Ballard, J. G. *High-Rise.* London: Harper, 2006.

Ballard, J. G. *Kingdom Come.* London: Harper, 2006.

Ballard, J. G. *Super-Cannes.* London: Harper, 2000.

Balzac, Honoré de. *Le Curé de Tours.* Paris: Garnier Flammarion, 1968.

Balzac, Honoré de. *Illusions perdues.* Paris: Gallimard Folio, 1974.

Balzac, Honoré de. *Père Goriot.* Paris: Garnier Flammarion, 1966.

Baridon, Laurent. *L'Imaginaire scientifique de Viollet-le-Duc.* Paris: L'Harmattan, 1996.

Barr, Alfred H. Foreword to *Modern Architecture: International Exhibition.* New York: Museum of Modern Art, 1932.

Barthes, Roland. *Sade, Fourier, Loyola.* Paris: Seuil, 1971.

Bataille, Georges. "Franz Kafka devant la critique communiste." *Critique* 41 (October 1950): 22–36.

Bataille, Georges. *La littérature et le mal.* Paris: Gallimard, 1957.

Bayley, Stephen. "Viollet-le-Duc et la restauration." In *Viollet-le-Duc: Centenaire de la mort à Lausanne.* Ed. Paul Auberson. Lausanne: Musée historique de l'Ancien-Evêché, 1979, 27–36.

Beckett, Samuel. *Endgame.* London: Faber and Faber, 1958.

Beckett, Samuel. *Proust.* Trans. Edith Fournier. Paris: Minuit, 1990.

Bekaert, Geert, ed. *A la recherche de Viollet-le-Duc.* Brussels: Pierre Mardaga, 1980.

Benjamin, Walter. *Illuminations.* Trans. Harry Zohn. New York: Schocken, 1969.

Benjamin, Walter. *Paris, capitale du XIXe siècle.* Trans. Jean Lacoste. Paris: Cerf, 2000.

Benjamin, Walter. *Das Passagen-Werk.* Ed. Rolf Tiedemann. 2 vols. Frankfurt am Main: Suhrkamp, 1983. Translated as *The Arcades Project.* Trans. Howard Eiland and Kevin McLaughlin. Cambridge, Mass.: Harvard University Press, 1999.

Benjamin, Walter. *Selected Writings, 1913–34.* Ed. Michael W. Jennings. 2 vols. Cambridge, Mass.: Harvard University Press, 1999.

Benjamin, Walter. "Über den Begriff der Geschichte." In *Gesammelte Schriften.* Ed. Rolf Tiedemann and Hermann Schweppenhäuser. Vol. 1:2. Suhrkamp: Frankfurt am Main, 1991, 691–704. Translated as "Theses in the Philosophy of History." In *Illuminations.* Trans. Harry Zohn. New York: Schocken, 1969, 253–64.

Benjamin, Walter. *Ursprung des deutschen Trauerspiels.* In *Gesammelte Schriften* Ed. Rolf Tiedemann und Hermann Schweppenhäuser. 1.1. Frankfurt am Main: Suhrkamp, 1991, 203–430. Translated as *The Origin of German Tragic Drama.* Trans. John Osborne. London: Verso 1998.

Bernstein, Susan. *Housing Problems: Writing and Architecture in Goethe, Walpole, Freud, and Heidegger.* Palo Alto: Stanford University Press, 2008.

Bizub, Edward. *La Venise intérieure: Proust et la poétique de la traduction.* Neuchâtel: La Baconnière, 1991.

Blakely, Edward J., and Mary Gail Snyder. *Fortress America: Gated Communities in the United States.* Washington, D.C.: Brookings Institution, 1999.

Blanchot, Maurice. *L'Entretien infini.* Paris: Gallimard, 1969.

Blanchot, Maurice. *Lautréamont et Sade.* Paris: Minuit, 1963.

Blanchot, Maurice. "Parole de fragment." In *L'Entretien infini.* Paris: Gallimard, 1969, 451–58.

Blavatsky, Helena Petrovna. *The Secret Doctrine: Synthesis of Science, Religion, and Philosophy.* 6 vols. Adyar, Madras: Vasanta Press, 1938.

Blondel, Jacques-François. *Cours d'architecture ou traité de la décoration, distribution, et construction des bâtiments.* 9 vols. Paris: Desaint, 1771–77.

Bloomer, Jennifer. *Architecture and the Text: The (S)crypts of Joyce and Piranesi.* New Haven: Yale University Press, 1993.

Boisserée, Sulpiz, and Melchior Boisserée. *Ansichten, Risse und einzelne Theile des Doms von Köln.* Stuttgart: Cotta, 1823.

Bornstein, George. *Material Modernism: The Politics of the Page.* Cambridge: Cambridge University Press, 2001.

Bourdieu, Pierre. *The Field of Cultural Production: Essays on Art and Literature.* New York: Columbia University Press, 1993.

Bourdieu, Pierre. *Outline of a Theory of Practice.* Trans. Richard Nice. Cambridge: Cambridge University Press, 1977.

Bourdieu, Pierre. "Postface." In Panovsky, Erwin, *Architecture gothique et pensée scolastique.* Trans. Pierre Bourdieu. Paris: Minuit, 1967.

Bové, Paul. *Destructive Poetics: Heidegger and American Poetry.* New York: Columbia University Press, 1980.

Boyd, William. *Ordinary Thunderstorms.* London: Bloomsbury, 2009.

Boyer, M. Christine. *The City of Collective Memory: Its Historical Imagery and Collective Entertainments.* Cambridge, Mass.: MIT Press, 1994.

Burke, Edmund. *A Philosophical Enquiry into the Origin of Our Ideas of the Sublime and Beautiful.* Oxford: Blackwell, 1987.

Byron, George Gordon, Lord. *The Complete Poetical Works.* Ed. Jerome McGann. Oxford: Clarendon Press, 1980.

Cacciari, Massimo. *Architecture and Nihilism: On the Philosophy of Modern Architecture.* Trans. Stephen Sartarelli. New Haven: Yale University Press, 1993.

Calasso, Roberto. *K.* Trans. Jean-Paul Manganaro. Paris: Gallimard, 2005.

Calvino, Italo. *Le città invisibili.* Milan: Eindaudi, 1973.

Carruthers, Mary. *The Book of Memory: A Study of Memory in Medieval Culture.* Cambridge: Cambridge University Press, 1990.

Casey, Christine. *Dublin: The City within the Grand and Royal Canals and the Circular Road with the Phoenix Park.* Buildings of Ireland series. New Haven and London: Yale University Press, 2005.

Cattaui, Georges. *Proust: Documents iconographiques.* Geneva: Pierre Cailler, 1956.

Cerutti, Toni, ed. *Ruskin and the Twentieth Century.* Vercelli: Mercurio, 2000.

Char, René. *Fureur et mystère.* Paris: Gallimard, 1967.

Chateaubriand, François René de. *Génie du Christianisme.* Paris: Flammarion, 1933.

Cianci, Giovanni, and Peter Nicholls, eds. *Ruskin and Modernism.* Basingstoke: Palgrave, 2001.

Coleridge, Samuel Taylor. *The Statesman's Manual* (1816). Vol. 6 of *The Collected Works.* Ed. R. J. White. 26 vols. Princeton: Princeton University Press, 1972.

Collier, Peter. *Proust and Venice.* Cambridge: Cambridge University Press, 1989.

Colonna, Francesco. *Hypnerotomachia Poliphili.* New York: Garland, 1976.

Conrads, Ulrich. *Programmes et manifestes de l'architecture du XXe siècle.* Paris: Editions de la Villette, 1991.

Le Corbusier [Charles-Édouard Jeanneret-Gris]. *Manière de penser l'urbanisme.* Paris: Denoël, 1946.

Le Corbusier [Charles-Édouard Jeanneret-Gris]. *Œuvres complètes.* 8 vols. Zurich: Artemis, 1971.

Le Corbusier [Charles-Édouard Jeanneret-Gris]. "Vers une architecture: Arguments." In *Programmes et manifestes de l'architecture du XXe siècle.* Ed. Ulrich Conrads. Paris: Editions de la Villette, 1991. 73–77.

Curtius, Ernst Robert. *Marcel Proust.* Trans. Armand Pierhal. Paris: Editions de la Nouvelle Revue, 1928.

Dällenbach , Lucien, and Christian Hart Nibrigg. *Fragment und Totalität.* Frankfurt am Main: Suhrkamp, 1984.

Damisch, Hubert. "Du Structuralisme au fonctionalisme." In *A la recherche de Viollet-le-Duc.* Ed. Geert Bekaert. Brussels: Pierre Mardaga, 1980, 117–30.

Dante Alighieri. *Convivio.* Torino: Garzanti, 2005.

Dante Alighieri. *La Divina Commedia.* Ed. C.H. Grandgent and Charles S. Singleton. Cambridge, Mass.: Harvard University Press, 1972.

Dante Alighieri. *The Divine Comedy.* Trans. John D. Sinclair. New York: Oxford University Press, 1961.

D'Avenant, William. *Gondibert: An Heroic Poem.* London: John Holden, 1651.

Deleuze, Gilles. *Proust et les signes.* Paris: Presses Universitaires de France, 1964.

Deleuze, Gilles, and Félix Guattari. *Anti-Oedipe: Capitalisme et schizophrénie.* Paris: Minuit, 1973.

Deleuze, Gilles, and Félix Guattari. *Mille plateaux.* Paris: Minuit, 1980.

de Man, Paul. *Aesthetic Ideology.* Minneapolis: University of Minnesota Press, 1996.

de Man, Paul. "The Rhetoric of Temporality." In *Blindness and Insight: Essays in the Rhetoric of Contemporary Criticism.* Minneapolis: University of Minnesota Press, 1983.

De Quincey, Thomas. *Works.* Ed. Grevel Lindorp. 21 vols. London: Pickering and Chatto, 2000.

Derrida, Jacques. "Before the Law." Trans. Avital Ronell and Christine Roulson. In *Acts of Literature.* Ed. Derek Attridge. London: Routledge, 1992. 181–220.

Derrida, Jacques. *Demeure: Maurice Blanchot.* Paris: Galilée, 1998.

Derrida, Jacques. "The Double Session." Trans. Barbara Johnson. In *The Derrida Reader.* Ed. Peggy Kamuf. New York: Columbia University Press, 1991, 169–99.

Derrida, Jacques. *De l'esprit: Heidegger et la question.* Paris: Galilée, 1987.

Derrida, Jacques. *Glas.* Paris: Galilée, 1974.

Derrida, Jacques. *Psyché: Inventions de l'autre.* Paris: Galilée, 1987.

Derrida, Jacques. "Des tours de Babel." In *Psyché: Inventions de l'autre.* Paris: Galilée, 1987. 203–35.

Destutt de Tracy, Antoine. *Mémoires sur la faculté de penser.* Paris: Institut national des sciences et arts, 1796.

Dickens, Charles. *Bleak House.* Oxford: Oxford World's Classics, 1998.

Dickens, Charles. *David Copperfield.* Oxford: Oxford World's Classics, 1999.

Dickens, Charles. *Dombey and Son.* Oxford: Clarendon Press, 1974.

Dickens, Charles. *Our Mutual Friend.* Oxford: Oxford University Press, 1998.

Dickens, Charles. *The Old Curiosity Shop.* London: Oxford University Press, 1951.

Diderot, Denis, and Jean le Rond d'Alembert. *Encyclopédie ou dictionnaire raisonné des sciences, des arts, et des métiers.* 17 vols. Paris: André le Breton, 1751.

Diderot, Denis, and Jean le Rond d'Alembert. *Ruines et paysages: Salons de 1767.* Ed. Else Marie Bukdahl, Michel Delon, and Annette Lorenceau. Paris: Hermann, 2008.

Dostoevsky, Fyodor. *Notes from Underground.* Trans. Richard Pevear and Larissa Volokhansky. New York: Vintage, 1993.

Eisenman, Peter. "Introduction." In *Writings,* by Philip Johnson. New York: Oxford University Press, 1979, 10–25.

Eisenman, Peter. "Architecture and the Problem of the Rhetorical Figure." In *Theorizing a New Agenda for Architecture*. Ed. Kate Nesbitt. Princeton: Princeton Architectural Press, 1996. 176–81.

Eisenstein, Sergei. "Piranesi, or the Fluidity of Forms." Trans. Roberta Reeder. *Oppositions* 11 (1978): 83–110.

Eliot, T .S. *Collected Poems, 1909–1962*. New York: Harcourt Brace, 1970.

Eliot, T. S. *Selected Prose*. Ed. Frank Kermode. New York: Harcourt Brace Jovanovich, 1975.

El Wakil, Leila. "Viollet-le-Duc à Genève." In *Viollet-le-Duc: Centenaire de la mort à Lausanne—exposition au Musée historique de l'Ancien-Evêché*. Ed. Paul Auberson. Lausanne: Musée Historique de l'Ancien-Evêché, 1979. 50–55.

Evans, Robert C. *Ben Jonson and the Poetics of Patronage*. Lewisburg, Pa.: Bucknell University Press, 1989.

Evans, Robin. *Translations from Drawing to Building and Other Essays*. London: Architectural Association, 1997.

Ficacci, Luigi. *Giovanni Battista Piranesi: The Etchings*. Trans. Bradley Baker Dick. Cologne: Taschen, 2006.

Fornara, Livio. "A propos de la restauration de 1889–1913." In *Saint-Pierre, Cathédrale de Genève: Un monument, une exposition*. Ed. Ruedi Wälti. Geneva: Musée Rath, 1982, 103–5.

Forty, Adrian. *Words and Buildings: A Vocabulary of Modern Architecture*. London: Thames and Hudson, 2000.

Foster, Hal. "Why All the Hoopla?" *London Review of Books* 23, no. 16 (23 August 2001): 3–5.

Fraisse, Luc. *L'Oeuvre cathédrale: Proust et l'architecture médiévale*. Paris: José Corti, 1990.

Frampton, Kenneth. *L'Architecture moderne: Une histoire critique*. Trans. Guillemette Morel-Journel. Paris: Thames and Hudson, 2006.

Frampton, Kenneth. "Modernisme et tradition dans l'oeuvre de Mies van der Rohe, 1920–68." In *Mies van der Rohe: Sa carrière, son héritage, et ses disciples*. Ed. John Zukowsky. Paris: Centre Georges Pompidou, 1987. 41–60.

Frampton, Kenneth. "Rappel à l'Ordre: The Case for the Tectonic." In *Labour, Work, and Architecture: Collected Essays on Architecture and Design*. London: Phaidon, 2002. 91–103.

Frampton, Kenneth. *Studies in Tectonic Culture: The Poetics of Construction in Nineteenth and Twentieth Century Architecture*. Cambridge, Mass.: MIT Press, 1995.

Frew, J. M. "Gothic Is English: John Carter and the Revival of the Gothic as England's National Style." *Art Bulletin* 64, no. 2 (June 1982): 315–19.

Frost, Robert. *Complete Poems*. London: Cape, 1967.

Frost, Robert. "The Figure a Poem Makes." In *Complete Poems*. Lorenceau. Paris: Hermann, 1995. 17–20.

Gadamer, Hans-Georg. *Esquisses herméneutiques: Essais et conferences*. Paris: J. Vrin, 2004.

Gadamer, Hans-Georg. *Truth and Method.* Trans. Joel Weinsheimer and Donald G. Marshall. New York: Crossroad, 1988.

Gage, John. Trans. *Goethe on Art.* London: Scolar Press, 1980.

Giedion, Siegfried. *Bauen in Frankreich: Bauen in Eisen, Bauen in Eisenbeton.* Berlin: Klinkhardt and Biermann, 1928.

Giedion, Siegfried. *Espace, temps, et architecture.* Trans. Irmeline Lebeer and Françoise-Marie Rosset. Paris: Denoël, 1990.

Gifford, Don. *Ulysses Annotated: Notes for James Joyce's Ulysses.* Berkeley: University of California Press, 1988.

Goethe, Johann Wolgang. *Briefwechsel zwischen Goethe und Reinhard in den Jahren 1807 bis 1832.* Stuttgart und Tübingen: Cotta, 1850.

Goethe, Johann Wolgang. *Goethe on Art.* Trans. John Gage. London: Scolar Press, 1980.

Goethe, Johann Wolgang. *Sämtliche Werke.* Ed. Gerhard Sauder. 31 vols. Munich: Carl Hanser Verlag, 1987.

Gold, Matthew K. "The Expert Hand and the Obedient Heart: Dr. Vittoz, T. S. Eliot, and the Therapeutic Possibilities of *The Waste Land.*" *Journal of Modern Literature* 23, nos. 3–4 (2000): 519–33.

Gottdiener, Mark. "Recapturing the Center: A Semiotic Analysis of Shopping Malls." In Mark Gottdiener and Alexandros Ph. Lagopoulos, *The City and the Sign: An Introduction to Urban Semiotics.* New York: Columbia University Press, 1986. 288–302.

Gout, Paul. *Viollet-le-Duc.* Paris: Edouard Champion, 1914.

Habermas, Jürgen. *The Philosophical Discourse of Modernity.* Trans. Frederick Lawrence. Cambridge, Mass.: MIT Press, 1987.

Hailey, Arthur. *Airport.* New York: Doubleday, 1968.

Hanchett, Thomas W. "U.S. Tax Policy and the Shopping-Center Boom of the 1950s and 1960s." *American Historical Review* 101 (1996): 1082–1110.

Hardwick, M. Jeffrey. *Mall Maker: Victor Gruen, Architect of an American Dream.* Philadelphia: University of Pennsylvania Press, 2004.

Harries, Karsten. *The Ethical Function of Architecture.* Cambridge, Mass.: MIT Press, 1997.

Hegel, Georg Friedrich. *Aesthetics: Lectures on Fine Art.* Trans. T.M. Knox. 2 vols. Oxford: Oxford University Press, 1975.

Hegel, Georg Friedrich. *Werke.* 20 vols. Frankfurt am Main: Suhrkamp, 1970.

Heidegger, Martin. "Bauen Wohnen Denken." In *Vortäge une Aufsätze.* Frankfurt am Main: Klostermann, 2000, 147–64. Translated as "Building Dwelling Thinking." In *Poetry, Language, Thought.* Trans. Albert Hofstadter. New York: Harper, 1971, 145–61.

Heidegger, Martin. *Einführung in die Metaphysik.* Frankfurt am Main: Klostermann, 1983.

Heidegger, Martin. "Die Frage nach Technik." *Vorträge une Aufsätze.* Vol. 7 in *Gesamtausgabe.* Frankfurt am Main: Klostermann, 2000.

Heidegger, Martin. *Holzwege. Gesamtausgabe,* Band 5. Frankfurt am Main: Klostermann, 1977.

Heidegger, Martin. "Letter on Humanism." *The Basic Writings.* Ed. David Farrell Krell. New York: Harper, 1977, 193–242.

Heidegger, Martin. *Poetry Language Thought.* Trans. Albert Hofstadter. New York: Harper, 1971.

Heidegger, Martin. *The Question Concerning Technology and Other Essays.* Trans. William Lovitt. New York: Harper, 1977.

Henderson, Thomas G. "Santayana Awaiting Death." *Journal of Philosophy* 50, no. 7 (1953): 201–6.

Hersant, Yves. "Hieroglyphica." In *Les Images parlantes.* Ed. Murielle Gagnebin. Seyssel: 2005. 29–38.

Heynen, Hilde. *Architecture and Modernity: A Critique.* Cambridge, Mass.: MIT Press, 1999.

Hines, Thomas J. *The Later Poetry of Wallace Stevens: Phenomenological Parallels with Heidegger and Husserl.* Lewisburg, Pa.: Bucknell University Press, 1976.

Holy Bible, King James Version. Oxford: Oxford University Press, 1997.

Homer. *Odyssey.* Trans. Richmond Lattimore. New York: Harper and Row, 1975.

Houellebecq, Michel. *La carte et le territoire.* Paris: Flammarion, 2010.

Houellebecq, Michel. *Extension du domaine de la lutte.* Paris: Maurice Nadeau, 1994. Translated by Paul Hammond as *Whatever.* London: Serpent's Tail, 1998.

Houellebecq, Michel. *Interventions.* Paris: Flammarion, 1998.

Houellebecq, Michel. *Interventions* II. Flammarion, 2009.

Houellebecq, Michel. *Les particules élémentaires.* Paris: Flammerion, 1998.

Hugo, Victor. *Notre-Dame de Paris.* Paris: Livre de Poche, 1988.

Huysmans, Joris-Karl. *La Cathédrale.* Paris: Stock, 1898

Iogna-Prat, Dominique. *La Maison Dieu: Une histoire monumentale de l'Eglise.* Paris: Seuil, 2006.

Iser, Wolfgang. *Walter Pater: The Aesthetic Moment.* Trans. David Henry Wilson. Cambridge: Cambridge University Press, 1987.

James, Henry. *The Art of Fiction and Other Essays.* New York: Oxford University Press, 1948.

James, Henry. *Collected Travel Writings on the Continent: A Little Tour in France, Italian Hours, Other Travels.* New York: Library of America, 1993.

James, Henry. *Notes on Novelists, with Some Other Notes.* London: J. M. Dent, 1914.

Jameson, Fredric. *The Cultural Turn: Selected Writings on the Postmodern, 1983–1998.* London: Verso, 1998.

Jameson, Fredric. *The Geopolitical Aesthetic: Cinema and Space in the World System.* Bloomington: Indiana University Press, 1992.

Jameson, Fredric. *Marxism and Form: Twentieth-Century Dialectical Theories of Literature.* Princeton: Princeton University Press, 1971.

Jameson, Fredric. *Postmodernism, or the Cultural Logic of Late Capitalism.* Durham: Duke University Press, 1991.

Johnson, Philip. *Writings.* New York: Oxford University Press, 1979.

Jonson, Ben. *Poems.* Ed. C. H. Hereford, Percy Simpson, and Evelyn Simpson. Oxford: Clarendon Press, 1965.

Joyce, James. *Critical Writings.* Ed. Ellsworth Mason and Richard Ellmann. Ithaca, N.Y.: Cornell University Press, 1989.

Joyce, James. *Finnegans Wake.* New York: Penguin Books, 1967.

Joyce, James. *Ulysses: The Corrected Text.* Ed. Hans Walter Gabler. London: Bodley Head, 1993.

Kafka, Franz. *The Castle.* Trans. Willa Muir, Edwin Muir, Eithne Wilkins, and Ernst Kaiser. London: Vintage, 1999.

Kafka, Franz. *The Complete Stories.* Ed. Nahum Glatzer. New York: Schocken Books, 1971.

Kafka, Franz. *Drucke zu Lebzeiten.* Ed. Wolf Kittler, Hans-Gerd Koch, and Gerhard Neumann. Frankfurt am Main: Fischer, 1994.

Kafka, Franz. *Nachgelassene Schriften und Fragmente.* Ed. Jost Schillemeit. 2 vols. Frankfurt am Main: Fischer, 1992.

Kafka, Franz. *Das Schloss.* Frankfurt am Main: Fischer, 1982. Translated as *The Castle.* Trans. Willa Muir, Edwin Muir, Eithne Wilkins, and Ernst Kaiser. London: Vintage, 1999.

Kafka, Franz. *Tägebucher.* Ed. Hans-Gerd Koch, Michael Müller, and Malcolm Pasley. Frankfurt am Main: Fischer, 1990.

Kermode, Frank. "Dwelling Poetically in Connecticut." In *Wallace Stevens: A Celebration.* Ed. Frank Doggett and Robert Buttel. Princeton: Princeton University Press, 1980. 256–73.

Kierkegaard, Søren. *Attack upon "Christendom."* Trans. Walter Lowrie. Princeton: Princeton University Press, 1968.

Kierkegaard, Søren. *Concluding Unscientific Postscript.* Trans. David F. Swenson. Princeton: Princeton University Press, 1944.

Kierkegaard, Søren. *Either/Or.* Trans. Howard V. Hong and Edna H. Hong. Princeton: Princeton University Press, 1987.

Klossowski, Pierre. *Sade, mon prochain.* Paris: Le Seuil, 1947.

Kooijman, Dion. "The Office Building: between Globalization and Local Identity." *Environmental and Planning B: Planning and Design* 27 (2000): 827–84.

Koolhaas, Rem. "Junkspace." *October* 100 (spring 2002): 175–90.

Kruft, Hanno-Walter. *A History of Architectural Theory from Vitruvius to the Present.* Trans. Robert Taylor, Elsie Callandar, and Antony Wood. Princeton: Princeton Architectural Press, 1994.

Landow, George. *The Aesthetic and Critical Theories of John Ruskin.* Princeton: Princeton University Press, 1971.

Lavalou, Armelle. *La Villette: Cité de la musique, parc et grande halle, cité des sciences.* Paris: Monum éditions du patrimoine, 2002.

Leniaud, Jean-Michel. *Viollet-le-Duc ou les délires du système.* Paris: Mengès, 1994.

Lentricchia, Frank. *Robert Frost: Modern Poetics and the Landscapes of Self.* Durham: Duke University Press, 1975.

Lerm Hayes, Christa-Maria. *Joyce in Art.* Dublin: Lilliput, 2004.

Levinson, Marjorie. "Insight and Oversight: Reading 'Tintern Abbey.'" In *Wordsworth's Great Period Poems.* Cambridge: Cambridge University Press, 1996, 14–57.

"Literary Supplement: From Work in Progress by James Joyce." *Transatlantic Review,* April 1924, 215–23.

Loos, Adolph. "Ornament und Verbrechen." In *Trotzdem, 1900–1930.* Vienna: Prachner, 1997. 78–88.

Lukacher, Ned. *Daimonic Figures: Shakespeare and the Question of Conscience.* Ithaca, N.Y.: Cornell University Press, 1994.

Lukács, Georg. *Theorie des Romans.* Neuwied: Luchterhand, 1962.

Marchand, Leslie. *Byron: A Biography.* 2 vols. New York: Knopf, 1957.

Marx Karl. *Selected Writings.* Ed. David McLellan. Oxford: Oxford University Press, 1977.

Miller, J. Hillis. "'O sole mio!' The Sun in Proust's 'Séjour à Venise.'" *Miscelanea: A Journal of English and American Studies* 18 (1997): 231–40.

Mitscherlich, Alexander. *Die Unwirtlichkeit unserer Städte.* Frankfurt am Main: Suhrkamp, 1965.

Moran, James. *Staging the Easter Rising.* Cork: Cork University Press, 2005.

Mortier, Roger. *La poétique des ruines en France.* Geneva: Droz, 1974.

Mortimer, Anthony. "The Feigned Commonwealth in the Poetry of Ben Jonson." *Studies in English Literature, 1500–1900* 13, no. 1 (1973): 69–79.

Muller, Marcel. "Proust et Flaubert: Une dimension intertextuelle du *A la recherche du temps perdu.*" In *Proust et le texte producteur.* Ed. John Erickson and Irène Pagès. Guelph, Ont.: University of Guelph, 1980. 57–71.

Musil, Robert. *The Man without Qualities.* Trans. Sophie Wilkins and Burton Pike. London: Picador, 1995.

Norberg-Schulz, Christian. *Meaning in Western Architecture.* New York: Rizzoli, 1981.

Obrist, Hans Ulrich. *Interviews.* Vol. 1. Milan: Charta, 2003.

O'Gorman, James. *Living Architecture: A Biography of H. H. Richardson.* New York: Simon and Shuster, 1997.

Panofsky, Erwin. *Abbot Suger on the Abbey Church of Saint-Denis.* Princeton: Princeton University Press, 1946.

Panofsky, Erwin. *Architecture gothique et pensée scolastique.* Trans. Pierre Bourdieu. Paris: Minuit, 1967.

Panofsky, Erwin. *Gothic Architecture and Scholasticism.* Latrobe, Pa.: Archabbey Press, 1951.

Pater, Walter. "Coleridge's Writings." *Westminster Review* 85 (1866): 47–58.

Pater, Walter. *Gaston de Latour.* London: Macmillan, 1896.

Pater, Walter. "Notre-Dame d'Amiens." In *Miscellaneous Studies: A Series of Essays*. London: Macmillan, 1895, 49–56.

Pater, Walter. *The Renaissance: Studies in Art and Poetry*. London: Macmillan, 1925.

Pavia, Sara, and Jason Bolton. *Stone Monuments Decay Study*. Dublin: Heritage Council, 2000.

Pérez-Gómez, Alberto. *Polyphilo, or the Dark Forest Revisited: An Erotic Epiphany of Architecture*. Cambridge, Mass.: MIT Press, 1992.

Pevsner, Nikolaus. *Ruskin and Viollet-le-Duc: Englishness and Frenchness in the Appreciation of Gothic Architecture*. London: Thames and Hudson, 1969.

Pinotti, Andrea. "Gothic as Leaf, Gothic as Crystal: John Ruskin and Wilhelm Worringer." In *Ruskin and Modernism*. Ed. Giovanni Cianci and Peter Nicholls. Houndmills, Basingstoke: Palgrave, 2001. 17–31.

Piranesi, Giovanii Battista. *Opere varie di architettura, prospettiva, antichità*. Rome: G. B. Piranesi, 1761.

Plato. *Timaeus*. Trans. R. G. Bury. Cambridge, Mass.: Loeb Classical Library, 1929.

Poe, Edgar Allan. "The Fall of the House of Usher." In *Selected Tales*. Ed. Diane Johnson. New York: Vintage, 1991. 54–73.

Poe, Edgar Allan. "The Man of the Crowd." In *Selected Tales*. Ed. Diane Johnson. New York: Vintage, 1991. 95–103.

Poe, Edgar Allan. "The Philosophy of Furniture." *Burton's Gentleman's Magazine*, May 1840, 243–45.

Poe, Edgar Allan. "A Review: Twice-Told Tales. By Nathaniel Hawthorne." *Graham's Lady's and Gentleman's Magazine* 20 (May 1842): 298–300.

Pope, Alexander. *Selected Poetry*. Oxford: Oxford University Press, 1994.

Poulet, Georges. *L'Espace proustien*. Paris: Gallimard, 1963.

Praz, Mario. *Mnemosyne: The Parallel between Literature and the Visual Arts*. Princeton: Princeton University Press, 1970.

Proust, Marcel. *Albertine disparue*. Ed. Nathalie Mauriac Dyer and Etienne Wolf. Paris: Grasset, 1987.

Proust, Marcel. *Albertine disparue*. Ed. Jean Milly. Paris: Honoré Champion, 1992.

Proust, Marcel. *Albertine disparue*. Ed. Anne Chevalier. Paris: Gallimard-Folio, 1990.

Proust, Marcel. *Lettres*. Sélection et annotation revue par Françoise Leriche. Paris: Plon, 2004.

Proust, Marcel. *Le temps retrouvé*. Paris: Gallimard-Folio, 1954.

Proust, Marcel. *A la recherche du temps perdu*. 4 vols. Ed. Jean-Yves Tadié. Paris: Gallimard, 1987.

Proust, Marcel. *A la recherche du temps perdu*. 3 vols. Ed. Pierre Clarac and André Ferre. Paris: Gallimard, 1954.

Proust, Marcel, trans. *La Bible d'Amiens* by John Ruskin. Paris: Mercure de France, 1947.

Pugin, Augustus Welby. *Contrasts, or a Parallel between the Noble Edifices of the Middle Ages and Corresponding Buildings of the Present Day; Shewing the Present*

Decay of Taste (London, 1841). Reprint; Leicester: Leicester University Press, 1969.

Pugin, Augustus Welby. *True Principles of Pointed or Christian Architecture.* London: Weale, 1841.

Pynchon, Thomas. *The Crying of Lot 49.* New York: Bantam, 1967.

Quatremère de Quincey, Antoine-Chrysostôme. *Encyclopédie méthodologique.* Paris: Henri Agasse, 1788.

Rasmussen, Steen Eiler. *Understanding Architecture.* 1st U.S. ed. Cambridge, Mass.: MIT Press, 1959.

Revel, Jean-Francois. "Viollet-le-Duc, précurseur de l'architecture moderne." In Geert Bekaert, ed. *A la recherche de Viollet-le-Duc.* Brussels: Pierre Mardaga, 1980, 131–42.

Rhys, Jean. *Voyage in the Dark.* London: Penguin, 1969.

Rickman, Thomas. *An attempt to discriminate the styles of English architecture, from the Conquest to the Reformation. Preceded by a sketch of the Grecian and Roman orders, with notices of nearly five hundred English buildings.* Liverpool: Longman, 1817.

Ricoeur, Paul. *Temps et récit.* Vol. 2: *La configuration dans le récit de fiction.* Paris: Seuil, 1984.

Riggs, David. *Ben Jonson, a Life.* Cambridge, Mass.: Harvard University Press, 1989.

Robson-Scott, W. D. *The Literary Background of the Gothic Revival in Gemany.* Oxford: Clarendon Press, 1965.

Rousseau, Jean-Jacques. "Lettre sur la musique française." In *Oeuvres complètes,* 26 vols. Paris: P. Dupont, 1824, 11:141–204.

Ryle, John Charles. *Practical Religion.* London: W. Hunt, 1878.

Sade, Donatien Alphonse François, Marquis de. *Les cent vingt journéss de Sodome.* Paris : Beauval, 1975.

Sade, Donatien Alphonse François, Marquis de. *Justine, ou les malheurs de la vertu.* Paris: Gallimard, 1981.

Said, Edward. "Thoughts on Late Style." *London Review of Books,* 5 August 2004, 3.

Sauder, Gerhard, ed. *Goethe: Sämtliche Werke.* 31 vols. Munich: Carl Hanser Verlag, 1987.

Savage, Jon. *England's Dreaming: The Sex Pistols and Punk Rock.* London: Faber and Faber, 1991.

Sbriglio, Jacques. *Le Corbusier: L'Unité d'habitation de Marseille.* Marseille: Parenthèses, 1992.

Scheerbart, Paul. *Glasarchitektur.* Munich: Wolfgang Pehnt, 1971.

Schier, Rudolf Dirk. "The Experience of the Noumenal in Goethe and Wordsworth." *Comparative Literature* 25, no. 1 (winter 1973): 37–59.

Schlegel, August Wilhelm, and Karl Wilhelm Friedrich. *Athenaeum.* Berlin: Heinrich Erdlich, 1798–1800.

Scott, George Gilbert. *Remarks on Secular and Domestic Architecture, Present and Future.* London: John Murray, 1857.

Simmel, Georg. *Brücke und Tür: Essays des Philosophen zur Geschichte, Religion, Kunst, und Gesellschaft.* Ed. Margarete Susman. Stuttgart: Köhler, 1957.

Simmel, Georg. "The Metropolis and Mental Life." In *The Sociology of Georg Simmel.* Trans. Kurt H. Wolff. Glencoe, Ill.: Free Press, 1964, 409–24.

Simpson, David. *9/11: The Culture of Commemoration.* Chicago: University of Chicago Press, 2006.

Soane, John. *Royal Academy Lectures.* Ed. David Watkin. Cambridge: Cambridge University Press, 2000.

Soullilou, Jacques. "L'architecte et le fantôme." *Revue d'esthétique* 29 (1996): 75–81.

Starobinski, Jean. "Les cheminées et les clochers." *Magazine Littéraire* 280 (September 1990), 26–27.

Starobinski, Jean. *L'Invention de la liberté, 1700–1789.* Geneva: Skira, 1987.

Stevens, Wallace. *Collected Poems.* New York: Vintage, 1990.

Stevens, Wallace. *Letters.* Ed. Holly Stevens. New York: Knopf, 1981.

Stevens, Wallace. *Opus Posthumous.* Ed. Milton J. Bates. New York: Knopf, 1989.

Sullivan, Louis. *The Public Papers.* Ed. Robert Twombly. Chicago: University of Chicago Press, 1988.

Tadié, Jean-Yves. *Marcel Proust: Biographie.* 2 vols. Paris: Gallimard Folio, 1996.

Tafuri, Manfredo. *Théories et histoire de l'architecture.* Trans. Jean-Patrick Fortin and François Laisney. Paris: Editions de la Société des Architectes Diplômés par le Gouvernement, 1976.

Tóibín, Colm. *The Master.* New York: Scribner, 2004.

van den Berg, Jan Hendrik. *The Phenomenological Approach to Psychiatry: An Introduction to Recent Phenomenological Psychopathology.* Springfield, Ill.: Charles Thomas, 1955.

Vasset, Philippe. *Un livre blanc.* Paris: Fayard, 2007.

Venturi, Robert, and Denise Scott Brown. *Learning from Las Vegas: The Forgotten Symbolism of Architectural Form.* Rev. ed. Cambridge, Mass.: MIT Press, 1977.

Vidler, Anthony. *The Architectural Uncanny: Essays in the Modern Unhomely.* Cambridge, Mass., MIT Press, 1992.

Vidler, Anthony. *Warped Space: Art, Architecture, and Anxiety in Modern Culture.* Cambridge, Mass.: MIT Press, 2000.

Viollet-le-Duc, Eugène-Emmanuel. *Entretiens.* 2 vols. Brussels: Pierre Mardaga, 1977.

Viollet-le-Duc, Eugène-Emmanuel. "Restauration." In *Dictionnaire raisonné de l'architecture française du XI au XVI siècle.* Paris: A. Morel, 1875–89. 31–36.

Virilio, Paul. "The Overexposed City." In *Lost Dimension.* Trans. Daniel Moshenberg. New York: Semiotext(e), 1991. 9–27. Reprinted in *Rethinking Architecture: A Reader in Cultural Theory.* Ed. Neil Leach. London: Routledge, 1997. 380–90.

Walpole, Horace. *Anecdotes of Painting in England.* 4 vols. New York: Arno Press, 1969.

Warburton, William. *The Divine Legation of Moses, Demonstrated on the Principles of a Religious Deist, from the Omission of the Doctrine of a Future State of Rewards and Punishments in the Jewish Dispensation.* London: Fletcher Gyles, 1741.

Wayne, Don. *Penshurst: The Semiotics of Place and the Poetics of History.* London: Methuen, 1984.

Westerhoff, Jan C. "A World of Signs: Baroque Pansemioticism, the Polyhistor, and the Early Modern Wunderkammer." *Journal of the History of Ideas* 62, no. 4 (October 2001): 633–50.

Wigley, Mark. *The Architecture of Deconstruction: Derrida's Haunt.* Cambridge, Mass.: MIT Press, 1993.

Wihl, Gary. *Ruskin and the Rhetoric of Infallibility.* New Haven: Yale University Press, 1985.

Wilde, Oscar. *The Picture of Dorian Gray.* Oxford: Oxford World's Classics. 1998

Williams, Raymond. *The Country and the City.* New York: Oxford University Press, 1973.

Wölfflin, Heinrich. *Prolégomènes pour une psychologie de l'architecture.* Trans. Jacques Bonniaud and Denis Perrin. Grenoble : Ecole d'Architecture, 1982.

Woolf, Virginia. *Mrs Dalloway.* Oxford: Oxford World's Classics. 1992.

Woolf, Virginia. *A Room of One's Own.* Oxford: Oxford World's Classics, 1992.

Woolf, Virginia. "A Sketch of the Past." In *Moments of Being.* New York: Harcourt Brace, 1985. 61–160.

Woolf, Virginia. *To the Lighthouse.* Oxford: Oxford World's Classics, 1992.

Wordsworth, Jonathan, Michael Jaye, and Robert Woof. *William Wordsworth and the Age of English Romanticism.* New Brunswick, N.J.: Rutgers University Press, 1987.

Wordsworth, William. *Poetical Works.* Ed. Thomas Hutchinson and Ernest de Selincourt. Oxford: Oxford University Press, 1969.

Yeats, William Butler. *Collected Poems.* New York: Macmillan, 1956.

Yeats, William Butler. *Essays and Introductions.* New York: Collier, 1961.

Yeats, William Butler. *W. B. Yeats and T. Sturge Moore: Their Correspondence, 1901–1937.* Ed. Ursula Bridge. London: Routledge, 1953.

Žižek, Slavoj. *The Fragile Absolute.* London: Verso, 2000.

Žižek, Slavoj. "You May!" *London Review of Books* 21, no. 6 (1999): 3–6.

Index